T0339705

Rules of Engagement ?

Rules of Engagement ?

A Social Anatomy of an American War Crime —

Operation Iron Triangle, Iraq

Stjepan G. Mestrovic

Algora Publishing
New York

Library of Congress Cataloging-in-Publication Data —

Mestrovic, Stjepan Gabriel.
    Rules of engagement? : a social anatomy of an American war crime : Operation Iron
Triangle , Iraq / S.G. Mestrovic.
        p. cm.
    Includes bibliographical references and index.
    ISBN 978-0-87586-672-7 (trade paper: alk. paper) — ISBN 978-0-87586-673-4 (case
laminate: alk. paper) — ISBN 978-0-87586-674-1 (ebook) 1. Operation Iron Triangle,
Iraq, 2006. 2. Iraq War, 2003—Atrocities. 3. Iraq War, 2003—Social aspects. 4. Iraq
War, 2003—Psychological aspects. 5. Prisoners of war—Iraq—Samarra' Region. 6. War
crimes—Iraq—Samarra' Region. 7. Soldiers—Iraq—Psychology. 8. United States. Army.
Airborne Division, 101st—Regulations. 9. Trials (Military offenses)—United States. I.
Title.

    DS79.766.T54M47 2008
    956.7044'3420973—dc22
                            2008027068

    Front Cover: Top: A US Soldier Guards a Detained Man. A U.S. soldier stands guard
over an Iraqi man who drove a car in a drive-by attack on U.S. soldiers. A second man was
killed after he had fired on their patrol with an AK-47 rifle from the passenger seat of the
car. © Stefan Zaklin/epa/Corbis
    Bottom: Iran-Iraq War: Situation Between Amarah & Bassorah © Jacques Pavlovsky/
Sygma/CORBIS

Printed in the United States

To my daughters

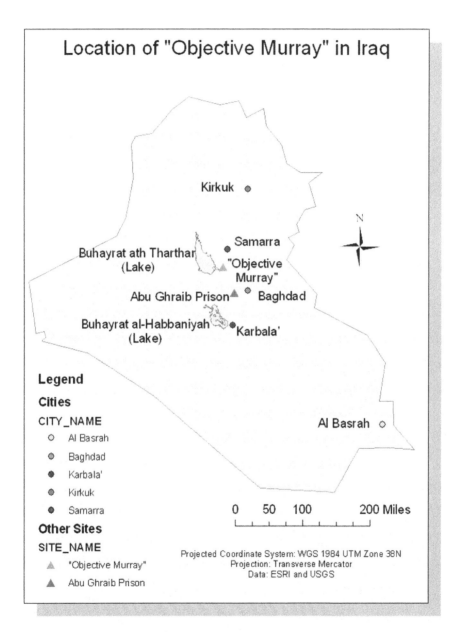

Location of "Objective Murray" in Iraq

Kirkuk ⊙

Samarra

Buhayrat ath Tharthar
(Lake)

"Objective
Murray"

Abu Ghraib Prison ▲   ⊙ Baghdad

Buhayrat al-Habbaniyah
(Lake)

Karbala'

N

Legend

Cities

CITY_NAME

○   Al Basrah

⊙   Baghdad

●   Karbala'

⊙   Kirkuk

●   Samarra

Al Basrah ○

Other Sites

SITE_NAME

▲   "Objective Murray"

▲   Abu Ghraib Prison

0   50   100   200 Miles

Projected Coordinate System: WGS 1984 UTM Zone 38N
Projection: Transverse Mercator
Data: ESRI and USGS

Map courtesy of Ronald Lorenzo

TABLE OF CONTENTS

Nowadays, perhaps partly because of the influence of postmodernism, contemporary readers feel more free than in previous generations to read any text in any way they choose, without concern for the author's intentions. Nevertheless, I will devote a few pages here to my intentions in writing this book, as well as to my background and experience in approaching this subject matter. Such disclosure of personal as well as professional motives in writing this book may be useful to some readers.

In its narrowest sense, this book is about a legal case that concerns the killing of four Iraqi males by US soldiers during a mission called Operation Iron Triangle that occurred on May 9, 2006, near Samarra, Iraq. The Rules of Engagement (ROE) for that mission were, in the words of the soldiers, to kill every military-aged male on sight. The soldiers applied the ROE to the killing of one elderly man but took four prisoners, three of whom they later shot and killed. Three soldiers were convicted of murder for killing the three prisoners, but not for the elderly man. I was asked to serve as an expert witness in sociology and psychology on the case. Have I given away the plot? In fact, this is not the central plot of the story at all.

In my view, the central plot concerns the ROE: whether it was related to other, similar ROE in Iraq and similar killings; the three distinct versions of what happened that are offered in sworn statements; and the ambivalence of the prosecutors and investigators in deciding exactly what was lawful versus unlawful in this case. Far from being a cut and dry legal case, it can be read as a mystery that is never fully resolved. Everything depends on which parts of the story are made central versus peripheral. I deliberately center my focus on the seemingly peripheral parts of the story.

My colleagues and students often ask me, "How did you get to be an expert witness in the case?" The answer is that I had built up experience as an expert witness in war crimes at The Hague in the year 1999 and in three Abu Ghraib courts-martial in the year 2005. It always started with an unexpected phone call from a lawyer. I had published several books on the war crimes in the former Yugoslavia in the 1990s, and an attorney who had read one of those books, telephoned me to come to The Hague and comment professionally on the case of Dario Kordic. I cut short a vacation at Big Bend, Texas, and made the flight to the Netherlands, and the next thing I knew, I was hired as an expert witness. That experience led several years later to a phone call from Paul Bergrin, attorney for Javal Davis in the Abu Ghraib abuse scandal, which led to another experience as expert witness, and so on for the cases of Sabrina Harman, Lynndie England, and finally, Corey Clagett in the Operation Iron Triangle case. It is still a mystery to me and my colleagues how, with my background in social theory (from classical theorists such as Emile Durkheim to postmodernists such as Jean Baudrillard) I would end up as an expert witness in war crime trials. Part of the reason is my surprise, and the surprise of attorneys, that I could withstand cross-examination. As a professor, one encounters apathy in students, and the annoying, standard question from them following any lecture, "Will this be on the test?" It does not matter how inspirational, brilliant, or passionate the lecture — it always comes down to the coldest pragmatism for the current generation of students, namely, which part of the lecture can be ignored and which part will get them the grade they seek to move up the career ladder. As an expert witness, one encounters a passionate attorney from the opposing side who yells "objection" every minute or so to anything one says, and whose aim during cross-examination is to "deconstruct" and tear apart everything the witness believes to be true. Again, it does not matter how cogent, truthful, or relevant the testimony — it always comes down to surviving the cross-examination. The most advice that I ever received from an attorney on how to handle cross-examination was, "Whatever you do, just don't crash and burn." The classroom and the courtroom are two different worlds. I never imagined being an expert witness in war crimes trials.

Part of the mystery is resolved when I look back on my friendship with David Riesman, a renowned sociology professor at Harvard University, which started when I was an undergraduate. I am not citing him to drop names or to impress others. He was not a snob, as evidenced by the fact that he sought out friendships with undergraduates such as myself, and I am not a snob either. I cite him to explain a subtle influence he exerted on me which I did not notice throughout our friendship but which lasted up to his death in the year 2002. Mark Twain, who was one of Riesman's heroes, defined a classic as "a book which people praise and don't read," and this statement applies to Riesman's classic, *The Lonely Crowd*. Even though I have read and re-read his classic many times, it was only after my experiences as an expert witness at The Hague that I realized Riesman had already prepared me for the witness stand over the course of a thirty-year-old friendship. He had graduated from Harvard Law School; he had clerked for Supreme Court Justice Louis Brandeis; and he had served for a time as Assistant District Attorney in Buffalo. He never earned a PhD in Sociology or any other field, yet this highly trained lawyer went on to write one of the most significant classics in sociology.[1] One of his central concepts is the "jury of one's peers," applied not to the courtroom but to society at large. He is best known for his theory that American society is moving away from the inner-directed type, who possesses a rigid, internal yet metaphorical "gyroscope" which would not change much despite changes in society, toward the other-directed type who looks to the "jury of one's peers" for guidance as to what is right, wrong, beautiful, ugly, or any other standard. Riesman was the lawyer who became the accidental sociologist, and I was the academic sociologist who became an accidental expert witness, but the two of us could relate to each other in the no-man's land between the professions of law and sociology. He was appointed to the sociology department by the President of Harvard University over the strong objections of his colleagues, and I was appointed as an expert witness at the Abu Ghraib trials over the strong objections of the military judge. For example, the judge allowed to me to serve as an expert witness in the Javal Davis case only if I agreed to do the work pro bono, to which I agreed readily. Riesman's colleagues objected to the fact that he was too popular to be a "real" academic, and the military judge objected to the fact that my testimony was putting the Army on trial, which, in a sense, it did. One of his most memorable lines was, "The Army is not on trial here!"

I discovered quickly that the way to survive a cross-examination is to be inner-directed, to be sincere, and to hold rigidly to one's gyroscope as to what is verifiably true no matter what the opposing attorney says or does. This is more complicated than it seems at first blush. A fanatic is also rigid, but a fanatic clings to unverifiable, private truths. The truth has to be publicly verifiable, that is to say, something that the jury of one's peers will accept, and sincere rigidity on behalf of such publicly verifiable truths is usually convincing. It thereby leads to consequences that go far beyond the particular event or exchange. Let me illustrate this with an example.

During the Sabrina Harman court-martial for the Abu Ghraib abuses, the military judge and prosecutor would not allow the words "Guantanamo"

---

1 See also Todd Gitlin, "David Riesman: Thoughtful Pragmatist," *Chronicle of Higher Education*, May 24, 2002.

and "Afghanistan" to be mentioned in any testimony. Perhaps both were following their inner-directed gyroscopes that the Army should not be put on trial, and only the soldier was on trial. Their publicly stated reasons were that the abuses at Abu Ghraib had no connection to abuses at Guantanamo and Afghanistan. In any case, Harman's defense hinged on the fact that she and the other so-called "rotten apples" did not dream up the abuse on their own but were following unlawful techniques that had "migrated" from US installations at Gitmo and in Afghanistan. When I mentioned on the witness stand that these abusive techniques did, indeed, originate in and migrated from Gitmo and Afghanistan, the military judge stopped the trial and asked the jury to leave the courtroom. I was startled! He argued with the defense attorney, Frank Spinner, at length as to whether I should be permitted to say this in open court. The judge demanded to know my evidence. Spinner responded that it came from a US government reported authored by James Schlesinger. The prosecutor argued that the Schlesinger Report is not a bona fide learned treatise, and is inadmissible as evidence. Spinner argued and cited the UCMJ (Uniform Code of Military Justice) that government reports are considered on par with learned treatises. This "hanging judge," as he was called by the courtroom staff (the phrase means simply that he was leaning toward the government's position), was put in the difficult position of adhering to his rigid and laudable love for the Army, the demands of his role to be rigidly objective, and considering the prosecutor's claim that statements in a US government report on Abu Ghraib might not true. The judge chose to allow my testimony, and the jury was called in. When I repeated my citation from this report, the prosecutor again objected, and this time the judge sent me out of the courtroom. I was genuinely perplexed at all this drama over a simple claim that is verified in the government's own reports,, but convinced myself again that a courtroom is nothing like a classroom. They argued some more, and eventually I was called back in and allowed to state an obvious truth which is verified by multiple sources, that the abusive techniques migrated from Gitmo and Afghanistan to Abu Ghraib and were part of a widespread pattern, not an idiosyncrasy dreamed up by the low-ranking soldiers. By this point, the jury was clearly attentive — because they also noticed the drama over a simple sentence — and the testimony visibly registered on their facial expressions. Harman received the lightest sentence of all the seven defendants in the Abu Ghraib scandal.

The parallel to the Operation Iron Triangle case is the following: The trial of the accused soldier, Corey Clagett, was cancelled and he made a plea bargain in which he pleaded guilty in order to avoid the possibility of a life sentence without parole. This situation is much more dramatic than asking the jury or a witness to leave the courtroom so as to avoid the disclosure of painful truths that would, indeed, albeit still metaphorically, put the Army on trial. The fact that Clagett's trial by military jury was cancelled meant that his Brigade Commander, who was scheduled to testify in the trial in exchange for immunity from prosecution, would not have to and did not testify concerning the strange and new ROE that he supposedly issued. There is no need to question the motives of any of the attorneys or officials involved in any of these decisions regarding the trial. All the various actors in the legal drama were doing their jobs as they saw them. Typically, judges and opposing attorneys jockey as to what information will be disclosed versus withheld from open trial. Based upon my experience as an expert witness, I can conclude that only a small fraction of the overall evidence is ever used during a trial; a smaller portion makes it through the filter of adversarial procedure and cross-examination; and the tiniest portion makes it through media filters to the public at large, the real "jury of one's peers." And an important aside is that I observed journalists in the Fort Hood courtroom compete with each other ferociously to be the first ones to "break the story" for that day's proceedings prior to lunch, but they rarely returned after lunch. The trials were held methodically from 8 am to 5 pm with a very short break for lunch, but journalists were uniformly present for a miniscule portion of the day's events. I was surprised that many journalists lacked even the minimal amount of what Thorstein Veblen called "idle curiosity" — since they were being paid to be at the trials for a week anyway, it is difficult to imagine what stopped them from following the trials more closely. Perhaps it is for this reason that the public is often shocked and outraged by verdicts. It is usually not privy to the process that leads to the verdicts and sentences, and the media is not as inner-directed about its obligations to capture the news as the public might imagine.

Yet the sworn affidavits and other documents that were made available to me by the government so that I could prepare to testify did not disappear even if the trial did vanish. The sworn statements now became "research data" in my more familiar domain of academic sociology. There is something truly wondrous about the transformation of these legal documents into data in the context of Army as well as American, inner-directed principles. A sworn statement is a solemn, legal document, admissible as evidence in trials and also the starting point for testimony, discovery, and cross examination. The Army's judicial system mandates that both the prosecutorial and defense teams have access to sworn statements. The First Amendment of the US Constitution is interpreted to mean that the government does not hold a copyright to the statements, because they belong to "the people." In these regards, it is clear that inner-directed standards derived from the Constitution still hold in the United States, which truly may be regarded as a free and open society in comparison with many other societies.

In quoting from the sworn statements as research data, I have kept the misspelled words, the colloquial expressions, the military jargon, and in sum, all the data as it exists without any changes. I felt that this was important for historical purposes, and also because the minute details of what the soldiers and officers said, wrote, and felt reveals aspects of the case whose importance may not be immediately evident but whose importance may come to be realized in the future. Some of the statements also include questions from the investigators as well as answers by the soldiers. Some are typed and some are handwritten. When read in sequential order over the course of three different time periods, the statements offer insight into the process of the social construction of the reality that was finally presented by the Army. At the same time, the statements offer insight into social constructions of reality the Army rejected.

In this book, I avoid scrupulously issues and questions as to what "really" happened or the "real" motivations of any of the actors. I accept from the outset the sociological premise that "reality" is socially constructed. Lawyers share this assumption, only they call it "building a case." Reality, whatever it is, can only be known through representations, and it never speaks for itself. There is no need to investigate or cite the many learned treatises on "reality" in sociology, philosophy, or related fields, which often come across as incomprehensible even to learned experts. The pragmatic, and important, point is simply this: The soldiers were apparently convinced that they were ordered to follow an ROE that compelled them to kill every military-aged Iraqi male on sight. Was the ROE lawful or unlawful, and if it was unlawful, who was responsible for following it?

One cannot escape the social construction of reality even in pursuing these pragmatic questions. By strict, inner-directed, gyroscopic standards, this new ROE was unlawful. However, it is well known that the Bush Administration has opted for malleable standards of what is lawful versus unlawful with regard to the Geneva Conventions. Ironically, this Republican, and ostensibly conservative, administration has used other-directed approaches to the laws of warfare. And when it comes to the doctrine of command responsibility, the situation seems to be even more flexible.

For example, at the Kordic trial at The Hague, as at all the other trials at the International Criminal Tribunal for the Former Yugoslavia (ICTY), the central issue was the doctrine of command responsibility. I know from personal observation and experience at this trial that the judges interpreted this doctrine to mean that a commander (civilian or military) was responsible for the war crimes committed by subordinates, even if the commander did not directly order or even know of the unlawful behavior by the subordinates. The ICTY took its cues from the Nuremberg trials and the Yamashita case, and pronounced that commanders were responsible even if they did not pull the trigger or give the order, by virtue of being commanders who should have known and should have taken steps to prevent the commission of crimes by their subordinates. Because I am not a lawyer, I am less interested in the legal precedents or consequences of the doctrine of command responsibility, and because I am a sociologist, I am more interested in the night-versus-day difference in US military courts-martial regarding the way that this doctrine is socially constructed. US military judges routinely hold the opposite standard, that it is the low-ranking soldier's duty to disobey an unlawful order.

The contrast in perceptions of responsibility for war crimes could not be more pronounced. At The Hague, the former President of Yugoslavia, Slobodan Milosevic, as well as many other high-ranking commanders, were put on trial for war crimes under the doctrine of command responsibility. In the United States, low-ranking soldiers were court-martialed under the principle enshrined in the UCMJ that obedience to unlawful orders is not a defense. Both attitudes are inspired by the Nuremberg trials, albeit in starkly divergent ways. The ICTY seems to reject the excuse for World War II atrocities, namely, "We didn't know," and insists that the commander should have known what his or her subordinates did unlawfully. The US military system seems to reject the excuse for World War II atrocities, namely, "We were just following orders," and insists that low-ranking soldiers are responsible for obeying unlawful orders. Which approach is more just? I will always remember one of the ICTY judges, Justice Patrick Lipton Robinson, saying to me, while I was on the witness stand, that perhaps both approaches are extreme and the most just perspective lies somewhere between these two extremes. This is an issue that will be resolved by judges, jurists, and legal scholars, and I will not venture into their domain. The more important point is that inner-directed, universal, gyroscopic standards for these crucial issues do not exist.

However, as a sociologist, I take note of the pragmatic consequences of the US approach to war crimes, which typically is to prosecute low-ranking soldiers for failure to disobey unlawful orders in military courts-martial rather than resorting to international tribunals that could prosecute high-ranking civilian and military leaders. This approach leads to a kind of Freudian compulsion to repeat historical errors since the Vietnam War such that commanders sometimes establish unlawful ROE that lead to "search and destroy" missions or wanton killing of civilians, and commanders generally escape responsibility for such policies. More importantly, American society as a whole is not compelled to examine or be responsible for the unlawful policies that are established in its name, because the resulting trials do not focus on the author of the unlawful ROE, but on the failures of the low-ranking soldiers.

From a narrowly legalistic point of view, the objection can be made that US officers have been reprimanded for abuses committed at Abu Ghraib and elsewhere, which was a point raised by the prosecutor in Harman's trial. But a written reprimand for an officer cannot be compared realistically to a prison sentence and dishonorable discharge for the low-ranking soldier. One could object that some officers, albeit not many, were put on trial, such as Captain Medina in the My Lai case and Lieutenant Colonel Steven Jordan in the Abu Ghraib case — but both were found not guilty, and both used the defense that they did not know or did not order the crimes committed by their subordinates. This defense would not and typically did not work at the ICTY. There seems to be no way to escape the conclusion that the doctrine of command responsibility is not a real, gyroscopic, rigid principle in the US military.

I seek to avoid legal or political considerations of the doctrine of command responsibility. In other words, I do not recommend and I do not consider in this book options such as impeaching the President or prosecuting the Brigade Commander who issued the unlawful order in this case or any other similar option. I also do not question the conviction of the accused in this case and do not argue for or against anyone's guilt or innocence in relation to the charges that were leveled. It is not necessarily true that either the US or European approach to war crimes, or any legal approach alone, will actually lessen the frequency of such crimes in the future.

My goal is to inform the reader of what occurred during Operation Iron Triangle in relation to the new ROE, and to try to engage in dialogue and imaginary discussion the readers I will never meet in person. In Riesman's words, "to be alone with a book, is to be alone in a new way." I have taken to heart Riesman's example as a mentor, which was to minimize lecturing and maximize discussion. It seems that the chief points for this imaginary discussion are the following: If the inner-directed type is fading away and is being replaced with the more shallow and malleable other-directed type, what will happen to the Geneva Conventions and the notion of the rules of war? It seems that the Geneva Conventions are already being perceived more as a quaint throwback to the past, and an impediment to effective warfare, and less as a rigid, gyroscopic principle that should never be weakened. The other-directed type is more interested in appearing moral, seeming to be just, and less committed to being moral and just vis-à-vis unshakeable standards. Riesman felt that society could never go back to being predominantly inner-directed, and that American society would become increasingly other-directed, which means, mindful of the approval of peers, media, and public opinion. Was he correct? Is there a way out of his seemingly gloomy prophecy?

I am grateful to David Riesman's inspiration in writing this book, and to my colleagues at Texas A&M University for comments on earlier drafts, Larry Oliver, John McDermott and David Rosen. Many attorneys from the several trials in which I served as expert witness taught me insights that went into this book: Paul Bergrin, Captain Jonathan Crisp, Captain Scott Dunn, Captain Catherine Krull, Mitko Naumovski, Captain Sasha Rutizer, Frank Spinner, and Captain Patsy Takemura, My research assistants and doctoral students were also helpful with regard to research and feedback: Ryan Ashley Caldwell, Keith Kerr, and Ronald Lorenzo. I am especially grateful to the research assistance of Rachel Romero. I am also grateful to the US Army prosecutorial and defense teams for making data available to me. Finally, acknowledgement is made of the elaboration of some previously published sociological theorizing regarding torture and abuse in Stjepan G. Mestrovic and Ronald Lorenzo, "Durkheim's Concept of Anomie and the Abuse at Abu Ghraib," *Journal of Classical Sociology*, Volume 8(2), May 2008 and Ryan Ashley Caldwell and Stjepan G. Mestrovic, "The Role of Gender in Expressive Abuse at Abu Ghraib," *Cultural Sociology*, Volume 2(3), November 2008. Thanks also to Ivy Mestrovic for her insights.

Chapter 1. Introducing an Apparently New Form of Combat

Terrorism was the subject of two scholarly conferences held at the John Jay College of Criminal Justice in New York City in May and November of 2006. In his keynote speech at the May conference, former senator and presidential candidate Senator Gary Hart made several points which, over the course of the year, came to take on special significance for this book and for issues related to terrorism, detention, law, and an apparently new form of combat. By November of 2006, I would be called to serve as an expert witness in a case that involved the murder of prisoners taken during one of these new raids.

First, Senator Hart said that, as a member of the 9/11 Commission, he was disappointed that the Administration had ignored most of the Commission's recommendations for making the United States safer from terrorists. One must keep in mind that in May of 2006, the Republicans controlled all three branches of the US government. Second, he claimed that military actions by the United States in the future would be less like conventional wars of the past and more like "surgical" police actions. Targets would be identified in precise locations, and the "bad guys" would be neutralized quickly and efficiently. Third, and in reference to present-day terrorist enemies of the United States, he wondered out loud, "Why do they hate us?"

Little did I know, as I sat in that conference room in Manhattan, in proximity to and in the shadow of the ruins from the terrorist attack that occurred on 9/11, that an incident was occurring in Iraq that would bring Senator Hart's words to life. On May 9, 2006, a "surgical" operation called Operation Iron Triangle was being conducted near Samarra, Iraq. (It would be an interesting digression to pursue the issue of how medical and military vocabularies overlap, as in "surgical air strikes," "operations," and so on.)

In this incident, soldiers from the 101st Airborne Division of the United States Army were ordered to kill every military-aged male that they encountered at a target they named Objective Murray.

Did this order imply that no military-aged male was to be left alive? Did the order imply that the perceived enemy was supposed to show hostile intent in order to qualify as a target? Was every Iraqi male on the island simply designated as hostile, whether or not he felt or showed hostility toward US soldiers? Above all: *Was this a lawful order, and was it part of a lawful policy?*

Ambiguity haunts this order and the story that unfolded as soldiers tried to carry it out, from the pre-raid pep talk to the ensuing plea bargains and one court-martial. Throughout the year 2006, the news media reported on several similar massacres committed by US soldiers and Marines at places like Haditha, Hamadiya, Baghdad, and elsewhere. The news was full of stories of US soldiers as well as contractors from Blackwater opening fire on noncombatants, with the United States frequently claiming that the Americans were following "rules of engagement" (ROE). Thus, the ambiguous incident known as Operation Iron Triangle is not an exception and may be perceived as part of a pattern.

Various soldiers and Marines were being charged with murder throughout the years 2006 and 2007 for their actions during some of these operations — including four soldiers who took part in Operation Iron Triangle. The problem lies in "connecting the dots" among seemingly disparate events and linking them to the issue of ROE. These connections are not obvious to the information media or the public.

On November 10, 2006, I returned to New York for the second conference on terrorism. Nine days later, I was asked to serve as an expert witness for the defense in the court-martial of PFC Corey Clagett, who, along with three other Army soldiers, was accused of pre-meditated murder in the deaths of three prisoners who were taken captive in Iraq during Operation Iron Triangle on May 9, 2006.

The most stunning part of the case was that the accused soldiers claimed they were following Rules of Engagement (ROE) which ordered them to kill on sight all the men at Objective Murray. An order may or may not be idiosyncratic to some extent based upon the officer who gives it, but a Rule of Engagement is a matter of public policy. Were the killings that resulted from the ROE murder, or were the soldiers following orders that were part of the new combat technique that Senator Hart had foretold? Closely related questions are the following: Do the orders they were following qualify as ROE in the Army's traditional way of conducting war? Are the "new" ROE truly new? Why would the United States establish a military policy that violates the Geneva Conventions? Were these new ROE a de facto policy handed down verbally or do documents exist to suggest a legal shift in the laws of warfare?

There is no clear or easy answer to any of these or related questions. Consider, for example, the wording of Article 3 of the Geneva Conventions, which was handed down on June 29, 2006, by the United States Supreme court in *Hamdan* v. *Rumsfeld* as being applicable as a matter of law to the conflict with Al Qaeda:

> In the case of armed conflict not of an international character occurring in the territory of one of the High Contracting Parties, each Party to the conflict shall be bound to apply, as a minimum, the following provisions:
>
> Persons taking no active part in the hostilities, including members of armed forces who have laid down their arms and those placed *hors de combat* by sickness, wounds, detention, or any other cause, shall in all circumstances be treated humanely, without any adverse distinction founded on race, color, religion or faith, sex, birth or wealth, or any other similar criteria.
>
> To this end, the following acts are and shall remain prohibited at any time and in any place whatsoever with respect to the above-mentioned persons:
>
> Violence to life and person, in particular murder of all kinds, mutilation, cruel treatment and torture;
>
> Taking of hostages;
>
> Outrages upon personal dignity, in particular, humiliating and degrading treatment;
>
> (d) The passing of sentences and the carrying out of executions without previous judgment pronounced by a regularly constituted court affording all the judicial guarantees which are recognized as indispensable by civilized peoples
>
> 2. The wounded and sick shall be collected and cared for.

The meaning and ramifications of Supreme Court decisions as well as the Geneva Conventions are debated by legal scholars, journalists, and the public as a whole. Ostensibly, *Hamdan* v. *Rumsfeld* concerned the rights of Osama bin-Laden's driver to a fair trial at Guantanamo, but the Court's ruling went far beyond this narrow issue and ruled that the third Geneva Convention applies to the entire "war on terror."[1] A memorandum from the Office of the Secretary of Defense dated 7 July 2006, sent to all the secretaries of military departments and various other military commanders, reads in part:

> The Supreme Court has determined that Common Article 3 to the Geneva Conventions of 1949 applies as a matter of law to the conflict with Al Qaeda. The Court found that the military commissions as constituted by the Department of Defense are not consistent with Common Article 3.... You will ensure that all DoD personnel adhere to these standards. In this regard, I request that you promptly review all relevant directives, regula-

1 www.supremecourtus.gov/opinions/05pdf/05-184.pdf

tions, policies, practices, and procedures under your purview to ensure
that they comply with the standards of Common Article 3.

It seems fairly certain that a "surgical" police action aimed at persons
who are not hostile would qualify as a violation of these standards. The present analysis is a study in sociology, which means that the social and cultural
implications of what appear to be narrow issues in military and international law shall be examined. Thus, regarding the limited context of what
occurred during Operation Iron Triangle in relation to this Supreme Court
decision and Article 3 of the Geneva Conventions, it seems clear that one
Iraqi male was killed in a manner that was deemed by the Army as lawful
under the new ROE but the killing may not have been lawful under the traditional laws of warfare; three prisoners were taken and killed in a manner
that undoubtedly violated Article 3 of the Geneva Conventions as well as
various provisions of the Uniform Code of Military Justice; and one prisoner
was allowed to live. In the larger, social context, one should note that prior
to this decision handed down by the Supreme Court on June 29, 2006, the
Bush Administration argued that many of the Geneva Conventions did not
apply to the conflict with Al Qaeda, while the Supreme Court ruled, albeit
late in the conflict, that they do apply.[1] Thus, in a larger context, the abuse
at Abu Ghraib and the irregular military commissions that were established
at Guantanamo Bay to try alleged terrorists were unlawful in relation to the
Geneva Conventions. The social significance of this widespread ambiguity
regarding which provisions of the Geneva Conventions did, did not, do or do
not apply and where they did, did not, do or do not apply is that soldiers as
well as ordinary citizens are confused as to the meaning of what is permissible versus forbidden in the current war on terror.

All these connections — terrorism and the conferences, New York City
and 9/11, murder and new ROE, Abu Ghraib and Guantanamo — and more
seemingly tangential connections to the Battle of Mogadishu which involved
similarly "surgical" operations that went awry in the year 1993, the 101st Airborne Division, and the commander Michael Steele (to mention a few at this
point; they will be developed more extensively later), are part of an intricate
synchronicity of ideas, dates, places, and events. Far from being some sort of
postmodern pastiche, all these diverse events and themes are bound together
by threads including the third Geneva Convention and the ROE.

The ROE must incorporate and be in line with this and other Geneva
Conventions and protocols to which the United States is a signatory. This
connection is not obvious, given that both the media and the government
repeatedly refer to prisoners — who have rights under the Geneva Conven-

---

1 See, for example, Seymour M. Hersh, *Chain of Command: The Road from 9/11 to Abu Ghraib* (New
York: Harper Collins, 2004); Richard Falk, Irene Gendzier and Robert Jay Lifton (eds.)
Crimes of War: Iraq (New York: Nation Books, 2006), among many other sources.

tions — from Abu Ghraib to Guantanamo to Operation Iron Triangle — as "detainees." The concept of "detainee" was invented, along with other euphemisms (such as PUC, or "person under control"), in order to avoid confronting the consequences of the Bush Administration's claim that the Geneva Conventions do not apply to enemies in the war on terror.

There exist other connections in this unhappy collage of events and themes. First, the 9/11 Commission made solid recommendations for taking political, economic, agricultural, and other widespread actions to protect the United States from terrorist attacks. Not only were their recommendations ignored until the Democratic-led Congress took over in January of 2007, but the Administration focused almost exclusively on military solutions to the terrorist threat, namely, killing or capturing as many so-called terrorists as possible outside the United States. The Administration's reasoning seemed to be that it was better to take the fight to the terrorists on their turf than to allow them to bring the fight to the United States. But here's the rub: Who was to decide on the battlefield whether a soldier should kill or capture the enemy? How does one recognize the enemy if he or she is not wearing a traditional uniform? Is the enemy one who expresses hostility, or who is merely tagged as the enemy prior to exhibiting any hostility? Under the traditional ROE, soldiers are permitted to engage an enemy who shows hostile intent but are required to take prisoners if the enemy is actively surrendering or does not show hostile intent.

Under the new ROE, the decision to kill versus capture is problematic. If the enemy is captured, are the soldiers disobeying the new ROE? Why bother taking prisoners, and if prisoners are taken — why not kill them anyway? To repeat, the killing of prisoners is clearly unlawful, but in trying to understand why and how highly-trained and motivated soldiers would engage in such unlawful behavior one is obligated to take the role of the other into account.

Far from being idle academic questions, these were precisely the issues that emerged in the cases of the four soldiers who were accused of murder in Operation Iron Triangle. The first sergeant on the mission, Eric Geressy, asked over the field radio why the soldiers had bothered to take prisoners since the new ROE stipulated that all military-aged males on the scene should have been killed, and his broadcast was heard far and wide over the battlefield. His remark is a chilling echo of LT Calley's infamous remark at My Lai concerning prisoners, "Why haven't you wasted them yet?" Perhaps Geressy was thinking out loud for the entire military unit, but he was also echoing an incoherent policy. Minutes after he broadcast this question over the radio, some of the soldiers killed three of the four prisoners.

If the new ROE violate the Geneva Conventions as well as the US military Laws of Armed Conflict, then it becomes difficult conceptually to shift all of the blame onto low-ranking soldiers who were trying to follow orders. Of course, the legalistic reply is that the soldier has an obligation to disobey an unlawful order. And in practice, US military courts-martial routinely do not recognize obedience to orders as a legal defense. The more important point is that society cannot and typically does not expect the soldier to be a legal scholar or expert in general and especially not in the heat of battle. On the contrary, and as articulated by the world's first professor of sociology, the French sociologist Emile Durkheim, society expects the soldier to obey orders and to be ready to sacrifice his or her life on behalf of society:

> Now, the first quality of a soldier is a sort of impersonality not to be found anywhere in civilian life to the same degree. He must be trained to set little value upon himself, since he must be prepared to sacrifice himself upon being ordered to do so. Even aside from such exceptional circumstances, in peace time and in the regular exercise of his profession, discipline requires him to obey without question and sometimes even without understanding.[1]

Second, the vision of the surgical police action that Senator Hart described seems in many ways to have been the model for the mission that was attempted during Operation Iron Triangle as well as for the daring raid in Mogadishu in the year 1993 that was immortalized in the book and film "Black Hawk Down." Perhaps it is true to some extent that a "new" form of warfare has already taken hold in the United States Army, even if the public seems mostly unaware of this fact.

Senator Hart apparently knew that the new technique was in use, but there seems to have been no open debate in Congress, the media, or any other public forum for this apparent shift in policy. One may argue that the murders committed during Operation Iron Triangle were an isolated case, not an illustration of existing policy. But that is a fundamental question: is the new policy de facto or a formally established policy? Moreover, in the formal, bureaucratic organization that is the United States Army, and in the rational-legal basis for democracy in America, ROE are required to be approved all the way up the chain of command. The brigade commander apparently *verbally* issued the new ROE to kill all military-aged males on sight — but who approved his decision? Who ordered him to give this unlawful order? If the ROE issued by the brigade commander was unlawful, and constitutes an isolated incident, why wasn't the brigade commander prosecuted instead of or in addition to four low-ranking soldiers? How many times in the history of the United States military have military commanders been held accountable for issuing unlawful orders? One may wish to retort that the brigade commander couldn't possibly have meant that prisoners should be killed. But a

---

1 Emile Durkheim, *Suicide: A Study in Sociology* (New York: Free Press [1897] 1951, p. 234).

non-prisoner, an unarmed man in his seventies, was also killed during this mission, and his death was not deemed to be a murder or to be problematic in any way by the United States Army. Yet he showed no hostile intent and according to traditional ROE he should not have been killed. Regardless of what the new ROE intended, it becomes clear from dozens of sworn affidavits that soldiers could not fully make out the difference between the "lawful" killing of the one elderly, unarmed Iraqi and the three restrained prisoners — the ROE was to kill every military-age male in the area.

The Iron Triangle case suggests that the new ROE has severe limitations. These include the fact that the choice of targets depends heavily upon informants, who are presumed to give accurate information. But given the language and cultural barriers between Americans and foreign informants, this presumption is open to question. I learned later that the Iraqi soldiers who were present during the joint US–Iraqi Army mission were extremely angry at the US soldiers for killing the elderly man while performing under the new ROE; these Iraqi soldiers were whisked away by helicopter prior to the subsequent killings of the three prisoners.

The negative reaction by Iraqi soldiers to the killings at Objective Murray suggests strongly that the Americans may have killed the wrong person. The multiplication of similar "mistakes," as reported in the media, had a counterproductive effect on any effort at winning the hearts and minds of the Iraqi people. News accounts revealed that soldiers involved in incidents from Haditha to Baghdad were claiming that they were following similar new ROE, so that in their view they were not committing murder. It seems that the more the US relied on such surgical police actions, the more insurgency and hostile action toward US soldiers increased.

By the end of the year 2006 the so-called "insurgency" was dominating the news, and was occurring in the midst of what some were calling a civil war in Iraq. The words "insurgent" and "insurgency" are euphemisms, like "detainees" and "Ant-Iraqi Fighters" (AIF) which do not hold a clear meaning. "Insurgents" could be terrorists, resistance fighters, common criminals, members of militias, various factions in civil wars, or other entities. For historical purposes, it should be noted that the Bush Administration denied repeatedly that the civil war was occurring even as it unfolded and grew steadily worse into the year 2008.

Furthermore, Senator Hart's statement also did not clarify whether the police action should be one of killing versus killing *or* capturing the enemy. This ambiguity in policy and ROE at the highest levels of the chain of command seems to have had disastrous effects for the soldiers who attempted to carry out their mission. They seemed genuinely perplexed by the decision to take prisoners when the ROE seemed to order them to kill the perceived enemy on sight.

The legal status of such "police" actions in warfare seems problematic in relation to both the Geneva Conventions and the LOAC (Laws of Armed Conflict). As noted previously, the Third Geneva Convention prohibits any military action against "persons taking no active part in the hostilities." Surgical strikes against persons who are designated as hostile but who, in fact, show no hostility seem to be obviously unlawful from a common sense point of view. Women, children, and innocent civilians in general may be present at the targets chosen for such action, and non-combatants are supposedly protected by the rules of war from being targeted. Women and children were present during Operation Iron Triangle, and their lives were spared by the US soldiers. But the more important point, as the sworn affidavits show clearly, is that the US soldiers on the mission encountered no resistance or hostility whatsoever.

At Haditha, women and children were apparently killed during episodes of "grazing fire" (which was also used during Operation Iron Triangle), episodes which are apparently lawful under the new ROE but which seem to violate the Geneva Conventions. "Grazing" or "suppressive" fire means US soldiers shooting directly into or in the vicinity of buildings or structures they are ordered to "clear" prior to entering the structures. The sworn statements regarding this mission suggest that this sort of unprovoked firing into structures is a common practice by US soldiers. The tactical function of this practice seems to be to reduce risk to US soldiers, but it raises the risk of killing non-combatants in the structures. In sum, and in abstract military theory, the chaotic reality that the Iron Triangle case revealed demonstrates that the police action model seems too neat and tidy to serve as guidance in a real-life situation.

Third, "Why do they hate us?" It is no longer clear to whom the word "they" refers. Right after 9/11, the question was rhetorical and was aimed at the terrorists who attacked New York City. In the year 2008, following five years of war — longer than World War II — and after the Abu Ghraib and Guantanamo fiascos, it seems that "they" could refer to millions of people throughout the world who oppose the human rights violations which have been part of the manner with which the US is conducting its global "war on terror." It was clear from the context that Senator Hart meant for his question to be rhetorical; the implicit reply was that there was no reason to hate Americans. But when one puts together Abu Ghraib, Guantanamo, and the new ROE to kill people on sight, a reasonable person may speculate that various people could have arrived at the decision to hate Americans as a result of "loose" ROE.

In any event, the question is important even if the answers are not clear. The question should become part of a wider public policy debate along with the meaning of the apparently new ROE. For with orders to shoot all military-age males on sight and to open fire on buildings before entering them, from Iraq and Afghanistan to Somalia and possibly elsewhere, some people have concluded that the true global threat in the global war on terror seems to be America itself.

Finally, what precisely is fresh about the supposedly new form of combat that relies on so-called surgical police action? Such actions have been around for a long time. Police departments seem to use some variations of this technique within the United States on people presumed to be domestic criminals, and sometimes with disastrous consequences. (Consider, for example, the attack on the Branch Davidians near Waco, Texas.)

One of the most famous military police actions occurred in Mogadishu, Somalia in 1991, as mentioned above. The book *Black Hawk Down*[1] emphasized that most of the residents of Mogadishu had already come to hate the US prior to the "police" action that took place, due to many previous similar incidents in which noncombatants were killed, strafed, or threatened. The truly "new" aspect seems to lie in the Rule of Engagement, not the technique, and more specifically in the order to kill on sight. The traditional rule to kill *or* capture an enemy who is exhibiting hostility is still old fashioned: the soldier is allowed to kill an enemy who shows hostile intent but is obligated to capture an enemy who is actively surrendering. This is part of the old ROE. What occurred on May 9, 2006 during Operation Iron Triangle was the result of a new ROE that was perceived by the soldiers as "strange," namely, to just kill the enemy on sight — minus the "or capture" — without taking into account whether hostile intent was shown by the enemy. Had they killed the five enemy targets on sight as they were ordered to do, it seems that none of the soldiers would have been accused of murder. Their actions would have been in accordance with the new ROE. But they killed one elderly person whom they perceived as an enemy, took four prisoners, and then killed three of the four captured prisoners. The soldiers thereby entered an ambiguous no-man's land between the new and the traditional rules of engagement.

The conceptual distinctions between warfare and murder, enemy combatants and prisoners, traditional ROE and new ROE, all became blurred. These and related ambiguities are the crux of the dilemma for the soldiers, for the story that will unfold in this book, and for public policy in the future.

Much of the story hinges on the tiny proposition "or," which, if taken seriously, obligates the soldier to follow the old-fashioned, traditional ROE but also makes the soldier seem derelict in duty for not following the new

---

1 Michael Bowden, *Black Hawk Down* (New York: Penguin, 1999).

ROE, which may assume the "or" but explicitly drops the proposition. This is the story of a public policy shift that is not fully public, from "kill or capture" to just "kill on sight."

Thus, questions this book will examine include:

- Why didn't the soldiers kill all the males on sight?
- Why did the soldiers spare the life of one of the prisoners?
- Why didn't the soldiers process all four of the captured males as prisoners?
- Why didn't the soldiers take five prisoners, since none of the men showed hostile intent?
- Why did the Army prosecute four soldiers for the deaths of three prisoners while it prosecuted no one for the death of the unarmed, elderly man?
- Why does the Army consistently fail to prosecute officers and civilian leaders for unlawful orders and policies, in contradistinction to precedents from Nuremberg to The Hague which are crystallized in the doctrine of command responsibility and which seek to punish the "big fish" in the commission of war crimes?

IMMERSION IN THE CASE

It was Sunday, November 19, 2006. A United States Army defense attorney named Captain Sasha Rutizer had telephoned me to ask if I would serve as an expert witness in sociology and psychology in the court-martial of Private First Class Corey Clagett. She was supposed to submit a list of potential witnesses to the government for approval on the following day. It was a similar last-minute rush regarding the courts-martial pertaining to Abu Ghraib in which I had testified previously for Javal Davis, Sabrina Harman, and Lynndie England at Ft. Hood, Texas. By now, I knew the drill: Rutizer would submit my name, along with the names of other potential witnesses, to the Commanding General of Ft. Campbell, Kentucky, for approval. He was the "convening authority" for setting a court-martial into motion, according to Army protocol as well as the Uniform Code of Military Justice (UCMJ). A similar procedure was followed by the CG (Commanding General) of Ft. Hood with regard to the trials of Abu Ghraib.

I asked for details about the case and soon realized that there were other, much more important similarities to the Abu Ghraib cases that were tried at Ft. Hood. The accused soldier, Private First Class Corey Clagett, was being charged with pre-meditated murder and conspiracy. Allegedly, he and three other soldiers had killed three suspected Al Qaeda "detainees" who were in their custody during a military operation, called Operation Iron Triangle, near the city of Samarra in Iraq. As usual, the US government was referring to prisoners of war as "detainees." The incident took place on May 9, 2006.

The attorney said that the soldiers were following a very explicit verbal order that was allegedly given by the regiment commander, Colonel Michael Steele: to kill every military-age Iraqi that they encountered.

I winced and gasped when I heard this. It sounded like the ghosts of the Vietnam War and its infamous search-and-destroy missions were rising up, including those from the massacre at My Lai.[1] Army defense attorney Sasha Rutizer added that this was the same Colonel Steele of Mogadishu fame. From the Vietnam era through the war in Somalia to the war in Iraq, the US military seemed to have a Freudian compulsion to repeat past mistakes and the American public was left out of the decision-making process and public policy debate — again.

Many of my students at Texas A & M University do not recognize the name "My Lai," and other massacres committed by American soldiers are even more obscure. For example, Son Thang was the Marine Corps equivalent of My Lai in Vietnam, as chronicled by the former military prosecutor and judge, Gary D. Solis in *Son Thang: An American War Crime*. At Son Thang, Marines who were part of "killer teams" were ordered to kill anyone they encountered, so they killed sixteen women and children. "There was no agreed definition [of the order], just that it meant to kill the enemy. The killer team had been told to 'Shoot first and ask questions later'."[2] Similarly, at No Gun Ri in Korea in 1950, US soldiers massacred unarmed, peaceful civilians who posed no threat to US forces.[3]

Going back further into history, Mark Twain was involved in the notorious case of General Frederick Funston, who ordered the massacre of prisoners during a raid in the Philippine–American War that lasted from 1899 to 1902. Twain's famous criticism of Funston's cowardice also raised questions about the reasons for American involvement in that war, which he regarded as a "quagmire" and as immoral.[4]

A careful reading of these and other accounts of similar massacres reveals that they were more than isolated incidents. Instead, the specific incidents of war crimes were parts of widespread policies to "search and destroy" anyone, including non-combatants. The point is that the incident at Samarra, which is the subject of this book, is *not* really new. The so-called new ROE that was used during Operation Iron Triangle is *not* really new. The incidents and policies are called "new" by those who do not know or who choose not to cite history.

---

1 Seymour Hersh, *My Lai-4: A Report on the Massacre and its Aftermath* (New York: Vintage, 1970).

2 Gary D. Solis, *Son Thang: An American War Crime* (New York: Bantam, 1997), p. ix.

3 See Charles Hanley, *The Bridge at No Gun Ri: A Hidden Nightmare from the Korean War* (New York: Henry Holt, 2001).

4 Mark Twain, "In Defence of General Funston," *North American Review* February 1901.

"Did Steele give the order in writing?" I asked. No, but many witnesses heard him give the order. And she added that the dozens of sworn statements made in writing by soldiers were consistent: the verbal order to kill on sight was given. Later, when I read the sworn statements, I was able to confirm that she was right. I never saw the real, written ROE (these are classified), but the sworn statements suggest that the soldiers perceived the verbal ROE as amounting to "kill every military-aged male on sight." It is worth digressing here to wonder out loud why the written version of the new ROE is kept secret and why I was told it is classified. Rules of engagement are supposed to be a matter of public policy.

Did the soldiers see the ROE or only hear them? CPT Rutizer gave me the phone number of a military attorney at Ft. Campbell who was an expert on ROE for the 101st Airborne Division. I telephoned him, and he was helpful with regard to some of my questions but evasive with regard to others. He said that there are several layers of ROE, from those issued by the Pentagon down to those issued by divisions and brigades, and finally to those practiced by soldiers. Many of these ROE are slightly different from each other, but supposedly all are approved by the chain of command. CPT Matt Lanseth emphasized that soldiers are repeatedly given verbal instructions of the ROE before going on a mission, but he tried to avoid the issue of written ROE. In fact, he said that he had not personally read the written version of the ROE that was used during Operation Iron Triangle.

In any event, CPT Rutizer saw no obstacle to proceeding with the trial even though the Army refused to disclose the written ROE, because the sworn statements are legal documents in themselves, and all of them verify that the unlawful ROE was given verbally. Sworn statements are admissible in court, and in fact are treated as the starting point for testimony. For the same reason, this book is based upon the sworn statements — which are considered as legal facts — even though they are only a part of the entire story.

Nevertheless, the secrecy of the ROE makes one wonder how the open trials would have been conducted. The short answer is that, of the four cases that were supposed to go to trial, only one actually did go to trial (that of SSG Girouard). Just as important, one wonders how soldiers can be punished for obeying or failing to obey lawful versus unlawful orders if they are not allowed to see them in writing and have to assume that the verbal orders given by their superiors are lawful orders. This is not only a legal issue — it is a common sense and public policy issue as well.

Yet Steele refused to testify at Clagett's Article 32 hearing (the equivalent of a civilian arraignment), and except for a written reprimand he would receive no punishment and would not be prosecuted. One should note that this tendency to prosecute low-ranking soldiers who follow unlawful orders but not to prosecute the superior officers who issue the orders is a clear tradition in the US military that can be traced back from Abu Ghraib to My Lai, Son Thang, No Gun Ri, and other similar cases. This tradition stands in sharp contrast to the prosecution of high-ranking military and civilian leaders at The Hague for war crimes committed in the former Yugoslavia under the doctrine of command responsibility. The doctrine of command responsibility holds that a commander is guilty of omission if he or she could or should have known that an order might lead to the commission of crimes by subordinates. In any event, the contents of the reprimand were never disclosed. In December of 2006, the military judge ordered Steele to testify at Clagett's trial, albeit Steele was given immunity from prosecution in exchange for his testimony against the low-ranking private. Similarly, in the trials of Abu Ghraib, the Commander of Military Intelligence, Colonel Thomas Pappas, was given immunity from prosecution in exchange for his testimony against some low-ranking soldiers. Why wasn't it the other way around? There seems to be a pattern here of the "grunts" in the United States taking all the blame and going to prison for questionable policy while officers are merely reprimanded.

Despite all this secrecy, the incident made it into the public domain to some extent via the information media. To be sure, the murders committed during Operation Iron Triangle were not covered as extensively as those at My Lai and Abu Ghraib. This may be part because the photographs from Iron Triangle were never leaked to the media (the sworn affidavits make references to photographs, but it is not clear whether the photographs still exist or were destroyed). If the soldiers were following the ROE as they perceived it, and were initially cleared of all wrongdoing, who or what happened that led someone to question their actions? How and why did the Army feel obliged to prosecute some of them? One may speculate that the Army felt compelled to prosecute to the extent that it would protect its image, but not necessarily to the extent that it would embarrass high-ranking officers and officials. It is as if the white-collar rule[1] applies to the Army as well as big corporations: White-collar crime is "invisible" and is more rarely published than crimes committed by blue-collar, ordinary, low-status persons.

Shortly after speaking with the defense attorney, I grasped further parallels to the Abu Ghraib cases: In both the Abu Ghraib abuse and the Iron Triangle murders, orders from high up in the chain of command were followed by soldiers who are trained to follow orders. Yet the lowest-ranking soldiers would become scapegoats for the effect of the unlawful orders. As

---

1 See the sociological classic on this topic, C. Wright Mills, *White Collar* (New York: Oxford University Press, 1951) and the earlier forerunner upon which it is based, Thorstein Veblen, *The Theory of the Leisure Class* (New York: Penguin, [1899] 2001).

the defense attorney spoke, and as I asked more questions, other similarities emerged. The soldiers involved in the Iron Triangle murders were confused as to what were lawful versus unlawful ROE. They knew that according to the old ROE it is unlawful to kill prisoners, but under the new ROE they were not sure if it was permissible to take prisoners.

The soldiers at Abu Ghraib were similarly confused as to lawful versus unlawful interrogation "techniques." The defense attorney volunteered the defense argument that a bad "command climate," which Steele might have created, might have contributed to the murders. This was similar to a phrase that Major General Fay had used to describe the social setting at Abu Ghraib, namely, a "poisoned social climate."[1]

Let me be clear about these similarities as well as differences: There is no public evidence that Colonel Pappas ordered soldiers to torture prisoners at Abu Ghraib. There is no public evidence that Colonel Steele ordered soldiers to murder prisoners near Samarra. Colonel Pappas issued ambiguous and new SOP (standard operating procedures) that set the stage for subsequent abuse according to the Army's own reports that were made public. Colonel Steele may have verbally issued ambiguous and new ROE that may have set the stage for the subsequent murders, although the Army's reports on Steele have not been made public.

Captain Rutizer said that the trial would begin on January 15, 2006. Two of the other accused soldiers would also be tried: William Hunsaker's trial was scheduled for February 5, and Raymond Girouard's was scheduled for March 5. I asked her to send me written material that described the incident as well as the command climate. She sent me scores of sworn statements. These were taken during three timeframes, on May 11, May 29, and at various dates in June 2006, and were submitted by all the soldiers who were on the mission.

The statements from each of the three timeframes give a different version of what happened, and the three versions vary dramatically. The first version is that the mission was accomplished and no crime was committed; the second version is that there were some irregularities in the mission; and the third version is that the four accused soldiers conspired to kill three prisoners but allowed one to live. Which version is correct?

That is a question that might have been settled, to some extent, during open trial — but only Girouard had a trial by jury, and by that time the other three defendants had signed plea bargains with the prosecution in exchange for testimony against Girouard. While this process of obtaining plea bargains in exchange for testimony is routine in criminal trials, and follows roughly

---

1 See S.G. Mestrovic, *The Trials of Abu Ghraib: An Expert Witness Account of Shame and Honor* (Boulder: Paradigm, 2007).

the paradigm known as the "prisoner's dilemma" in the social sciences (none of the defendants can be sure which if any of the others will stick to the original story and avoid betraying one or more of the others), it nevertheless precludes a truly open airing of what occurred according to a common sense perception. Obviously, three of the defendants had already been coerced into giving testimony that was stacked against the fourth. And COL Steele never testified in Girouard's trial, although he was scheduled to testify in Clagett's trial. Thus, the issue of the new ROE was never fully aired in public.

Just as important, the fact that there are three versions of what happened begs the question: Why did the story change? And why did the story change drastically, from soldiers being completely cleared of all wrongdoing to some soldiers being sent to prison?

To repeat, the focus of this book is less on the legal procedures or aspects of what occurred and more on the common sense perspectives, or more precisely the perspectives of what sociologists call the common or collective consciousness. Lawyers have their established procedures for fixing responsibility for crimes. But the sociological perspective holds that, ultimately, it is society that is responsible for what occurred, and in this case it is not clear that society had much knowledge of what was done in its name. Again, quoting Durkheim:

> An act is criminal when it offends strong and defined states of the collective consciousness. In other words, we must not say that an action shocks the common conscience because it is criminal, but rather that it is criminal because it shocks the common conscience. We do not reprove it because it is a crime, but it is a crime because we reprove it.[1]

This passage from Durkheim has inspired literally thousands of research studies on crime, but it is in some ways the opposite of what lawyers do in practice. Lawyers and judges seem to reprove acts because they are crimes, that is, because certain acts violate specific laws. But the sociological perspective, which is more in line with public opinion, examines why some laws are cited while others are not. In this case both the new ROE and the behavior of some of the soldiers were unlawful, but the public consciousness has precious little access to the new ROE so it has no realistic basis for a reaction.

As the trial dates approached, events began to turn suddenly. On January 9, 2007, Specialist Justin Graber (the fourth co-accused soldier) struck a deal with the prosecution in which he would be sentenced to nine months for aggravated assault in exchange for testimony against the others. In plain language, he confessed to a "mercy killing" of one of the three prisoners who were shot and who had not yet died when Graber came upon the scene. On January 11, 2007, the civilian defense attorney for Clagett, Mr. Paul Bergrin,

---

1 Emile Durkheim, *The Division of Labor in Society* (New York: Free Press, [1893] 1933, p. 81).

was indicted in New York City for charges relating to money laundering and prostitution. On that same day, William Hunsaker was sentenced to 18 years as part of a plea bargain with the prosecution, in exchange for testimony against Clagett and Girouard. Once the prosecutors had obtained promises of testimony in exchange for leniency, and Clagett's attorney had been arrested, the pressure was on Clagett to turn against his comrades in exchange for leniency. Clagett would never have his scheduled court-martial. As of Martin Luther King Jr. Day (January 15) in 2007, two of the accused soldiers had pleaded guilty to lesser charges and the two remaining trials (for Clagett and Girouard) had been postponed.

From one point of view, this rapid and surprising turns of events can be construed as the normal procedure that prosecutors use to make defendants "roll over" on other defendants. On the other hand, the tendency to reach plea bargains also has the effect — whether it is unintended or deliberate is open to debate — of preventing cases from going to public trial by a military panel of jurors. Not going to trial in this instance also meant that the issues surrounding the ROE would not be publicly aired and would not become accessible to the news media.

On January 18, 2007 Bergrin was released from jail on a $1 million bond. On January 19, 2007, Bergrin announced that Clagett would plead guilty to some of the charges against him, because Graber and Hunsaker would testify against him as part of their plea bargains. On January 25, 2007 Clagett was sentenced by the judge, COL Theodore Dixon, to 18 years of prison for premeditated murder and related crimes — there was no trial, only a court session to accept a plea bargain.

Why would soldiers make plea bargains for such severe sentences? CPT Rutizer explained to me that all of the accused were facing maximum sentences of life imprisonment without parole, and that in the Army no parole truly means no parole. The Army apparently operates under a genuine "truth in sentencing" system. Given this state of affairs, an eighteen-year sentence is preferable to the sentence that could have been imposed following a trial.

CHAPTER 2. LAYING OUT THE CONCEPTUAL TOOLS FOR THE SOCIAL ANATOMY THAT FOLLOWS

In making my analysis for this book, I have relied upon both psychological and sociological approaches, but I am also mindful of legal issues. These social scientific approaches do not encroach upon and are distinct from the legal and military issues and approaches that are involved in courts-martial. In other words, I am not concerned in this analysis with the legal guilt or innocence of the accused or other suspects or any of the actors in this drama. However, the social scientific perspective does comment on the psychology and sociology of law, social climate, command climate, personality, individual as well as social character, and social behavior, all of which are relevant for evaluating various understandings of what occurred with regard to the incident of May 9 and subsequent developments. I focus more on the fact that the Army resolved these apparent crimes through the ancient method of obtaining confessions from the accused rather than presenting factual evidence in open court in separate trials for all of the accused.

These and related issues are sociological and psychological, and they involve public policy in the name of a public that is forbidden to see that very policy (the secret new ROE) and that hardly noticed the incident. Moreover, social scientists take the approach that reality is socially constructed through the interaction of multiple participants, ranging from the soldiers themselves to the various investigators, interrogators, psychiatrists, special agents, lawyers, convening authorities, and others who become involved in any discourse, including the discourse at hand.

Moreover, sociology, and to a lesser extent psychology, are such vast and untamed domains that it is impossible to refer to anything like "the" sociological or psychological theory of anything. Instead, these disciplines choose from traditions established by Freud, Durkheim, Weber, Marx, Simmel, and Veblen, among others, and an even more crowded field of more recent theorists such as Parsons, Riesman, Baudrillard, Foucault, and others. The sheer quantity of different theories and theorists is disconcerting to the student in an introductory course. In order to minimize the disorientation of this wilderness effect of the social sciences, I shall limit myself primarily to relying upon Durkheim and Riesman in this analysis.

An excellent entry point into the differences between the divergent styles typically used by lawyers versus sociologists in analyzing crime is offered by David Riesman, a graduate of Harvard Law School who worked for a time as an assistant district attorney in Buffalo, New York. He went on to become an eminent sociologist, best known for his best-selling treatise in sociology, *The Lonely Crowd.* Riesman observes that "no pure theory of law has won anything like universal assent,"[1] because the law is based upon precedents, whereas sociology does strive for general, even grand, theories of how societies operate universally. Moreover, "one can graduate from law school without having ever read any major abstract or theoretical works in the social sciences — neither Plato nor Max Weber nor Durkheim nor Marx." The lawyer builds his or her reputation by winning cases, whereas the sociologist builds his or her reputation by explaining events in relation to universal principles. Riesman bemoans "how hard it is to interest law students in knowledge for its own sake" (p. 474). Lawyers believe that "Sociology is a goal or an attitude in the minds of men; law exists *out there*" (p. 475), but Riesman believes that this perceived difference is exaggerated.

Another difference, seen clearly in this and other legal cases, is that lawyers "play it by ear" and rely on their gifts as showmen (or women) in the courtroom whereas the sociologist patiently points to traditions and social "laws" of determinism. Thus, lawyers reading this book would focus on proving or disproving the relative guilt or innocence of the accused in relation to "the law," whereas the sociologist will focus on the interpersonal drama for any soldier in any similar case requiring him or her to decipher and respond to an unlawful order. "Moreover," according to Riesman, "the lawyer's 'play it by ear' tendency supports the wish most of us have, as adults, that we will not have to learn anything really new" (p. 476).

The analysis of sworn affidavits in the remainder of this book demonstrates clearly that lawyers and investigators were "playing by ear" the decision as to which way they would go: whether they would charge the commanders or charge the grunts for the crimes that occurred. The sociologist is able to predict that the white-collar, leisure class structure of the Army and

---

1 David Riesman, *Abundance for What?* (New Brunswick: Transaction Publishers, 1993, p. 456).

to some extent American society as a whole will tend to protect the high-ranking officials and shift the blame onto the low-ranking soldiers. Again, I am not referring to the blame for the murders that occurred but to the social climate generated by the new ROE.

Yet another difference between the lawyer's and the sociologist's respective styles is that the lawyer breaks down the crime and the criminal into what is intended to look like a set of crystal-clear points and citations of case law whereas the sociologist uses jargon that is often incomprehensible to the lawyer. I am mindful of this tendency in my profession to repel laypersons and will attempt to keep the jargon to a minimum. The lawyer feels compelled to do his or her job — indeed, regards defending or prosecuting an individual, no matter how heinous the crime, as just a job — whether or not the case is important to society as a whole, and they are generally less interested in what is important to society versus what is important in regard to "the law." By contrast, sociologists "will be interested in what is important, and what is important will be interesting to them" (p. 479). Another way of phrasing this distinction is that lawyers tend to think in terms of "a government of laws and not of men [and women]" whereas sociologists tend to think in interpersonal terms — how people respond to and interpret laws (p. 485). For example, in my role as a sociologist, I am more interested in this book in what various lawyers and investigators said, and what they did in relation to what the soldiers said and did, than in the guilt or innocence of anyone relative to "the law." *How* are the ideas of guilt, innocence, responsibility, guilt, and blame socially constructed relative to how others construct these ideas in other societies and eras? — This is the domain of the sociologist.

To summarize briefly, my approach in this book is to be self-consciously mindful of the differences between lawyers and sociologists, without mixing them up. I show how prosecutors and investigators arrived at their conclusions and decided to prosecute some of the soldiers but not to prosecute the commanders. But I also show how such decisions echo similar decisions regarding Abu Ghraib, Son Thang, My Lai, and other, similar cases. Thus, the event at Operation Iron Triangle becomes a social type and a compulsion to repeat the past; it was not a unique event. I focus on the interpersonal dynamics among the members of the military unit involved in Operation Iron Triangle, including but not limited to a sense of loyalty to each other, confusion as to the new ROE, and mixed emotions about the mercy as well as criminal inclinations which they showed. Above all, I strive to link the events in this one case to broader issues of culture, policy, and universal dynamics.

How to Distinguish Real Sincerity from "Fake Sincerity" in This Case

In the social sciences, the social construction of reality must be consistent with what Emile Durkheim called perceptions of the "average" or "common" and sometimes "collective consciousness" Another illustrious sociologist referred to this collective consciousness as the "Generalized Other."[1] In other words, the social construction created by any elite group (within the Army, the media, or any other specialized entity) is not regarded as true, in the long run, unless it is validated by the viewpoints of the "reasonable," average person. Riesman — who was, to repeat, a famous sociologist who began his career as a lawyer — used the phrase "jury of one's peers" to refer to most of society, not just the real members of a real jury panel. The presence of the information media at trials and courts-martial typically transfers information from the courtroom over the heads of the real jury of one's peers to the metaphorical jury of one's peers that is society. In the case of Corey Clagett, neither "jury of one's peers" — not the real one in the courtroom and not the metaphorical one in society at large — became involved because the Army canceled his scheduled trial. Nevertheless, the major difference between my sociological approach and the approach taken by a lawyer is that I am addressing the metaphorical jury of peers in society at large, whereas lawyers primarily address the jury of peers in the courtroom or other lawyers who will use the outcome of the trial as precedent and case law. Typically, lawyers who aim to involve society at large are labeled as "media hounds," which is considered something of a pejorative.

The average, collective or common consciousness involves many layers of society from the most micro-sociological unit of analysis involving two people (formally known as a dyad) to the most macro-sociological unit of analysis that involves culture as well as society's commonly held norms, values, sanctions, and beliefs. A vast subfield of sociology, known as the sociology of knowledge, offers guidance on how people arrive at what is commonly perceived as "truth." The consistency required for a social construction of reality to be regarded as "true" by the average or collective mind is such that it must fit into a social "cosmology"[2] of sorts, in addition to meeting the requirements of formal logic. This cosmology in latter-day society in the United States is part of a vast and interlocking system of beliefs and values that include but are not limited to the following: Americans are the "good guys" in wars, the rule of law prevails over the power of individuals and elites, all Americans are equal before the law, and so on. Americans also value sincerity, or at least

---

1 George Herbert Mead, *Mind, Self and Society* (Chicago, University of Chicago Press, [1903] 1995).

2 See Emile Durkheim, *The Elementary Forms of the Religious Life* (New York: Free Press [1912] 1965).

the appearance of sincerity, in their celebrities, political leaders, military commanders, and others who command the stage of public attention.

Given the several distinct versions of what happened on the troubled mission dubbed Operation Iron Triangle, one must wonder who is being sincere regarding the facts, issues, motives, and policies surrounding this case. It is obvious that some soldiers lied at some points in the narrative, but lying is not the same as insincerity. Lawyers, judges, and juries decide who is lying and who is telling the truth. But the average person and the average collective conscience decide who is being sincere. In *The Lonely Crowd*, Riesman[1] claims that modern Americans have invented "fake sincerity" as a new but ever-changing standard for evaluating the social world: "Just because such a premium is put on sincerity, a premium is put on faking it" (p. 196).

One may think of collective parallels to the "false self" that psychiatrists attribute to the individual narcissist and also the seemingly constant emphasis in American culture on spin, irony, simulacra, and other postmodern phenomena which are summarized by the phrase, "end of truth." However, Riesman differs from the postmodernists in that he is less concerned with simulacra such as fake breast milk or other fake things and more concerned with fakely-sincere emotions. To be sure, "fake sincerity" seems like an oxymoron, but it is intriguing precisely because it implies the capability to manipulate one's self as well as others. In other words, the person who is fakely sincere comes to believe his or her own "lies" and is thereby different from the ordinary liar, hypocrite, con-artist, exaggerator, and so on. Riesman writes:

> In a study of attitudes toward popular music we find again and again such statements as, "I like Dinah Shore because she's so sincere," or, "that's a very sincere record," or, "You can just feel that he [Frank Sinatra] is sincere." While it is clear that people want to personalize their relationships to their heroes of consumption and that their yearning for sincerity is a grim reminder of how little they can trust themselves or others in daily life, it is less clear just what it is that they find "sincere" in a singer or other performer....But the popular emphasis on sincerity means more than this. It means that the source of criteria for judgment has shifted from the content of the performance and its goodness or badness, aesthetically speaking, to the personality of the performer. He is judged for his attitude toward the audience, an attitude which is either sincere or insincere, rather than by his relation to his craft, that is, his honesty and skill (p. 194).

It is easy to substitute the names of contemporary celebrities such as Oprah for Dinah Shore and conclude that Riesman's assessment is still relevant. More important, the quest for sincerity the tendency to be taken in by "fake sincerity" also applies to politics:

> Viewing the political scene as a market for comparable emotions, it seems that the appeal of many of our political candidates tends to be of this sort. Forced to choose between skill and sincerity, many in the audience prefer

---

1 David Riesman, *The Lonely Crowd* (New Haven, CT: Yale University Press [1950] 1992).

the latter. They are tolerant of bumbles and obvious ineptness if the leader tries hard (p. 195).

Again, one may update Riesman's claims with references to President Bush — who was judged to be sincere at the beginning of his first term by most Americans — and the rivalry between Senators Barack Obama and Hillary Clinton for the Democratic Party nomination for President. It does seem to be true that, more than other societies, Americans value sincerity — or at least, the appearance of sincerity — in their celebrities as well as leaders more than other attributes.

This insight is directly relevant to the case being analyzed here. The killings at Operation Iron Triangle can and will be analyzed from many different legal and social perspectives, but the bottom line question is the following: Was the brigade commander sincere in issuing the new ROE? Were the soldiers sincere in trying to carry out the orders? Was the US government sincere in the reasons it laid out for waging war in Iraq? A negative reply to these and related questions is sufficient to sour public opinion, whether or not any of these given "performances" is objectively "successful" or not. Thus, the various "missions" in Iraq, Mogadishu, Abu Ghraib, Guantanamo and elsewhere may or may not have been "successful." Pro and con arguments have been and will continue to be made by pundits, analysts, and scholars regarding all these "missions," on macro- as well as micro-sociological levels. But despite the overwhelming military victory in Iraq, public opinion turned against the war when the sincerity of President Bush's motives came to be questioned by American society as a whole.

One needs to place Riesman's insight into "fake sincerity" into the context of his overall social theory. All societies begin as tradition directed, in which there is very little change from the way things have usually been done or perceived. The inner-directed type emerges with modernization and industrialization, and it is characterized by the metaphorical planting of an equally metaphorical "gyroscope" by parents and other authorities into their children. Inner-directed types were and some still are generally rigid with regard to the beliefs, values, and norms they hold. They assume that what they believe to be true will last for at least their lifetime and possibly the lifetimes of their children. The third social type, which begins to emerge in the United States in the 1950s, is labeled by Riesman as the other-directed type. The other-directed type uses a metaphorical "radar" to take his or her cues as to what is right or wrong from the peer-group and the media more than from his or her parents or authority figures. However, the peer group and the media are constantly changing, and this type does *not* assume that any belief or value will last for a period of time approaching a lifetime. Rather, an other-directed society and the individuals in it change their minds, collectively and privately, very often about almost everything. Inner-directed parents taught their children that "honesty is the best policy," for example, whereas other-directed parents teach their children to "do the best you can under the circumstances," and they take their advice in raising children from self-help books, the media, and peers. Sincerity is assumed for the first two social types, but the other-directed type is more cynical and therefore more sensitive to the fine distinction between "fake sincerity" and real sincerity.

To phrase this sociological insight in another way, one may point to an emerging "personality market" in contemporary, other-directed societies. There are no hard-and-fast lies versus truths in such a market, only emotional responses that various marketplaces support for consumption. When the market changes, one must alter one's personality in order to survive. In the case of the Iron Triangle murders, there are at least two distinct markets: one which supports a certain emotional commodity in the Army, and another which supports public perception on the home front and in the court of international public opinion.

Army commanders would find it very costly indeed to have their ROE scrutinized by society, especially if some of these ROE are unlawful. Consider the doublespeak that ensued after the publication of the photographs of torture at Abu Ghraib (the marketplace at Abu Ghraib), which were dismissed with the phrase, "America does not commit torture" (the marketplace of public opinion). One can go back in history to Son Thang and other massacres and find a similar "split personality" geared for different emotional markets: in Vietnam, the civilians were frequently referred to as "gooks" and dehumanized as such, but the prosecution of some soldiers for atrocities upheld values enshrined in the Geneva Conventions. Which versions were, and are, sincere?

The average person is confused by fake sincerity, which causes tremendous cognitive dissonance. Is the Army really using a new ROE that orders soldiers to kill on sight? Are such orders in line or out of sync with American values? Were the soldiers in this case really cold-blooded murderers? How will the international community perceive US values and intentions if these new ROE really exist?

Using these insights as a starting point for discussion, I wish to suggest that the details of the Iron Triangle murder incident are indicative of a general shift in social character in US society as a whole that has been slowly and imperceptibly occurring at least since the 1950s. In Riesman's terminology, our ancestors were raised to be inner-directed: parents and societies tried to instill values in children that would last for at least a lifetime. The Geneva Conventions, which were incorporated into the UCMJ in 1950, were also intended to last for at least a lifetime. But the current generation is raised to be other-directed, which means that they are raised to attend to ever-changing signals from the peer group (including the news media) and they do not commit themselves emotionally to any person, place, thing, or idea with the permanence of their ancestors. Nowadays, the Geneva Conventions and the LOAC are perceived by some as "quaint" and as placing too many restrictions on commanders and soldiers. For the inner-directed, values and norms were set in stone. For the other-directed, life offers a Milky Way galaxy of choices, including moral choices in war. There can be little doubt that modern Americans switch partners, religions, diets, residences, and jobs at a dizzying pace that our ancestors could not have imagined. But this reluctance to commit to anything also applies to moral standards, in general and in war.

When I teach Riesman's theory, my students make it clear that they seek to be or at least to *seem* to be inner directed. Who would not admire the inner-directed type's sure commitment to moral values? Conversely, who would not be reluctant to be judged as a shallow manipulator when it comes to moral standards? Yet the most intriguing aspect of Riesman's theory is the suggestion that most people in the contemporary world will seek to *seem* inner directed — as if they had morals cast in stone, and as if they had an inner gyroscope of values — precisely because they are unsure of what they would do in a situation such as the one that confronted the soldiers during the mission called Operation Iron Triangle.

The many, diverse meanings of the tragedy that occurred on May 9, 2006 near Samarra go beyond the dry, legalistic compendium of the facts that have already been disclosed by the news media: four soldiers apparently shot and killed one elderly man "lawfully" and three prisoners unlawfully while they allowed one prisoner to live. The deeper one gets into the incident, the less one can discern the difference between what was lawful versus unlawful. The accused soldiers went to the trouble of making it seem as if the prisoners whom they killed were fleeing, and thereby *seem* like they were following inner-directed standards — the prisoners would have posed a threat to the soldiers had they escaped. Even in this exercise in fake sincerity, they did not calculate the old-fashioned ROE which calls for a gradual escalation of force in dealing with escaping prisoners. And why didn't they just go through the arcane but standard procedure of keeping and processing prisoners? They did process one prisoner lawfully and did not kill him. Why the inconsistency? One reason seems to be that they were swayed by the new ROE, which said nothing about taking prisoners, yet were confused by the traditional ROE, which is based upon the Geneva Conventions. Old standards were evaporating but new standards had not yet crystallized into firm referents.

The reactions by bloggers and the news media are equally ambivalent. To some, the soldiers were heroes doing their job, and the Army was perceived in a negative light by prosecuting them. The media's reaction to My Lai was similar. Others felt that the soldiers came across as cold-blooded killers who tarnished the image of the Army. The most difficult question to settle in all these competing points of view is the one implied by Riesman: Who is being sincere in this narrative? This question applies to the US government, Army, soldiers, media, and others who were directly or indirectly involved in this incident.

Applying Riesman's Theory to Motives for Wars

Thus far, I have examined the perplexities in determining who is being sincere in the many diverse accounts of what actually happened during the incident in question. But there is also the larger cultural context. Riesman's linkage of tradition-, inner-, and other-directedness to wars is directly relevant to the present discussion. In summary, Riesman holds that inner-directed societies are motivated to go to war for the sake of their nation's honor while other-directed societies are motivated to go to war by arguments that suggest they are fighting for "their way of life." He writes:

> Wars and technological changes, as well as the shift from inner-direction to other-direction, have brought the moralizing style, in either its indignant or enthusiastic versions, into disrepute. The Civil War, itself a complex catharsis of the moral indignation that accompanied the political sphere in the preceding years, initiated a process that has since continued. Probably the few living veterans of the Civil War still retain a fighting faith in the righteousness of their cause. The veterans of World War I are less involved in their cause, though still involved in their experience. The veterans of World War II bring scarcely a trace of moral righteousness into their scant political participation. These men "ain't mad at nobody." It looks as though since the Civil War there has been a decline in the emotionality of political differences (p. 179).

Riesman's overall point seems to be that inner-directed types are emotionally involved in what they believe to be the righteousness of their cause in a war — applicable to soldiers as well as the country as a whole — whereas other-directed types are less committed to the cause (which is difficult for them to discern) and more committed to the "experience." He elaborates:

> In the nineteenth century, most journalistic treatments of international politics drew on such parochial slogans as "national honor" — in the case of Mason and Slidell, for instance, or the *Maine*. Today, however, the mass media, although with many exceptions, appear to discuss world politics in terms made familiar by psychological warfare, and events are interpreted for their bearing on the propaganda of one side or the other.... Some may find current talk about our "way of life" reminiscent of national honor. But the change is not merely one of phrasing. ...However vague the content of the national enemy was quite specific. "Our way of life," on the other hand, has many more psychological connotations; it is fairly specific in domestic content but highly unspecific as to what the consequences in foreign policy are, or should be, of this slogan. "National honor" sometimes strait-jacketed our foreign policy by establishing a moral beachhead we were neither willing nor prepared to defend. As

against this, "our way of life" gives almost no moral guidance to foreign policy, which seems, therefore to be left to Realpolitik. Only seems to be, however. For just as the phrase "national honor" calls to mind a Victorian form of hypocrisy, so the phrase "our way of life" reminds us that the other-directed man conceals from himself as well as from others such morality as he possesses by taking refuge in seemingly expediential considerations (p. 186).

Riesman's examples are dated, but the principles are not. Let us pose the question: Is the current war on terror seen as a matter of national honor or a means to preserve "our way of life?" The 9/11 attack could be construed as an attack on America's honor, in line with historical events such as the attacks on the *Maine* or Pearl Harbor. But in the first place, America's response to 9/11 by attacking Iraq — which had nothing to do with 9/11 — seems incoherent in comparison with direct retaliation at the nations who were held responsible for the attacks on the *Maine* and Pearl Harbor. Second, the Bush Administration phrased its initiatives in the wars against Afghanistan and Iraq — loosely framed as responses to the tragic event of 9/11 — not in terms of revenge but, indeed, in terms of fighting for democracy or "our way of life." But after five years of war, the public has begun to doubt the connection between the failure (up to now) of establishing democracy in Iraq and Afghanistan and "our way of life."

The end result seems to be, sadly, as Riesman predicted: expedience with regard to the laws of warfare, which, in turn, has soured much of the world's opinion of America's image and its way of life. And as of this writing, in the year 2008, opinion polls suggest that Americans are deeply divided and confused about the meaning, motives, and reasons for the wars against Afghanistan and Iraq. Undoubtedly, historians will not find many traces of a democratic way of life in actions taken at Operation Iron Triangle, Abu Ghraib, Guantanamo, and other sites that have already become infamous.

For the soldier on the ground in Iraq, the situation must be even more confusing. Why were they supposedly fighting al Qaeda in Iraq when Osama bin Laden, who is considered responsible for 9/11, was hiding safely in the border region between Afghanistan and Pakistan? There was no al Qaeda influence in Iraq until it was invaded by the United States. Thus, the soldier who might want to imitate inner-directed standards such as fighting for honor and holding to gyroscopic principles enshrined in the traditional ROE was confronted by a situation in which the Iraqis lost their initial high regard for Americans as liberators from Saddam Hussein. The unexpected hostility from an enemy that did not wear formal uniforms and resorted to devastating tactics such as the use of IEDs (improvised explosive devices) led, in turn, to the expediency of resorting to new, unlawful roes, which further tarnished America's self-image as well as its image abroad as a democratic nation.

I have already mentioned the connection between COL Steele and the battle in Mogadishu in the year 1993. When the United States entered Somalia in 1993 under the Clinton Administration it was also touted as a humanitarian effort, and the mission in Mogadishu was deemed a fiasco by pundits and opinion-makers. President Clinton withdrew US forces the day after the failed raid which involved Steele, who was a captain at the time. But *Black Hawk Down* transformed this veritable military failure into a stunning victory of sorts. As Riesman predicted, the movie and the book focused on the *experience* of the battle and the other-directed camaraderie among the American soldiers, not on the fact that the battle and the mission as a whole were regarded as failures.

Hardly any media coverage of Operation Iron Triangle fails to mention Steele and the link to Somalia, so that this connection cannot be ignored. But how can we explain this compulsion to repeat the past and recast defeat into victory? In order to explain this tendency, one has to build upon Riesman's social theory but also move beyond it.

Postemotional Wars

In *Postemotional Society*, I developed further Riesman's central ideas concerning "fake sincerity" in the context of a cultural shift toward other-directedness. Postemotional society harks to the past in order to create synthetic emotional responses in the present, and I defined postemotionalism as "the tendency for emotionally charged collective representations to be abstracted from their cultural contexts and then manipulated artificially by self and others in new and artificially contrived contexts."[1] This definition comes perilously close to the sort of jargon that lawyers and laypersons abhor, so it may be more fruitful to illustrate the definition. Examples range from the Serbs invoking their "glorious defeat" (victory) at the Battle of Kosovo which was fought in the year 1389 in order to justify their violence in Yugoslavia in the 1990s, Greece using the memory of Alexander the Great in order to block the existence of Macedonia in the 1990s and again in the year 2007 to block Macedonia's entrance into NATO, to France and England still nursing their wounds at losing their stature as founders of civilization and the Enlightenment. In Texas, the Battle of Alamo is another such "glorious defeat" reformulated as victory for American democracy. Most of my students in Texas are stunned when confronted with the historical fact that Texans lost the Battle of Alamo. Similarly, the United States used the moral code of America as the beacon of democracy set upon a hill, found in Alexis de Tocqueville's *Democracy in America*,[2] to justify war against Iraq when the real enemy was Osama Bin Laden. A moral code that used to evoke genuine emo-

1 Stjepan G. Mestrovic, *Postemotional Society* (London: Routledge, 1997).
2 Alexis de Tocqueville, *Democracy in America* (New York: Library of America, [1848] 2004).

tions among the inner-directed Puritans was used at the beginning of the present millennium in an attempt to depict US motives in the war against Iraq as noble even if the means involved disregard for the Geneva Conventions. Again, the connection to Tocqueville tends to overlook the uncomfortable fact that he devotes several hundred pages to slavery, extermination of the Native Americans, and other crimes committed by Puritans. In a book with the provocative title *Lies My History Teacher Told Me*,[1] James Loewen deconstructs further the mythology of the Puritans. To the average US citizen, the fact that Puritans persecuted Native Americans, and that the kindergarten image of Puritans and Native Americans sitting down to a Thanksgiving dinner together is false, are as disturbing as the more recent finding that Pluto is not a planet.

Similarly, in the Abu Ghraib scandal of the new millennium, the postemotional US public does not see a de facto policy of torture, abuse or even criminality in the old-fashioned, inner-directed moral indignation and emotional outrage at and desecration of the Geneva Conventions or United States Army. Despite the plethora of books that demonstrate that the soldiers were following de facto policy, most Americans seem to believe the government and the media that it was the result of a handful of "bad apples." The public responded with a blasé attitude, not moral indignation, when it considered these matters at Abu Ghraib relative to US policy. The proof is that after the abuse at Abu Ghraib was revealed, and blamed on a handful of low-ranking soldiers, abuse continued at Guantanamo and various other prisons throughout Afghanistan and Iraq. Another postemotional irony is that Abu Ghraib was supposed to represent the democratic values of the United States and was supposed to be a model to the Iraqis, but it ended up reflecting a compulsion to repeat some of the negative connotations of the prison from Saddam Hussein's regime. Why didn't the United States Army build a completely new facility and run it as a model prison? Even the documentary "Standard Operating Procedure," produced by the award-winning filmmaker Errol Morris, failed to penetrate the pre-existing belief that Americans do not commit torture so it must have been the result of a few bad apples. His film was a box office flop and failed to generate much interest.

The other-directed type has mutated from Riesman's description of a shallow conformist and manipulator of self and others into the sophisticated, postemotional voyeur of emotional drama considered as text, not reality. The Geneva Conventions are simply too inner-directed and old-fashioned to have a genuine impact on other-directed society: they were authored by individuals who possessed internal moral "gyroscopes" or a moral compass and

---

1 James Loewen, *Lies My History Teacher Told Me: Everything Your American History Textbooks Got Wrong* (New York: Touchstone, 2007).

who believed that moral standards should last for at least their lifetimes. The other-directed, postemotional type is resigned to the conclusion that moral standards can and do change so rapidly that the individual can do little or anything in response that could not be re-interpreted later as good or bad.

Richard Rorty calls this tendency in contemporary life "irony."[1] One of the postemotional ironies regarding the Abu Ghraib fiasco is that the soldiers claimed they were taking photographs in order to document the abuse, yet the photographs were used by the government as evidence against them.

In David Riesman's terminology, the other-directed or what I call the postemotional type has become the ultimate "inside-dopester:"

> The inside-dopester may be one who has concluded (with good reason) that since he can do nothing to change politics, he can only understand it. Or he may see all political issues in terms of being able to get some insider on the telephone. That is, some inside-dopesters actually crave to *be* on the inside, to join an inner circle or invent one; others aim no higher than to *know* the inside, for whatever peer-group satisfactions this can bring them (p. 181).

Riesman's depiction of the helplessness of the observer to change politics applies also to the American soldier's sense of helplessness in challenging unlawful policies at sites of abuse, from Abu Ghraib to Operation Iron Triangle. But this sense of apathy and helplessness extends to the United States electorate as a whole. In the presidential campaign of 2008, as of this writing, the torture and abuse at Guantanamo and Abu Ghraib, and the mass killings at Haditha and elsewhere, and the shootings by Blackwater contractors, have not become political issues. To bring them up as issues is to risk being labeled as un-American, but it also exposes the sense of helplessness in restoring America's image as a nation that respects the rule of law. And it might open up too many uncomfortable questions about the meaning of "our way of life." Riesman sensitizes the reader to the fact that the other-directed or postemotional type feels helpless to do anything about matters that might touch on his or her genuine emotions.

Consider, as illustration, one of the most iconic photographs from Abu Ghraib, that of a prisoner who was named "Gilligan" by the US soldiers and who is shown standing on a box, hooded, waiting to be electrocuted. One of the most eerie moments of the courts-martial at Ft. Hood, Texas was the testimony by several soldiers that Gilligan was friendly, liked the soldiers, and that they liked him too. (Riesman emphasizes that other-directed society favors the veneer of events being "nice" and fakely agreeable to the peer group.) This photograph of what appears to be old-fashioned "torture" was re-described in the courtroom as a friendly incident in which soldiers were *doing their job* trying to keep Gilligan awake and that he understood this so that he laughed and joked with them during the torture. The defense attor-

---

1 Richard Rorty, *Contingency, Irony, and Solidarity* (New York: Basic Books, 1989).

ney insisted that Gilligan and the soldiers who tortured him "were friends." This iconic incident was re-described as a sort of "nice," postemotional torture — again, the behavior and the emotions were not connected. I learned later through interviews with the soldiers involved that they felt anxious and depressed doing their "jobs" of inflicting suffering on Gilligan, and one may surmise that Gilligan was experiencing a form of Stockholm Syndrome.

In this context, one of the most remarkable things about the abuse at Abu Ghraib is that it was framed by the culture industry primarily as an "interrogation technique." Some of the following were listed as such techniques: yelling, shouting, inducing fear, playing loud music, bringing in military working dogs, and deception — among others. If one reads this list of behaviors, without knowing that it comes from an approved list of interrogation techniques, one might think that they were descriptions of what angry people do in abusive relationships. The postemotional soldier is put in the position of being able to yell, shout at, and abuse prisoners while rationalizing whatever emotions he or she might be feeling — even friendly feelings — as just doing one's job of inflicting suffering. Moreover, the soldier is convinced by the peer-group that the job of inflicting suffering is beneficial to the national cause because it might save the lives of US soldiers in the future by obtaining information (which, in reality, did not exist).

Similarly, the sworn affidavits from Operation Iron Triangle show that soldiers attended what amounted to a sort of "pep rally" the night before the mission, in which they were convinced by their superiors that the entire island was full of terrorists who were bent upon their destruction. This presumed fact justified the "strange" and "new" ROE to shoot every military-age male on sight and not wait for signs of hostility. One must ask the question: How did the soldiers feel about these strange, new orders? All of them had presumably been trained in the traditional rules of warfare, which demand that one shoots only at enemy who shows hostile intent. The cognitive dissonance in their minds must have been immense. Presumably, like the soldiers at Abu Ghraib, they resigned themselves to apathy and to doing their "jobs." Their genuine emotions must have been disengaged while they kept up the postemotional veneer that they were performing their mission to the best of their ability.

What were the alternatives? Despite efforts by scholars such as Philip Zimbardo,[1] who sermonize that soldiers have a duty to be heroes and disobey unlawful orders, and who criticize the tendency for soldiers to obey orders, in reality, a military unit could not function if the only alternatives to following an unlawful order are desertion and mutiny. And how could the

---

1 Philip G. Zimbardo, *The Lucifer Effect: Understanding How Good People Turn Evil* (New York: Random House, 2007).

soldiers determine that the order was unlawful? Apparently, it was given by the brigade commander, and soldiers are taught that they must obey orders handed down the chain of command.

The soldiers who testified during the Abu Ghraib courts-martial exhibited this careful control of passion and "fake sincerity" that postemotional society demands. They all expressed regret for the harm that their behavior caused to the *image* of the United States Army, but none exhibited empathy for the emotional and physical harm inflicted upon Iraqi prisoners. Remarkably, the courts-martial were primarily about the American soldiers and American image: Neither the prosecution nor the defense ventured into the lives, suffering, or fate of the Iraqi prisoners. Everyone in the courtroom was careful to avoid any harshly negative words against Muslims, even though soldiers were on trial primarily for abusing Muslims. Soldiers did not come across as bitter, hysterical, or otherwise passionate in their descriptions of what had happened. On the contrary, their accounts of horrific abuse came across as bland and dull. Both the US Government reports and testimony concerning abuse at Abu Ghraib depicted it primarily as the result of "confusion" as to what was permissible versus prohibited behavior. It may well be true that soldiers were confused for cogent reasons. What appeared to be intensely emotional, hateful abuse was reformulated in postemotional terms as an issue of trying to follow confusing guidelines as part of one's job expectations. In what could be read as an appendix to David Riesman's *Lonely Crowd*, the soldiers opened themselves up to the jury of their peers in the larger society in exactly the manner that the postemotional jury of their peers sought: without passion yet with the appearance of carefully crafted sincerity.

All of these observations about the soldiers vis-à-vis the abuse at Abu Ghraib apply to the soldiers involved in the killings committed during Operation Iron Triangle. They were confused by the discrepancy between the new versus the traditional ROE. They were trying to do their jobs. Their performance does not betray a trace, not even a hint, of prejudice against Iraqis or Muslims (except for their suspiciousness of Iraqi Army soldiers who were part of the joint mission). The Iraqis who were taken prisoner or killed are practically invisible in the sworn affidavits — nothing is known about who they were, whether any were or were not, in fact, terrorists, or anything factual about them. As the reader will see in the coming chapters, the sworn affidavits are factual, dull, and bland. And as with Abu Ghraib, the blame was shifted entirely onto a handful of soldiers who were convicted, when the more important fact is that the entire unit — all the soldiers on the mission that day — were involved in the cover-up as well as the confusion.

CONCLUSIONS

The analysis, or more properly, social anatomy, that follows is similar to previous analyses, written primarily by lawyers but also some journalists, of My Lai, Son Thang, and other sites of US war crimes. The distinctive element in the present analysis is the use of sociological concepts and especially the idea of "fake sincerity" in relation to David Riesman's overall theory in *The Lonely Crowd.* The careful "dissection" of the sworn statements and other documents that follow in the rest of this book are intended primarily to answer the question, "Who is being sincere?" with regard to the numerous legal, military, and public policy issues that are raised by the killings that occurred during Operation Iron Triangle.

CHAPTER 3. THE FIRST VERSION OF EVENTS — MISSION ACCOMPLISHED

The various sworn statements made by many soldiers on May 11, 2006 who were directly or indirectly involved in *US* v. *Clagett* suggest the following: The brigade commander issued verbally an "operational" and "new" ROE that was apparently interpreted the same way by most of the soldiers and officers. In the words of one of the soldiers, Brandon Helton, they were to proceed, "with the ROE given directly by the brigade commander to kill every military-age male on the island." Some, but not all, of the subsequent sworn statements that were made on May 29 and around June 15 of 2006 suggest that the order may have been "kill or capture" all military-aged males, even to just "kill those son-of-a-bitches." The important point is that the initial memories by the soldiers in the May 11 statements made no mention of the option to capture — just to kill on sight.

The ROE to kill on sight can be construed as being a new departure from customary ROE while at the same time being an ancient practice. Consider, for example, William Shakespeare's immortal play, *The Tragedy of Julius Caesar*. In Act 5, Scene 5 of this masterpiece, Brutus and Clitus discuss briefly the whereabouts of Statilus, who is either "taken or slain" — a prisoner or killed. Similarly, Brutus asks his friends to kill him rather than to allow him to be taken captive. If this fundamental question — whether captives should be kept as prisoners or killed — continues to animate contemporary art that harks back to Shakespeare's times, which in turn harks back to the Roman Empire, then one can assume that it has been a fundamental issue in all wars in all centuries. The emotional power of the ancient warrior's dilemma, whether to show mercy or succumb to hatred (and fear) of the enemy, is what drives this particular narrative of the incident at Samarra. The matter-of-fact, cold, legalistic tone of the sworn statements should not distract the reader from the fundamental and emotional nature of this issue: it is simultaneously new and age-old. Moreover, it is not the behavior that is at issue, but the motive. The tradition-directed type will kill or capture based upon adherence to custom, and failure to comply with customary practice will result in shame. The inner-directed type will kill or capture based upon the internalization of a "gyroscope" or "moral compass" and the wrong choice will result in guilt. The other-directed type will kill or capture based upon signals from the peer group, and the wrong choice will result in anxiety. But the postemotional type will confuse these styles, and with a sense of fake sincerity will try to present an other-directed decision as principled and inner-directed. The fake sincerity will be betrayed by a distinct sense of emotional apathy. Fake sincerity can never fully replicate the spontaneous sense of effervescence that accompanies genuine emotions in any aspect of social life.

The initial investigation and report that were conducted in May of 2006 conclude that PFC Clagett and the other accused soldiers acted in accordance with the ROE and that no crime was committed. The Company Commander, CPT Hart, writes: "The bottom line is that the Soldiers acted within the ROE when responding to the attacks by the AIF [Anti-Iraqi Forces] personnel." AIF is a curious euphemism. Were some of the Anti-Iraqi Forces, in fact, Iraqis? How many were foreign fighters? One can imagine an "anti-Iraqi Iraqi fighter," but one has to strain one's brain in order to imagine such an entity. Weren't the AIFs more properly anti-American forces or fighters? The name that one gives to one's enemy is very important in any war, because it is supposed to distinguish friend from foe. The term AIF, used by the US military in Iraq, has to be one of the most ambiguous labels for an enemy that one could ever dream up. On this particular mission, soldiers were forced to engage an "enemy" that was not necessarily a threat to them and that certainly showed no hostile intent. With perceived hostility by an enemy removed from the equation, what is the difference between a potential enemy that is captured and one that is free but in one's gun sight? Practically, from the perspective of the common person — there is no difference.

In any event, the nationality or ethnicity of the killed captives is never disclosed in any of the sworn statements, although their full names are disclosed. CPT Hart as well as the other soldiers and officers did not address such subtleties in their common usage of the term AIF to refer to the enemy that was supposed to be killed on sight. As of May 11, the case seemed to be closed almost as soon as it was opened.

On May 29, and especially around June 15, 2006, some of the soldiers changed their accounts of what happened, suggesting a crime that involved pre-meditation, cunning, irresponsibility, senseless aggression, and disregard for the consequences affecting each other, their unit, or the prisoners. These latter statements are noteworthy for their inconsistency, highly varied interpretations of the ROE, and contradiction with the accounts by other witnesses. I will elaborate on these inconsistencies, contradictions, and apparent cognitive distortion in some of the post-May 11th statements throughout this book.

At this point in the analysis, it is important to note that the narrative or text that underlies this case is remarkable for its initial consistency — internal with regard to statements made and external with regard to perceived roes — in sharp contrast to its extraordinary inconsistency (both internal and external) in and following May 29, 2006. This sharp contrast in the accounts begs the questions: What really happened during Operation Iron Triangle on May 9, 2006? Why was there remarkable consistency at first, followed by a total loss of consistency in subsequent statements? Perhaps some soldiers were lying — but why? Were they protecting each other or their commanders or the image of their unit? Was pressure put on the soldiers to change their stories? If so, who or what was the origin of the social pressure? If the pressure existed, was it exerted in the initial statements or subsequent ones, or throughout the narrative for different reasons?

The nine individual sworn statements that were taken on May 11, 2006 — just two days following the incident — come across as almost exact replicas of each other with regard to the ROE and some other details. The consistency is due partly to the fact that the investigators and platoon leader had written the key elements of the story on a chalkboard. A possible secondary reason is the "band of brothers" motive in which the soldiers were already covering up the incident out of a sense of loyalty to each other. One soldier's account is representative of the other accounts, and reads as follows:

> On 09 of May 2006 me and my OG attached to 3rd squad and 2nd squad arrived at grid #_____ at approximately 0640 hrs. Upon arriving at the house, SSG Girourard engaged 1 male standing in the window in accordance with the ROE given directly by the brigade commander to kill every military-age male on the island (obj Murray). They proceeded into the house detaining 3 other males and dragging the 1 KIA out of the house. We proceeded to house 2 where I used suppressive fire above the house not striking the house or any personnel inside. 1 male came outside holding a baby in front of him as a shield so he would not be shot. They detained that one male at approximately 0646. The platoon and 2nd squad with the 1 KIA pushed to another obj. My gun team attached to 3rd squad stayed back at the house with the detainees. My gunteam, SPC Graber, SGT Lemus and I secured the LZ while SPC Hunsaker and Private Clagett changed zip ties on the 3 detainees because they had broke once before on the detainees. At approximately 0844 I heard "oh shit" come from the house. I looked back to see the 3 detainees, 2 with blindfolds down and 1 in the process of taking his down running full speed from the house and then were shot from the

soldiers in the house, killing all three. I ran to the house to see if everyone was OK. PVT Clagett said he had been punched by 1 detainee in the jaw and that SPC Hunsacker had been stabbed. I proceeded into the house to see Hunsaker on the ground with a cut across his face and a deep cut across the arm. SPC Bivins evaluated the 3 males and said they were all dead. We bagged all 3 bodies and called it up to Choppin 5 & 6 bodies and 1 detainee to the tac. Our birds arrived at approximately 1308 and met up with Choppin 36 at another obj.

Euphemisms and a separate military language were used routinely by all soldiers describing the incident. Prisoners are called "detainees." Prisoners have rights under the Geneva Conventions while "detainees" do not necessarily have such rights. The military refers to prisoners as "detainees" in situations ranging from Abu Ghraib and Guantanamo to this and similar incidents in Iraq. To "engage" someone is to kill him — at least with regard to this particular ROE and the May 11 version of events.

In the first version of events, the one person who was killed "lawfully" is described simply as a male. In subsequent versions, he would be described as an elderly man in his 70s who showed no hostile intent and did not point a weapon. "Suppressive fire" means to shoot at a target in order to flush out everyone inside a structure. Once persons come out of the house due to the suppressive fire — if they come out at all, alive or wounded — it is not clear whether they may be killed or captured. It is also not clear whether suppressive fire would be regarded by the common conscience as a lawful or unlawful procedure. Perhaps the average consensus would depend on the perception whether the "targets" inside the house were "bad guys" (terrorists) or "good guys" (women and children), or some mixture of "good" and "bad" people. Indeed, the most puzzling aspect of the sworn statements is the attribution to the brigade commander of the order to kill every military-age male. Are these the precise words that the BC used? The order is not described by the soldiers as kill or capture — just to kill. This leaves many questions unanswered: what are the parameters of the category "military-age male?" How old and how young does the enemy have to be in order to not qualify as a target? How do soldiers determine the age of a target in the heat of battle? And what about the women and the children in the area? The order to shoot males excludes them, but the order to use "grazing fire" on houses exposes women and children to deadly force.

Corey Clagett's statement is worth reading in its entirety because he was one of the four soldiers charged in the murder. Here is his account of what happened:

> On this day 09 May 2006 I was involved in an air assault on an island that was labeled obj. Murray which was a known insurgent strong hold. My unit was briefed with the new ROE by the brigade commander which was to kill any military-aged males on the island. After already clearing our first objective my squad and 2nd squad loaded up ... and flew to our

second objective.... 3rd squad (which includes me) began to approach the first house. I was last in order, because my ammo became delinked from my SAW (squad automatic weapon). I fixed my ammo, and began to try to catch up with the rest of my squad. As I came to the house I heard gun shots, and by the time I had got there they had already had one KIA, and three detainees. At that time my squad leader (SSG Girouard) told me to go to the top of the nearest hill and do a recon. I spotted one male run into the house. At that time one of the gun teams that was attached to 3rd squad CPL Helton and SGT Ryan came to my location and took over my position so that I could link back up with my squad. SSG Girouard and I proceeded to the second house while CPT Helton was providing grazing fire over the house while half of 3rd squad and myself ran to the second house. As we approached the house a military aged man came outside of the house using a baby as a shield. We took the baby away, and detained [him]. We brought the detainee along with the AK47 we found to the other house with the other detainees. At approximately 0841 our platoon leader and 2nd squad left the objective. After they left SPC Hunsaker and myself began to move the detainees to LZ [landing zone] when I picked up one detainee and the thin flex cuffs broke. So my squad leader told us to change the flex cuffs with thicker ones. So I cut their cuffs off so their hands became free. Hunsaker and myself were talking to each other, and getting ready to recuff the detainees when I was struck in the head with either a fist or a blunt object, and my vision went black, and when I came to, two detainees were running and behind was the other detainee. Then Hunsaker shot first, then I began to engage the fleeing detainees, and we eliminated the threat. I felt this action was necessary, because I believe the life of my friend (Hunsaker) and myself were in danger because thee individuals used deadly force against us. So in preservation in our own live we had no choice to use deadly force against them. When this incident was over I checked myself and Hunsaker and saw he was bleeding and had a significant cut on his arm, and then our squad leader came to see what happen. Then 2nd platoon came and bagged and tagged the knife and helped move the bodies to PZ posture. We then exfilled that location at about 1300 hrs.

If four prisoners were taken, and three were killed, what happened to the fourth prisoner? Why would weak cuffs be used on a mission? Were the soldiers following procedure in releasing two prisoners at a time in order to re-cuff them? Common sense leads one to ask basic questions as such as these, but only if one is suspicious about what occurred.

Most of the soldiers were careful to include in their statement not only the wording of the verbal ROE but the assertion that it was given by COL Steele. Later statements would elaborate that several officers in the chain of command reinforced this ROE. For example, note William Hunsaker's reference to the "new" ROE:

On this day 09 My 2006 I was involved in an air assault on an island that was labeled obj. Murray which was a known insurgent stronghold. My unit was briefed with the new ROE by the brigade commander which was to kill any military-age males on the island.

A slightly different version is given by Leonel Lemus, with particular emphasis that the platoon leader, LT Wehrheim, ordered that structures, women, and children were not to be "engaged":

Our ROE was that every male on the OBJ was hostile. SSG Girouard shot at the window where the hostile male was standing. I identified SSG Girouard's target and also engaged, shooting 4x rounds, throughout the window. We entered the building and found 3 other males holding their wives as shields. Further clearing of the house we found 1 male wounded in the room with the window that we shot into. Myself and SPC Hunsaker reported 1 enemy WIA and carried him outside for our medic Bivins to attend to. 2 women were taken to a different room, away from the detainees and the 1 wounded.... Our gun team, CPL Helton and SGT Ryan, were set on top of a hill overwatching the next building. As we moved across the hill, SSG Girouard requested that the gun team provide suppressive fire at the birm behind the house. 1LT Wehrheim gave the "OK" only that no structures or women or children were engaged.... Once we gave the signal the guns ceased fire and we entered the building. 1 male ... exited the house holding a baby as a cover and shield. SSG Girouard put the baby down and I took the male down to the floor and zip-tied him.... I heard a yell at the building and seen the 3 detainees run. They fell as they got shot, and SSG Girouard contacted me to inform me that they (the detainees) had fought PFC Clagett and stabbed SPC Hunsaker. SPC Bivins attempted to provide aid to the hostile men. They were pronounced dead after a few minutes. The 3 dead males were put in body bags and were prep'd for exfil. We left the island at 1308, 4 enemy KIA, 1 detainee.

Subsequent affidavits later in May and in June would change this version of events considerably. But on May 11, the consensus was unanimous that 4 "enemy" were killed in action, not that 3 were killed as prisoners. Note also that the males who were killed are labeled as "hostile" even though, as later affidavits would suggest, none of the actual behaved in a hostile manner. They were all pre-designated as hostile. Another soldier, Bradley Mason, gave the following account of what happened:

Upon arriving to the house, SSG Girouard, SGT Lemus, SPC Hunsaker and myself engaged 1 male in the window in accordance with the ROE given directly by the brigade commander. The ROE was to kill every military-aged male on the island (obj. Murray). We proceeded into the house and detained 3 other males that were hiding behind 2 women so we would not shoot them. We then dragged the KIA outside. From there 3rd squad with Gun 6 proceeded to the 2nd house, leaving 2nd squad and the platoon leader with the detainees. As 3rd squad ran to the 2nd house while Gun 6 laid down suppressive fire over the house so they would not hit anyone in the house. When third squad got to the door a man came out holding a baby so that he would not get shot.... SPC Hunsaker and PFC Clagett were changing the zip ties on the detainee to bigger ones because the one we had on them broke earlier on the obj. I heard "oh shit" come from the front of the house followed by gun fire. SSG Girouard and I ran around to the front of the house, where I found PFC Clagett holding his face from where he had been struck by one of the detainees. When I asked him what happened he told me that when they were changing the zip ties one of the detainees stabbed Hunsaker and another one punched PFC Clagett. So they were forced to use deadly force. When I went inside I found that Hunsaker had been stabbed but was going to be ok. I then returned to the room where the women were at and remained there till we left at 1308.

Kevin A. Ryan made the following sworn statement:

0086-06-CID469-75447

SWORN STATEMENT
For use of this form, see AR 190-45; the proponent agency is Office of The Deputy Chief of Staff for Personnel.

LOCATION COB Spiecher, Tikrit APO AE 09393	DATE *MBB* 29 May 2006	TIME *MB* **1026**	FILE NUMBER Seq #
LAST NAME, FIRST NAME, MIDDLE NAME BIVINS, Micah Brandon	SOCIAL SECURITY NUMBER		GRADE/STATUS SPC/AD

ORGANIZATION OR ADDRESS
C Company 3-187 IN BN, Brassfield Mora, Iraq (Fort Campbell, KY)

I, ___ *MBB* ___ Micah Brandon Bivins ___, WANT TO MAKE THE FOLLOWING STATEMENT UNDER OATH:

After supper chow we were sitting around our humvees when Colonel Steele started making rounds. He would stop and talk to groups of soldiers, shake hands, and just shoot the shit for a little while. Before he left the parking area he gave a pep talk. He told us how proud he is of us and how we are doing a good job. Then he started talking about the mission, he said that a couple objectives were going to be hot LZs. Later my squad had a meeting, and we were told that apachies were going to light the objectives up. An hour or so later word got around that we didn't have AWT for the objective that we were going to. We were later told that all military aged males were to be considered hostile. On 9 May 06, we left for objective Murray. On the first objective we found an empty house and sheep pen. At the second objective we landed maybe 150 to 100 meters a way from a house. Most of third squad formed a line and started at the house, I was the last person in that line. By the time some of the squad cleared the house I was told that an Iraqi had been shot. He was brought outside and I started to work on him. He had two bullet wounds to the lower chest. He died about two minutes after the first shots were fired. There were three military aged males and two adult females. Someone detained the males and stayed to guard them. SSG Girourd, SGT Lemus, SPC Hunsaker, PFC Mason, and I ran to the berm where SGT Ryan and CPL Helton had an m240 placed for overwatch. SSG Girourd told CPL Helton to provide grazing fire into the berm on the other side of the second house. He was told to not stop firing until we got to a feeding trench next to the house. We started running down the berm towards the house and rounded the corner I saw the detainees lying on the open holding a small child in front of his head and chest. Someone took the child from him and gave it to one of the females. The house was cleared and we found an AK 47 and several mags. We moved the detainee back to the first house and started the detainee packets. While a couple of soldiers were working on the detainee packages someone else started putting the KIA into a body bag. SPC Graber and myself started searching the house and found some AK 47 parts and several mags. SPC Graber found a 9 mm pistol in a woman's purse. We finished our search of the house and started taking pictures of the weapons and detainees. About this time second squad and Lt Weirheim went to secure the PZ. An UH60 came and took them to the next objective. After they left we were suppose to have an UH60 come back in a few minutes to pick us up. So Sgt Ryan, Cpl Helton, SPC Kemp, Sgt Lemus and the detainee, and myself went into PZ posture. After a few minutes I heard gunshots at the house, I got up and grabbed my aid bag and ran back to the house. As I rounded the corner I saw the detainees lying on the ground about 20 to 30 feet away from the house. I saw PFC Claggett standing up in the yard by the doorway. He didn't seem to have any obvious life threatening injuries so I went to the detainees I did a quick assessment and two were dead right there and the third was having agnail breathing. Before I could do anything he had stop agnail breathing and I called him in dead. About that time I went check on SPC Hunsaker and PFC Claggett and I saw SPC Hunsaker's arm was bleeding to where I applied a pressure dressing and I clean up his wounds in his face. I then went to PFC Claggett and he told me he had been hit so I check for fractures in his face and found no fractures. I gave him a Tylenol for a headache. After that we started taking pictures of what was left of the detainees and pictures of the wounds. About that time 2nd PLT walked up and SSG Girourd and LT Young had a conversation, but I didn't hear it. Then 2nd PLT took the remaining detainee and KIAs on UH60s. They put all of the KIAs and detainee on the same bird and left. We sat in PZ posture for three to four and a half hours before the next helicopter came for us. We went to a different objective, but I don't remember the name of it. This all that happened on OBJ Murry that I can recall. *MBB*
Q: JONES *MBB*
A: BIVINS *MBB*
Q: Did you type the above narrative?
A: Yes, except for the last few lines. *MBB*
Q: Why did SA JONES type the last few lines?
A: Cause the computer went haywire. *MBB*
Q: Did you hear COL Steel say the ROE was to kill all military age males on OBJ Murry?
A: No *MBB*

EXHIBIT	INITIALS OF PERSON MAKING STATEMENT *MBB*	
		PAGE 1 OF ___ 4 ___ PAGES

ADDITIONAL PAGES MUST CONTAIN THE HEADING "STATEMENT OF ____ TAKEN AT ____ DATED ____CONTINUED."
THE BOTTOM OF EACH ADDITIONAL PAGE MUST BEAR THE INITIALS OF THE PERSON MAKING THE STATEMENT AND BE
INITIALED AS "PAGE ____ OF ____ PAGES." WHEN ADDITIONAL PAGES ARE UTILIZED, THE BACK OF PAGE 1 WILL BE
LINED OUT, AND THE STATEMENT WILL BE CONCLUDED ON THE REVERSE SIDE OF ANOTHER COPY OF THIS FORM.

DA FORM 2823
1 JUL 72

SUPERSEDES DA FORM 2823, 1 JAN 68, WHICH WILL BE USED.
FOR OFFICIAL USE ONLY - LAW ENFORCEMENT SENSITIVE   EXHIBIT _____

Sample of a portion of the sworn statement by Micah Branden Bivins

> On 09 May 2006 I was an assistant gunner attached to 3rd squad, 3rd plt, C Co. 3-187 In. That morning we were conducting raids on OBJ Murray, a known insurgent stronghold. The ROE for OBJ Murray as set by the brigade commander was to kill any military-age male.... Upon landing we proceeded 50m to the north to a single house. Before entering the house a male appeared in the window and was engaged by 3rd squad. Me and CPL Helton stopped short at the corner of the house and provided security. Shortly thereafter the house was cleared with 3 male detainees.... The man that was engaged by 3rd squad died less than 5 minutes later. Myself and CPL Helton proceeded to the hill north of the house. We relieved PFC Clagett on overwatch on another mud hut to the north. CPL Helton was instructed by SSG Girouard to lay grazing fire over the top of the hut into a berm behind it while he and his squad approached from the south. Upon using grazing fire and 3rd squad approaching house, a single male of military-aged male came outside holding a baby.... Approximately 3 hours later we were exfilled.

The platoon leader, LT Justin Wehrheim, who was leading the mission on the ground, gives a very similar account of the new ROE and the mission:

> On 09 May 2006 at LC ____, 3rd squad and 2nd squad of 3rd platoon were dropped off by 2 UH-60 helicopters in order to raid the two housing compounds in the vicinity of that grid. The ROE given by our chain of command was to kill every military-aged male on the objective. Upon proceeding north to the first house, Staff Sergeant Girouard engaged one military-aged male standing in the window. I then began to check the M-240 placement. After being satisfied with the gun placement, I proceeded towards the house where there were 1 KIA and 3 male detainees who had used the women in the house as shields. After they were properly detained, we proceeded north to the next house and got 1 more male detainee who used his baby as a shield. After the houses had been searched and the 1 KIA was put in a body bag, I took 2nd squad and proceeded to the next objective. I then was called on the radio and told that the detainees we had left with 3rd squad were now KIA after they had stabbed SPC Hunsaker in the face and wrist with a knife and punched PFC Clagett in the face and attempted to flee after breaking their flex cuffs.

REACTIONS FROM THE COMMANDING OFFICERS

On the same day that the soldiers were making their sworn statements, Steele issued a written order that called for an investigation into the deaths of the three prisoners:

> To perform an informal investigation IAW AR 15-6, obtaining details pertaining to the circumstances surrounding the deaths of three (3) insurgents by elements of C/3-187 IN on 9 May 06. Your investigation should answer the following questions:

> What are the facts surrounding the deaths of the insurgents? How was an insurgent able to attack a soldier with a knife? Is there physical evidence of the attack? Why were the other insurgents killed?

> Were the shootings justified under the current Rules of Engagement? What threat did the Soldiers perceive from the insurgents? Was this threat reasonable under the circumstances?

> Was there a violation of the Law of Armed Conflict (LOAC)?

The memorandum is signed "MICHAEL D. STEELE, COL, IN Command-ing." Note that the prisoners who were called detainees by the soldiers are referred to by Steele as "insurgents." This is an important discrepancy be-cause "insurgents" could conceivably fall under the ROE to kill all military-age males, whereas detainees and prisoners hold some rights under the laws of war. In any case, how did Steele know they were insurgents? CPT Hart referred to them as terrorists. Terrorists and insurgents are not necessarily the same category of people. Note that Steele refers to "the current Rules of Engagement," not *the* ROE.

Also on this same day, the 11 of May 2006, CPT Daniel C. Hart, the Com-pany Commander wrote a memorandum to the brigade commander. Hart's report covers much the same information as the sworn affidavits, albeit, with some greater detail, and with a conclusion that no crime was committed:

> While detaining three individuals after an attack on OBJ Murray in the vicinity of _____ CPL Hunsacker and PFC Clagett shot and killed three prospective detainees after being attacked by them with deadly force dur-ing the detainment process. The purpose of this memorandum is to com-municate the findings regarding the facts behind the shootings and to rec-ommend actions for the benefit of future performance.

> Background: During all planning and preparation for Operation Iron Tri-angle, I and the battalion and brigade commanders over me reinforced the Rules of Engagement noting *that positively identified personnel in known affiliation with terrorist organizations were legitimate military targets* [my emphasis]. The Soldiers knew that OBJ Murray was full of Al Qaeda members and associ-ates of Al Zarqawi. OBJ Murray had also been the target of at least one SOF raid in the past two months. After exiting their UH-60 Blackhawks, the 3rd Platoon element consisting of 1LT Wehrheim, SSG Girouard, SGT Lemus, CPL Hunsacker, CPL Helms, SPC Kemp, SPC Bivins, and PFC Clagett ran to the nearest building to begin clearing it. Seeing a man through an open window, the Soldiers shot him as they approached. Three military-aged males named _____ remained in the house and used their wives as shields as they cowered behind them. The Soldiers moved the ladies to the side and brought the men outside the house. They searched, separated, zip-tied and blindfolded each detainee and prepped them to move. The majority of the platoon bypassed the house and continued toward one more, where they captured an additional detainee. The Iraqi Army Soldiers who were on the objective engaged the US Soldiers in a heated argument about killing the first man and detaining the other three. Although they had been briefed nu-merous times the night prior that the people of the area were responsible for beheadings, kidnappings, murders, IED operations and other terrorist activities, they reached the point of belligerence in their argumentation. 1LT Wehrehim dealt with them and calmed the situation. Then, 1LT Weh-rheim and members of the platoon moved toward the PZ with the final detainee and flew to their next objective. A few minutes later as CPL Hun-sacker was prepping his detainees to move to the helicopter, he noticed that the detainees' handcuffs were very weak and needed to be replaced by actual zip ties. In fact, one of the detainees had apparently already bro-ken his zip ties. As the Soldiers began to change the zip ties, one of them brandished a knife and slashed CPL Hunsacker and another punched PFC

Clagett in the face. CPL Hunsacker and PFC Clagett responded to these attacks with deadly force and shot the men as they attempted to escape. Other soldiers heard the yelling and turned to see them shooting the AIF as they turned to run. SPC Bivins arrived on the scene and checked CPL Hunsacker's wounds determining that he had sustained a four inch superficial cut on his left cheek, an inch long superficial cut on his right cheek and a three inch long laceration on his left forearm. He treated CPL Hunsacker's wounds and bandaged him. The platoon then bagged the mission and continued mission.

Findings: The Soldiers understood the ROE and had been told many times that this area was populated with AIF. They went into the mission with an expectation to fight upon arrival. On this and other missions during Operation Iron Triangle, known insurgents used non-combatants like women and babies as shields to avoid being shot. This further confirmed in the minds of the Soldiers that the three detainees they had taken from OBJ Murray were in fact AIF. The AIF had been searched for weapons already and it is not clear how one of them secured a knife and broke his zip-ties. I am exploring and will investigate the possibility of one of the Iraqi Soldiers slipping him a knife thinking that he could use it to escape. The bottom line is that the Soldiers acted within the ROE when responding to the attacks by the AIF personnel. They observed a hostile act and reacted with deadly force, killing the AIF.

Actions: At the point of detention, the number of detainees outnumbered the number of Soldiers. Although this is normally the case at a hasty detainee collection point, Soldiers must take care in any situation where the detainee is unrestrained (eating, using the latrine, or changing flex-cuffs) that they are only permitting one detainee at a time to be uncuffed. The fact that all three were uncuffed at the same time is a large contributing factor to their attempt to escape. Furthermore, the zip-ties used initially were indeed weak and will not be used again in this company. The company will use only prussic cuffs or wider flex-cuffs. In addition to these, I will continue to condition my Iraqi Army company to understand the nature and severity of the conflict and to prevent them from having similarly adverse reactions to the killing and detention of AIF. This is a serious issue that must be overcome if our units will ever work well together. I recommend no further action after completion of the Article 15-6 investigation that is currently ongoing.

Note that both Hart and Steele use the term "ROE" in their statements, but they do not define what it is, and only Hart paraphrases it as "positively identified personnel in known affiliation with terrorist organizations were legitimate military targets." Steele refers to it as the "current" ROE. Hart's and Steele's care in choosing their words stands in sharp contrast to the sworn statements by the soldiers, as well as the platoon leader LT Wehrheim who defined the ROE very precisely and attributed it to Steele. Given that the tone of Steele's memorandum suggests that he wants to make sure it is understood that the undefined "current" ROE was followed, and Hart's memorandum suggests that it was — it seems odd that the ROE is not stated verbatim.

0086-06-CID469-75447

SWORN STATEMENT
For use of this form, see AR 190-45; the proponent agency is Office of The Deputy Chief of Staff for Personnel.

LOCATION	DATE	TIME	FILE NUMBER
COB Speicher Tikrit, Iz, APO AE 09393	29 May06	1548	

LAST NAME, FIRST NAME, MIDDLE NAME: WEHRHEIM, Justin Richard
SOCIAL SECURITY NUMBER: [redacted]
GRADE/STATUS: O-2/AD

ORGANIZATION OR ADDRESS: C Company, 3/187th INF BN, FOB Brassfield-Mora, Samarra, Iz, APO AE 09394

I, 1LT Justin R. WEHRHEIM, WANT TO MAKE THE FOLLOWING STATEMENT UNDER OATH:

On 08May06 my platoon, 3/C/3-187 arrived at FOB Remagen at or about 1500 for operation Iron Triangle. We then began to conduct rehearsals with out IA counterparts for this mission. I was called aside by Chappin' 6, CPT. HART, who told me that the ROE for this mission was that all military aged males on this objective (objective Murray) were positively identified as being affiliated with Al-queda in Iraq and they could there-fore be shot/engaged immediately upon Identifying them as a military aged males on objective murray. We then went to chow with our Iraqi counterparts. After chow we had a backbrief in a warehouse to the south west of the parking lot we had staged in. Squad leaders and above attended this backbrief. The ROG was reinforced that all military aged males on objective murray (the whole island) were positively identified as al-queda in Iraq and could be engaged on sight/positive identification that they were a military aged male and that all structures were hostile structures. We were also briefed that pre-assault fires had been approved for this objective. I then went back an reinforced this ROE to my Platoon. Soon after that, Col Steele came and gave a speech to C/3-187 and reinforced that every military aged male on objective Murray was to be killed. He again reinforced, verbally, that this objective had engaged gun

EXHIBIT	INITIALS OF PERSON MAKING STATEMENT	PAGE 1 OF 11 PAGES

ADDITIONAL PAGES MUST CONTAIN THE HEADING "STATEMENT OF ___ TAKEN AT ___ DATED ___ CONTINUED." THE BOTTOM OF EACH ADDITIONAL PAGE MUST BEAR THE INITIALS OF THE PERSON MAKING THE STATEMENT AND BE INITIALED AS "PAGE ___ OF ___ PAGES." WHEN ADDITIONAL PAGES ARE UTILIZED, THE BACK OF PAGE 1 WILL BE LINED OUT, AND THE STATEMENT WILL BE CONCLUDED ON THE REVERSE SIDE OF ANOTHER COPY OF THIS FORM.

DA FORM 2823
1 JUL 72
SUPERSEDES DA FORM 2823, 1 JAN 68, WHICH WILL BE USED.
For Official Use Only – Law Enforcement Sensitive   EXHIBIT_____

Sample of a portion of the sworn statement by Justin P. Wehrheimer.

Since the ROE is the main focus of Hart's and Steele's documents, why didn't they define the ROE? One possible reason is that the two command-ers may have already suspected that there was something wrong with the ROE. Defining the ROE would have exposed the commanders to the same legal jeopardy that some of the soldiers experienced precisely because they did define the ROE — namely, the ROE is unlawful. Hart's report concludes that the undefined but paraphrased and "current" ROE was followed, and that the obedience to this new ROE was lawful.

Hart refers to the three dead men variously as "prospective detainees" and "detainees." Were they, in fact, prisoners or potential prisoners? And which of these two categories did the soldiers use to perceive them? Hart mentions that the soldiers "knew" (or at least perceived) the prisoners to be Al-Qaeda terrorists. And the soldiers were given verbal orders repeatedly to kill all military-age males, who were perceived as terrorists or insurgents or AIF, on sight. It would have been difficult for the soldiers to make the switch mentally that the three captured males were "prisoners," and that separate ROE as well as sops (standard operating procedures), in addition to the Ge-neva Conventions, apply to prisoners. While Hart concludes that the pris-oners were killed lawfully under existing yet undefined ROE, he does not mention the Laws of Armed Conflict which state that a gradual escalation of force must be used against escaping prisoners. The precise definition of the social status of the captured men — in fact, as well as a matter of collective perception — makes all the difference in the world in understanding and judging what happened. Moreover, a precise understanding of which ROE (the traditional one which allows for taking prisoners and specifies precisely the gradual escalation of force in dealing with hostile prisoners versus the new one which is virtually unknown except for how it was perceived by soldiers) applied, and to which social status (non-combatant, combatant, prisoner), is also important for rendering judgment.

The issue of the Iraqi soldiers who were present at the scene haunts the narrative and will haunt this analysis from beginning to end. Soldiers verify Hart's observation that the Iraqi soldiers were angry at the Americans for shooting the first presumed AIF. Why were they angry? Hart implies that it was because they were not thoroughly briefed in the ROE or were not suf-ficiently trained. The platoon leader, LT Wehrheim, would claim later that they were briefed thoroughly. Clagett told me that the Iraqi soldiers said the man who was killed was old and "was a good man" and an Iraqi policeman. In other words, one possible explanation for the anger of the Iraqi soldiers was that they thought that the Americans had made a mistake in killing the elderly man. The platoon leader, 1LT Wehrheim, confirmed Clagett's claim, and told me that he took the Iraqi soldiers away from the scene because they were extremely upset. A few minutes after Wehreim flew away with the Iraqi soldiers on a Black Hawk helicopter, the prisoners were killed. Were the Iraqi soldiers trying to protect the prisoners? For their part, the American soldiers were suspicious of the Iraqi soldiers.

It is not clear, from Hart's statement, why the fact that the men on the island used women and babies as shields confirmed in the minds of the soldiers that the men were, in fact, terrorists. Perhaps the American soldiers perceived terrorists as cowards; this particular image, of dark-skinned bad guys hiding behind women and children, is enshrined in "Black Hawk Down." But terrorist or not, it is possible that any man who thought he would be shot on sight and who was unarmed would resort to any means to save his life — including the use of women and babies as human shields. Another possible interpretation is that the US military believes that Iraqi forces are infiltrated with the enemy; thus it is conceivable that, once the Iraqi soldiers were briefed on the ROE, the "insurgents" were told what to expect from US soldiers, and therefore they hid behind the only thing that would protect them from the ROE as well as American bullets, namely, women and children. This might also explain why the Iraqi soldiers were so upset: they knew that the "insurgent" prisoners were likely to be killed under the new ROE. If the situation on the ground during the "battle" (there was no enemy fire) was insecure and operations were still ongoing, why would the Army remove its allied Iraqi forces from the battlefield? Had the relationship between the US and Iraqi soldiers been one of genuine alliance, surely the Americans would have put the Iraqi soldiers in charge of the prisoners, freeing up its own soldiers to clear and control the rest of the area. It seems very odd that the Iraqi soldiers were whisked away by the platoon leader in a helicopter while the mission continued.

But the bottom line, as Hart puts it, is that the US soldiers acted properly in killing the prisoners. The issue of the type of handcuffs, zip-ties, or flexi-cuffs that were used on the prisoners is a diversion from the issues at hand. Would the prisoners be alive had they been handcuffed with the sturdiest material used by the Army? Moreover, subsequent versions of what happened suggest that the soldiers cut the prisoners free, and told them to run, so that they could shoot them with the pretense that the prisoners were hostile toward the soldiers, which in turn justified the use of deadly force in their minds. We shall examine these alternate scenarios later. At this point in the analysis, it is important to note that the matter could have been and almost was closed with Hart's report.

Indeed, Hart's conclusion became the basis for subsequent media reports of the incident. It was also the fundamental narrative with which the defense attorneys approached the case, the media, and me. If Hart's conclusion were true, then one would have to explain why the Army was prosecuting US soldiers for following the new ROE. The soldiers apparently assume in their May 11 sworn statements that the new ROE were lawful, but some of them express doubts in subsequent statements. Hart assumes that the new ROE were lawful and that the killings were as well. The Army, as well as the information media, had to make a choice in framing the events being described. Either the new ROE were unlawful, or the soldiers broke the law. The consequences of pursuing one path versus the other are enormous. The first path would have put the Army on trial, metaphorically speaking, but also would have raised questions as to why soldiers failed to disobey an unlawful order. The second path would have put the soldiers on trial, but then questions would arise as to *which* law they broke, the new ROE or the traditional ROE. The killing of the man in the window was "lawful" under the new ROE but unlawful under the traditional ROE. The killing of the prisoners is problematic under either version of the ROE. The safest path for the Army was to ignore the killing of the man in the window and charge soldiers with violating the traditional ROE with regard to the prisoners.

But too much public exposure of these issues would still raise questions about the ROE. That fact put pressure on the Army to obtain plea bargains and try to avoid going to trial. The government and the media took the path more traveled by — shifting the blame onto the low-ranking soldier and not the government that established the unlawful policies.

Conclusions

Mission accomplished? This bold and premature claim by the Bush Administration has been a source of irony and criticism ever since those infamous words were posted on a banner on the *USS Abraham Lincoln* in the year 2003. Five years later, the Bush Administration would admit reluctantly that it was a poor choice of words. But the phrase "mission accomplished," in both cases (the initial victory in Iraq and Operation Iron Triangle) leads to several questions: What was the mission? How does one measure the success of the mission? Had the mission in Iraq been solely the inner-directed one, a swift military victory, then indeed it was accomplished. But, and in addition to military victory, the goal was the other-directed one of pacification and bringing democracy, which clearly was not accomplished (as of this writing). Similarly, in Operation Iron Triangle, the mission would have been successful had the soldiers carried out the order to kill every military-aged male on the island — the new ROE would not have been questioned had that occurred. But the taking of prisoners, and subsequent killing of prisoners, raised suspicions and questions.

The questions are not only about the facts of the case but about the military's principles, rules, and code of honor. And of course, the minor discrepancies among the soldiers' sworn affidavits and the commander's memorandums immediately raise suspicions as to the sincerity of all the accounts.

Similar questions have been raised about the infamous mission in Mogadishu, Somalia in 1993. Was it a fiasco, as some have claimed, that resulted in the needless deaths of 18 US soldiers and over a thousand Somali civilians? Or was it a success in the ways portrayed in "Black Hawk Down," in that US soldiers showed courage and determination against tremendous odds? The same Michael Steele who was the commander during the mission in Mogadishu was the commander during Operation Iron Triangle. By inner-directed standards, courage has to be measured in relation to the value of the goal that is being pursued, so that demanding courage from soldiers in pursuit of a dubious goal is considered reckless. By other-directed standards, one person's perception of fiasco is another person's perception of a glorious victory, if victory is measured by narrow standards that are valued by specific peer groups and media. Thus, the mission in Mogadishu was portrayed in the film as a success because the two warlords were eventually captured and the US soldiers behaved as a "band of brothers." Nevertheless, the day following the successful-or-failed mission, depending upon one's point of view, President Clinton ordered US troops to withdraw from Somalia.

Ambiguity, ambivalence, and an uneasy perplexity follow attempts to recast inner-directed defeats into other-directed victories. Similarly, regarding Operation Iron Triangle, the letters and affidavits that tried to present a successful mission raised more questions than answers and led to suspicions. The "joint" US–Iraqi Army mission suggests that the two sides were suspicious of each other. The US soldiers met no resistance on the island; was the "intelligence" about terrorists valid? Shooting prisoners under any circumstances immediately raises questions about the laws of warfare.

CHAPTER 4. THE MEDIA'S SPIN ON THE EVENTS AND THEIR ECHOES IN THE PAST

It is a truism that since the 1950s, the media, ranging from newspapers and television to films and Internet blogs, has exploded in influence, variety, and quantity. If our recent ancestors were thrilled to be able to choose between two channels on a black and white television set (or between Tide and Cheer in detergents, Coke and Pepsi in colas, and so on), the contemporary postemotional type often has the option of choosing among hundreds of television programs (and ever-increasing choices in detergents or colas or other consumables, many of which add further agony in decision making by adding varieties of flavors, scents, accents, and other tiny details of marginal differentiation). Ironically, the contemporary viewer is often bored and uninterested in current events, despite or perhaps because of the Milky Way Galaxy of choices that are available. Like a child who cannot choose what to wear precisely because his or her closet is crammed full of clothes, the contemporary consumer of information is often paralyzed by the huge quantities of seemingly disparate bits of information. In previous generations, a recognizable figure such as Walter Cronkite was trusted and believed partly because he or she was a consistent and predictable figure in one's life, which was already far more consistent and stable in contrast to the constant shifts we experience now. Nowadays, people choose their favorite source of news — although the loyalty is fleeting, as in all other aspects of life — but even then are confused by the various angles, perspectives, takes, and spin on the information. The typical human response to over-stimulation and an embarrassment of choices is apathy.

For example, the Operation Iron Triangle killings received their fair share of media coverage. But these killings were reported in 2006, in which a plethora of other apparently similar crimes were reported from Haditha, Baghdad, and elsewhere. Was this an indication of a pattern — that a new set of ROE had become de facto policy in the war in Iraq — or a remarkable set of coincidences?

I have observed lawyers in war crimes trials to use the analogy of a widespread fire versus a series of individual brushfires to make either point, depending upon whether the lawyer was arguing for the defense or the prosecution. A fire is an empirical, verifiable fact, but it can be cast as one huge fire (an overall pattern) or a series of small, individual, unrelated fires. A similar question arises in the Abu Ghraib abuse: were these actions perpetrated by a few "rotten apples," or were they part of a de facto policy that was put in place at Guantanamo, Bagram prison in Afghanistan, and detention centers run by the US military in general since 2003? Journalists seem to be as confused as analysts, lawyers, and laypersons who consume this overload of information.

Even when the media concentrates on one specific site of abuse, such as the Iron Triangle murders or Abu Ghraib, it can confuse itself and its consumers by choosing to focus on one aspect of the case versus another and also by focusing on "distractions." For example, should the emphasis be on COL Steele's alleged ROE to kill all military age Iraqis or on the bitter in-fighting and betrayal among the soldiers in the squad as they attempted to cope with an investigation that was going to send some of them to jail? With regard to Abu Ghraib, the media alternated between focusing on MG Geoffrey Miller's infamous trip from Guantanamo to Abu Ghraib as an effort to "Gitmo-ize" Abu Ghraib versus the details of Lynndie England's sex life at Abu Ghraib. "Distractions" have become an integral aspect of contemporary media coverage because many consumers *are* interested in details which would have been regarded as irrelevant by the inner-directed type, such as what sorts of cuffs the soldiers used to restrain captives during Operation Iron Triangle, the name of Lynndie England's baby, or more remotely, why Senator Barack Obama didn't always wear a flag pin (which was inflated into a divisive issue in the presidential campaign in the year 2008). In contemporary society, deciding on what is "the" news is as difficult as agreeing on what "the" law means.

CPT Hart's version of events (mission accomplished, no crimes were committed) was reproduced in some form by the so-called mainstream media in August 2006 and right up to the scheduled trials that were canceled in January of 2007. This is significant because by August 2006, the Army already possessed sworn statements that were drastically different from the May 11 version of events and had already charged some of the soldiers with premeditated murder.

Also, in June 2006, the Supreme Court re-affirmed that Article 3 of the Geneva Conventions *does* apply to the war against al Qaeda. Theoretically, that ruling would have made the shooting of the man in the window as unlawful as the shooting of the three prisoners. But ironically, the killing of the Iraqi man in the window, which was a war crime by standards enshrined in the Geneva Conventions and re-affirmed by the Supreme Court, drew hardly any notice or focus from the media.

Instead, the media chose to focus on the glamour of COL Steele's reputation, not from the actual battle of the Battle of Mogadishu, which is regarded as a military fiasco, but from "Black Hawk Down," which recast it as a tale of courage. The media also focused on the in-fighting between the soldiers, who were unable to live up to expectations based on the stereotype of the "band of brothers." In the end, the heart of the matter — the serious legal ramifications as well as the social implications of the war crimes committed during Operation Iron Triangle and elsewhere in Iraq — was diluted by media coverage into a disconnected series of "distractions."

It is in this context that ABC's "Nightline" ran a segment on August 2, 2006 entitled "Shoot to Kill: The Band of Brothers Unravels." One of the most important norms followed by the media in contemporary times is to present opposing viewpoints in the coverage of any story. It is an open question whether this approach truly promotes objectivity or just the appearance of objectivity, but there is no doubt that the norm is real. By pitting COL Steele's version against that of the soldiers, and some of the soldiers against other soldiers, the media comes across as seemingly sincere in striving for objectivity, even if at the end of the broadcast the consumer of information is left without firm referents for deciding which version is correct and who is actually being sincere.

It is more important that, in this particular case, the news media performed the substitute function of putting the accused on trial — in its own way — given that the trial never took place. The "jury" in the substitute media trial is our society, but also to some extent the international audience in the background — and these two "juries" often arrive at different verdicts based upon the same evidence. The peer group jury of public opinion has increasingly come to rival the importance of the traditional jury of one's peers in a real courtroom. Obviously, there is no cross-examination in a news segment, and other traditional aspects of a jury trial are missing as well. Nevertheless, Nightline's airing of opposing viewpoints would be as close as Clagett would ever get to a real trial.

Finally, the media routinely "frame" issues, even as they present opposing viewpoints, through the emotionally-laden words they choose carefully
and just as scrupulously omit, and other techniques of centering versus de-
centering and marginalizing issues. What ideas and emotions are evoked
by the phrase, "shoot to kill?" What feelings are created in the consumer
of news with the phrase, "band of brothers?" The role of the Army and the
government is left out of the frame. To be sure, real judges and lawyers also
frame issues by referring to their interpretations of various laws that are invoked. Frames of reference and social constructions of reality are used in
all attempts at "objectivity," whether these are used by lawyers and judges,
journalists, or social scientists and other academics.

But, again, objectivity is not necessarily the information media's major
goal in the other-directed age — even though projecting the appearance of
objectivity is paramount. Again, Riesman observes that contemporary media
seek to present themselves as tolerant and "cannot help being aware of those
attitudes that may offend their complex constituencies." He continues:
"Whereas the early nineteenth-century editor could gamble on a crusade that
might bring him both a libel suit and a circulation, the twentieth-century
publisher often cannot afford to let his editor gamble on an increased circulation" (p. 192). The media in the twenty first-century seems to be even
more mindful of seeking to avoid offending specific audiences and thereby
losing money from advertising. Thus, we will see that ABC News and other
media were careful *not* to appeal to inner-directed types who were indignant that United States Army was charging its own soldiers with shooting
people who were presumed to be terrorists. At the same time, it tolerated
their voices to some extent, but not too much. The way that the story was
presented is a typical example of the balancing act that goes into presenting
a contemporary news story. The segment began as follows:

> Good evening. We begin, tonight, with a group of soldiers, part of one of
> the most-respected divisions within the American army accused of con-
> spiracy and murder. Military misconduct in Iraq has been an increasing
> source of controversy and the US has made it clear that it will punish any
> soldiers found guilty of wrongdoing. And in Iraq today, there was an Ar-
> ticle 32 hearing, the military equivalent of a grand jury, to decide whether
> these soldiers should be court-martialed. Tonight, we're going to hear from
> one of the soldiers accused of murder. He spoke exclusively to "Nightline."
> And his side of the story raises some serious questions.

Nightline uses relatively neutral descriptions such as "misconduct" and
"controversy" to refer to the government's role in this and related cases. It uses
"shoot to kill" as the somewhat familiar and sensationalistic title for the segment, but fails to mention the term ROE. Even when ROE is mentioned later
in the segment, the overall focus is shifted away from the government's role
and toward the "unraveling" of the alleged "band of brothers" or soldiers in

the unit. In this way, the information media mirrors the government's overall thrust and approach to the case. Few if any questions are raised about the extent to which these ROE (which are interpreted by "Nightline" as "shoot to kill" but not as "kill on sight," which are two different things) are policy in the war in Iraq, and most questions focus on the minute details of how the soldiers turned on each other and changed their version of what happened.

In a sense, the public is distracted away from the serious policy issues and toward issues that it has been socialized to recognize in Reality TV shows — the private lives, bickering, accusations, and counter-accusations of any group of people in almost any situation. It is as if one were watching a yacht race but was more concerned with what the people on the boats were saying to each other and how they got along than with the outcome of the race. American audiences have already been thoroughly socialized by the media to concentrate on insignificant details or "distractions" as opposed to "the big picture" through a plethora of television shows, especially "reality" shows which concentrate on insider bickering and disagreements.

Moreover, the use of the phrase "band of brothers" refers indirectly to a bestselling book by Stephen E. Ambrose, which is subtitled "E Company, 506th Regiment, 101st Airborne from Normandy to Hitler's Eagle's Nest." It is ironic that Clagett was also assigned to the 101st Airborne Division. This phrase also invokes a television series by the same title that featured Hollywood director Steven Spielberg and actor Tom Hanks: "Band of Brothers — They Depended on Each Other and the World Depended on Them." To what extent was the media playing on these postemotional connections — the manipulation of synthetic emotional affinities — in order to suggest that Saddam Hussein was like Adolph Hitler, and the 101st Airborne soldiers in both wars were saving the world from tyrants? One significant difference is that the "band of brothers" in this particular case, in the year 2006, turned on each other.

The soldier in question in the "Nightline" segment was "our accused," as CPT Rutizer referred to him, namely — Corey Clagett. Clagett's mother came on the air: "I have begged God, I have prayed. I stood out in the rain for an hour and a half just talking to him and telling him, 'I will never ask him for anything, ever. But please, bring my son home." Next, the lead defense attorney (who is a civilian but is a former commissioned officer) Paul Bergrin, said: "If my client is found guilty, he's facing the death penalty. Capital punishment. They shouldn't be put through this. And I'm going to prove to the American public, the United States military, that they are innocent." These were the inner-directed voices of indignation at the military having the audacity to put heroic soldiers on trial.

ABC's journalist Martin Bashir summarized the situation as follows: "On May the 9th, the detachment of soldiers from the 3rd Battalion 101st Airborne Division, landed on an island close to the Iraqi border with Syria. They were in a state of highly charged readiness. We spoke to Private Clagett by telephone from his jail cell in the presence of his lawyer." Following this broadcast, most media accounts of this incident referred to the location in this vague way as being close to Syria, and sometimes as being close to the city of Samarra. Very few accounts stated that the site of the mission was some sixty miles north of Baghdad. The negative connotations of Syria play immediately upon the emotions. The televised exchange between Bashir and Clagett went as follows:

> Clagett: "I was told that we were going into an al Qaeda and in an Iraqi–anti-Iraqi Force training area and when we were coming in, to expect fire before we got on the ground. They were gonna shoot the bird and said we're gonna go in hot.
>
> Bashir: "Members of the unit say they were given their rules of engagement the day before the mission. And on this occasion, those rules were highly unusual. What, specifically, were you told?"
>
> Clagett: "We were told that everybody on this island was hostile. They were known al Qaeda insurgents and we're going to kill all military-aged males. So be prepared."
>
> Bashir: "So you were told specifically to kill all military-aged males?"
>
> Clagett: "Correct."
>
> Bashir: "Were you ever told on any other mission that you were to kill all military-aged males? Did that ever happen prior to this event?"
>
> Clagett: "No."
>
> Bashir: "Never?"
>
> Clagett: "Never."
>
> Bashir: "Private Clagett's statement is supported by other soldiers, whose testimony has been obtained by 'Nightline.' We showed their statements to Professor Gary Solis, a former military judge and prosecutor.
>
> Professor Gary Solis: "Several of the statements mentioned that there was an order from the regimental commander that all military-aged males that were encountered could be shot and killed on sight. If it's correct that a commander gave such an order, that order would, in itself, be a violation of the law of armed conflict."

This was the one and only time in the broadcast that any reference was made to the alleged unlawfulness of the ROE. The speaker is the same Gary Solis who published the book, *Son Thang*, about the Marine Corps equivalent of the My Lai massacre. This expert was accorded the least amount of time in the program. After all, if the commander had issued such an unlawful order, most people, presumably, would be inclined to blame the commander as well as the accused soldier for following orders. Albeit the "picture frame" (metaphorically speaking) of a soldier following unlawful orders is itself complex and raises serious issues: Should the soldier have disobeyed the unlawful order? How would the soldier know or perceive that the order was unlawful? Such questions echo similar dilemmas and legal issues from the My Lai massacre.

The incident also harks back post emotionally into history to the Nuremberg trials and beyond. However, at least two points must be kept in mind in assessing this frame of reference. First, Clagett's version of the order is, indeed, supported by numerous other sworn statements by other soldiers. The sworn statements that I had read do correspond to the particular version of the order that was broadcast by ABC News. In other words, there is a remarkable consistency in the reported perception of the verbal order that was given, regardless of what the written order may have said (which was kept secret in any event).

However, some of the soldiers stated that this was not the first time they had received such an unusual ROE. Second, the frame of reference touched on by the media — that Clagett was following an unlawful order to kill all military-aged males on sight — is one that the Army would regard as most unwelcome. This frame of reference, had it been pursued at trial and by the media, would have raised many troubling questions, including the following: Is the Army repeating the mistakes of My Lai? How widespread is the usage of these unlawful ROE? How far up the chain of command does one have to travel to find the person or persons responsible for issuing the unlawful ROE?

Note also that Clagett refers to the enemy as both al Qaeda and anti-Iraqi Iraqis — we have already touched on the ambiguity of labeling the enemy during this operation. The "enemy" were AIF. He also refers to them as al Qaeda insurgents, but this only confounds an already confusing state of affairs. Presumably, there is a difference between al Qaeda terrorists and various types of insurgents. News accounts suggest that some insurgents in Iraq have no links to al Qaeda and that other insurgents are involved in a civil war that has nothing to do with the United States. The accused is clearly echoing the confusing terminology that was used by Steele and Hart, which was examined in Chapter 3.

One may speculate that Bergrin wanted Clagett's version of events to be broadcast on ABC News as a message to the Army that the public is watching, and to give notice that he would not allow the Army to run roughshod over the accused.

Allegedly, Clagett was put in solitary confinement shortly after this broadcast. Was this the Army's punishment for Clagett and Bergrin going to the media? Bergrin was arrested a week prior to first scheduled date of the trial, January 15. One may speculate further that, if Bergrin had wanted to put the Army on notice, the Army was sending Bergrin its own message through its actions. It is understandable that the Army would not want Bergrin's frame of reference to stand as the final version of events. His version taps into submerged reservoirs of inner-directed indignation at the government due to the suggestion that it does not honor the sacrifice of soldiers and veterans.

Perhaps it is for this reason that the Army changed the frame of reference drastically following this broadcast: away from a focus on the new ROE and Colonel Steele and toward a focus on a small group of soldiers who allegedly conspired to kill prisoners; away from public policy issues and toward the more easily recognizable and tolerated soap-opera bickering among the soldiers, away from open trials that would necessitate an airing out of issues pertaining to the legal status of the ROE and toward plea-bargains that would avoid trials.

Noam Chomsky's[1] publications on how the information media in the US tend to follow the government's lead — what he calls the manufacture of consent — already prepare the reader for the tentative conclusion that the media mirrored the government in this case. Most media accounts followed ABC's and the government's frame of reference by placing the accent on the unraveling of the band of brothers, not the unlawfulness of the new ROE.

Had ABC News stopped the segment at this point, the contrast between the two competing frames of reference (a soldier following an unlawful order versus a conspiracy by bad soldiers to kill prisoners) would have been stark. Had the Army held open trials for each of the four accused soldiers, the contrast between the two paths of inquiry would have been even more pronounced, because it would have forced the media to stay focused on the contrast between the two versions. The elite, mainstream media and the Army elite avoided the path less traveled by (to examine government policy on ROE) and took the easy path — the bickering and betrayal among the soldiers.

Taking the Easy Path

Martin Bashir of ABC News continues:

> According to several of the soldiers, the order came from Colonel Michael Steele. Colonel Steele had refused to testify at Private Clagett's hearing. After landing, they advanced towards a house. And a man was observed looking out of the window. He was shot on sight. They then approached another property, and found three men hiding, using women and children as human shields. *What happened next has become the subject of bitter dispute between soldiers of the elite combat unit known as the "band of brothers"* [my emphasis]. Initially, all the soldiers in the unit gave accounts of what happened that were remarkably consistent, including the four accused. Private Clagett,

---

1 Noam Chomsky, *The Chomsky Reader* (New York: Pantheon, 1987).

> Staff Sergeant Ray Girouard, Specialist William Hunsaker, and Specialist Juston Graber, all say that the Iraqis were detained and had zip ties binding their wrists. They said Girouard, the squad leader, then ordered the zip ties be changed to more secure restraints. It was then, the soldiers claimed, the detainees tried to break loose. And Clagett says he and Specialist Hunsaker were attacked.

The man who was shot in the window is mentioned once, but clearly his death is not deemed significant in relation to the ROE. Steele's refusal to testify is accorded one sentence, but the "bitter dispute" is treated at length.

It is not entirely accurate to frame the contradictions in the later sworn affidavits as a bitter or any other sort of dispute. If the soldiers had been allowed to testify in an open trial, then perhaps one could have said that they were disputing each other's accounts in some ways, although they would have corroborated each other to some extent as well. Without the cross-examination of witnesses in a public trial, there is no way to accurately portray the states of mind of the soldiers. The allegedly bitter dispute among the soldiers can be framed also in terms of the government returning to the soldiers on repeated occasions and requesting additional sworn statements along the lines of the previously mentioned strategy of invoking "the prisoner's dilemma," in which suspects inevitably turn on each other. But a focus on the Army's interrogation techniques, which caused soldiers to betray each other out of fear, might be a cause for indignation; so it is ignored. Bashir then moved to the next part of the story:

> All three detainees were killed. The bodies recovered, *the mission accomplished* [my emphasis]. Two days later, there was a commander's enquiry into the killings. The conclusion was unequivocal. "The bottom line is that the soldiers acted within the rules of engagement. They observed a hostile act and reacted with deadly force." A second internal inquiry confirmed these findings. But then, in June, the army's Criminal Investigative Division began re-interviewing the soldiers and some began to give an entirely different version of events. Private Micah Bivins, the unit's paramedic, entered the house immediately after shots were fired. His first duty was to examine Clagett and Hunsaker. Private Bivins spoke to us by telephone from Iraq.
>
> Bashir: What did you think of those cuts?
>
> Bivins: At first, I didn't really think about it but after a little bit of speculation, I kind of thought it — something was a little bit strange because of how light the cuts were.
>
> Bashir: What do you mean by that?
>
> Bivins: I believe that — possibly someone — if someone was going to try to fight for their lives, they would have done more than what happened.
>
> Bashir: One of the accused soldiers would soon offer an explanation for why the wounds were superficial and suspicious. Specialist Juston Graber recalled a conversation shortly after the shooting had taken place. Staff Sergeant Girouard said, "Hunsaker punched Clagett first. Clagett said, 'He hit me, too light. So he hit me again. Then, I was good.' But Staff Sergeant Girourad came out of nowhere and sucker punched me. Staff Sergeant Girouard said, "Then, I slashed Hunsaker's face once. Looked at it then cut

him on the other side of the face." Specialist Graber claims that the injuries were self-inflicted in order to create a cover story for the premeditated murder of the detainees. Graber has admitted to the mercy killing of one of the Iraqis.

Bashir confronted Clagett with Graber's statement. Clagett used a very interesting choice of words when he replied to Bashir: "So, I mean, I just followed my original rule of engagement." Could it be that some of the soldiers interpreted the new ROE as "originally" meaning that all the military-aged males should be killed, whether or not they were prisoners? But if this were the case, why would they think they needed to fake self-inflicted wounds in order to make it seem as if the prisoners were escaping?

There is no easy answer. I will demonstrate later that some soldiers made sworn statements to the effect that they thought the prisoners should have been killed as part of the new ROE. Bashir responded to Clagett: "But that view is not shared by other personnel who took part in the operation on May the 9." In fact, Clagett's view is shared by some of the other personnel on the mission, albeit not Graber and Bivins, who were interviewed live on "Nightline" and who had already promised to testify on behalf of the Army against the accused. Presumably, this choice of soldiers to be interviewed is part of the news media's typical way of creating the appearance of objectivity: the constant introduction of opposing points of view, albeit carefully edited, so as not to risk a direct confrontation with the government or tap into the indignation of the inner-directed types.

Bashir asked Bivins, "Do you believe that these detainees should have been shot?" and Bivins answered "No." At one point in the discussion, Bashir asked: "So, why were these detainees shot? It's long been rumored that divisions in Iraq are competing against each other, to kill as many high-valued targets, insurgents, as possible. But no soldier has ever confirmed this, until now. Is it true that amongst certain divisions of American personnel in Iraq, there's like, a list, a tally of how many high-value targets are killed in Iraq? Is that true?" "Yes, it's true" Bivins replied.

Bashir asked: "Do you think having a list like that is helpful? Doesn't that generate a sense of competition?" Bivins replied: "Yes, it does. And pretty much, there was a competition. Everyone's saying there wasn't, but there was."

In sociological and military terms, Bivins is describing a dysfunctional "command climate" which set the stage for the killings. But without a trial, the issue of command climate could not be forced into open discourse. Note also that Bashir seems to be equating "high-value targets" with "insurgents" — the two categories are not equivalent. Not all insurgents are high-value or terrorists. Again, the focus shifts subtly but effectively from the unlawfulness of such presumed kill contests — if they exist — to metaphors of healthy competition, as if an Army unit were something like a football team.

Nightline's segment ended with the following words by Bashir: "And sources familiar with the inquiry tell us that Colonel Steele has been reprimanded for failing to follow investigative procedures, and he remains under scrutiny. Meanwhile, sources close to Colonel Steele say he denies all the allegations, including the order to kill all military-aged males." One wonders: Who were these anonymous "sources" close to the brigade commander? According to CPT Rutizer, and following this broadcast by ABC News, Steele was granted immunity from prosecution by the Army. In effect, he did not testify at the pre-trial hearings, the trials that were canceled, and he was not confronted on this ABC News program. Perhaps he did not give this order, but the many sworn statements to the effect that he did give the order show the perception of his order by his soldiers — unless one assumes that the entire military unit was lying about the new ROE. The frame for apprehending the events at hand have been established by the government as well as the media: The issues surrounding the ROE, the exact orders that Steele gave, kill-contests, and military policy have been fire walled from the public discourse. On the other hand, and with regard to the low-ranking soldiers, the issues surrounding who said what to whom, who denied what was said, and the many competing and contradictory versions of what happened based upon soldier's perceptions and statements — but not facts that would be required in a trial — were put on the front stage. The front stage performance inevitably became a distraction. Without facts based upon written documents, forensic evidence, and first-hand evidence under oath from the witnesses, including the Iraqi soldiers, that would have emerged during trials, the narrative boils down to confessions made by some soldiers under conditions of fear and intimidation, and plea bargains made with specific soldiers who were prepared to testify against fellow-soldiers.

OTHER COVERAGE BY THE MEDIA

Four days after this broadcast on Nightline, on August 6, 2006, Paul von Zielbauer published an article in the *New York Times* with the title, "4 G.I.'s Tell of How Iraqi Raid Went Wrong." The opening lines of the article dramatize the other-directed "experience" of the events in question:

> When the burst of machine-gun fire stopped, two of the three Iraqi men were dead, their bodies chewed by bullets sprayed at them by two American soldiers a few yards away. But a third man, brains spattered on his face, was somehow still alive, and with eyes closed, was gasping for air. Specialists Juston R. Graber and Thomas A. Kemp, surprised to hear gunfire after securing the rural swatch of land northeast of Baghdad, ran over to find the three Iraqis lying in the dirt....Then, according to sworn statements of what Specialists Graber and Kemp later told Army investigators, Sergeant Girouard said, "Put him out of his misery."

The article proceeds to mention the order the soldiers were given, without ever mentioning the phrase ROE:

> Several soldiers have said in sworn statements or testimony at the hearing that senior officers, including the Third Brigade commander, Col. Michael Steele, told them in a gathering the night before the raid to kill any military-age male they encountered on the island, where 20 fighters loyal to Al Qaeda were thought to be. In a statement to investigators, Colonel Steele has denied giving any such order. On Friday, he declined, through his military lawyer, to comment for this article.

The journalist performed his duty by giving both sides of the issue (an order versus murderous impulse by soldiers) but deftly avoids one of the key issues: an "order" or having "told" the soldiers something is not the same as an ROE. An ROE carries the weight of the entire chain of command and of the United States Army and government. An order could conceivably be idiosyncratic.

The rest of the story notes the detail that "Six Iraqi Army soldiers accompanied" the American soldiers, but the sworn statements contradict each other on how many IA soldiers were actually present. The journalist offers no conceptual scaffolding as a basis by which the reader can judge who is telling the truth or what really happened. Instead, the reader is left satisfied at the role of acquiring some "inside dope" (which may or may not be true) but with no basis for making a rational or emotional reaction of any consequence.

An Associated Press article written by Ryan Lenz, entitled, "Soldier Pleads Guilty to Iraq Murders," dated January 25, 2007, also manages to summarize the complex events under discussion here without ever mentioning the phrase ROE:

> A soldier was sentenced Thursday to 18 years in prison for killing three detainees during a raid on a suspected al Qaeda compound last year in Iraq. Spc. William B. Hunsaker, 24, pleaded guilty earlier Thursday to murder, attempted murder and obstruction of justice....Hunsaker was one of four 101st Airborne Division soldiers charged in the killings during a raid at the Muthana chemical complex near Samarra, about 60 miles north of Baghdad. The soldiers told investigators they shot the detainees because they were attempting to flee — a story they now say they made up — and that commanders told them to kill all military-age males....Hunsaker said he knew it was illegal but felt he was doing a greater good by killing detainees who might have been al Qaeda agents in Iraq. "In his mind, he believed it was a lesser evil for a greater good," defense attorney Michael Waddington said.... Under the plea agreement, Hunsaker got a life sentence but will not serve more than 18 years in prison ... provided he cooperates with prosecutors bringing cases against other soldiers accused in the killings. Girouard, 24, and Pfc. Corey R. Clagett, 21, are awaiting courts-martial in the coming months. Girouard's military attorneys have declined to discuss the case with the media. Clagett's lawyer, Paul Bergrin, was charged Wednesday with involvement in a New York City escort agency. He did not immediately return an e-mail Thursday, and his voice mail was too full to accept

messages. Prosecutors at Fort Campbell said it wasn't clear whether Bergrin's legal troubles would affect Clagett's court-martial, set for Jan. 29. Spc. Juston R. Graber, 21, pleaded Tuesday to a lesser charge of aggravated assault and agreed to cooperate with prosecutors. He was sentenced to nine months in military jail.... Four other soldiers from the division's 2nd Brigade Combat Team are accused of raping and killing an Iraqi teenager and killing three others in her family last March. A former Army private also faces federal murder and rape charges.

By January of 2007, the issue of the ROE had disappeared completely from the discourse. The journalist's brief mention of other, seemingly ordinary crimes in the context of the war crimes committed during Operation Iron Triangle falsely equalizes them. ROE involve the Geneva Conventions. Also, Bergrin was the only defense attorney who had won permission from the military judge to have COL Steele testify. With Bergrin's arrest, and the fact that none of the other defense attorneys was able to persuade the military judge to force Steele to testify, the Army effectively erased the issue of the ROE from this narrative.

Was it a coincidence that Bergrin was arrested just days before the scheduled trial of his client? I raised this question with the military defense attorney for Clagett, CPT Rutizer, who told me I was "into conspiracy theories." Nevertheless, even the most uninformed reader may perhaps wonder about the coincidence of the timing of Bergrin's arrest with a trifecta of plea bargains that followed.

Bergrin came with a reputation from the Abu Ghraib trial of Javal Davis as the attorney who convinced the military judge to stop President Bush's order to raze Abu Ghraib prison to the ground, in order to preserve evidence. Bergrin was clearly the most aggressive lawyer in the Abu Ghraib trials, and there can be little doubt that the prosecutors in the Iron Triangle cases perceived him as a serious threat.

Finally, it is noteworthy that the journalist uses the carefully-crafted phrase that the "detainees" (prisoners) "might have been al Qaeda agents." In fact, it was never determined whether the Iraqis who were killed were terrorists or not. What is an "agent" as opposed to an "insurgent," "terrorist," "AIF" or any other label that has been used?

On August 3, 2006, Ryan Lenz wrote another story that was published in *The Washington Post*, entitled, "Accused US soldiers Refuse to Testify." Covering the pre-trial hearing for the four accused soldiers in Tikrit, Iraq, Lenz notes that "the four invoked their right not to testify for fear of incriminating themselves at the hearing to determine if they should be court-martialed for the May 9 shooting deaths." Lenz goes on to write that "the shootings have raised questions about the Army's rules of engagement during combat and dealt another blow to the reputation of US soldiers, fueling anger against the coalition presence."

The news story that covered Clagett's sentencing is even more cryptic. In an Associated Press story written by Beth Rucker, entitled "Soldier Admits Murdering Iraqi Detainees," she writes:

> A 101st Airborne Division soldier pleaded guilty Thursday to murdering three detainees in Iraq last year, saying he went along with a plan to make it look like they were escaping.... In an agreement with prosecutors, Clagett, of Moncks Corner, S.C., pleaded guilty to charges of murder, attempted murder, conspiracy to commit murder and conspiracy to obstruct justice... The soldiers first told investigators they shot the detainees because they were attempting to flee — a story they now say they made up — and that commanders had given them orders to kill all military-age males on the mission.... Clagett's lawyer, Paul Bergrin, has insisted Clagett was following orders, but sought the plea agreement after Hunsaker, 24, told a military judge that Clagett helped him shoot the detainees. Military prosecutors would not discuss the case.

Again, the journalist fails to use the phrase Rule of Engagement, which is used by the soldiers from the first to the last set of sworn affidavits. The wording by the journalists hints — in an extremely subtle manner — that the soldiers may have been lying about the "order" since they lied about the prisoners trying to escape. But officers in the unit freely admit the existence of the ROE. Without the context of the ROE, the reader is left with the conclusion that this was an ordinary case of murder.

Connections to Other Misuses of ROE in Iraq

Regarding the massacre at Haditha, "Sgt. Asad Amer Mashoot, a 26-year-old Iraqi soldier who was in the Marine convoy, told investigators he watched in horror as the four students and taxi drivers fell" from gunshot wounds. "We were afraid from Marines and we saw them behaving like crazy." Note the similarity to the incident at issue here, wherein the Iraqi soldiers expressed anger and horror at the killing of the Iraqi man in the window who was considered an AIF.

Another similarity is that the accused Marines "have argued that they behaved appropriately while taking fire in an especially dangerous area." While the similarity is not exact (the Army soldiers were not taking fire), it lies in the perception by the soldiers that they were in an especially dangerous area. Moreover, "Defense attorneys have argued that the men were following their 'rules of engagement.'" "Several Marines said they quickly cleared the home, shooting through dust, debris and darkness to eliminate what they believed was a threat." Again, while the similarities are not exact, they do lie in the observations that several Iraqis were killed under the widespread perception by Marines that they were following ROE, even though some of the Iraqi victims ostensibly posed no visible threat to them.

According to a newspaper story, "Iraqis know it is within the US 'rules of engagement' to shoot at them when using mobiles, and that US troops enjoy impunity whatever they do." The use of cell phones is a very common behavior throughout the world, but in Iraq, it has apparently become a widespread perception that using a cell phone in public might get one killed, due to ROE. "The human costs are so high that many Iraqis believe that had there been a competition between Saddam's regime and the Bush–Blair occupation over the killing of Iraqi minds and culture; the latter would win by far."[1]

In an article entitled "Changing the Army for Counterinsurgency Operations" published in *Military Review* in November–December 2005, British Brigadier Aylwin-Foster argues that since 2003, the United States Army has been slow to adapt to the policy of winning the hearts of minds of the Iraqi people. Instead, he remarks that "US Rules of Engagement (ROE) were more lenient than other nations', thus encouraging earlier escalation." "Too much of the force remained conceptually in war fighting mode in the post combat phase, and failed to understand that every soldier becomes a CIMIC [civil–military cooperation] operator." "Conversely, some US officers held that their allies were too reluctant to use lethal force." The brigadier goes on to cite various problems in the United States Army's "heavy-handed" approach in Iraq: doctrinal issues in not doing enough to gain popular support; training issue, in that most soldiers are not aware "of the importance of influencing the population through appropriate interaction"; and cultural insensitivity and engaging in behaviors that "served further to alienate the troops from the population." In general, the author accuses the Americans of "institutional racism" against Iraqis. Institutional racism refers to rules and policies that are established by formal groups such that, in this case, virtually any Iraqi is considered to be suspicious or potentially dangerous to the United States.

Regarding the operation to "pacify" Fallujah, BBC reports that "Humanitarian workers speak of US soldiers firing at ambulances and civilians."[2]

According to the Voice of America, 8 March 2005, "Questions remain about the March 4 death that Bulgarian officials say was an accidental killing by US forces. . . . He died around the same time that US forces also accidentally shot and killed an Italian secret-service agent in Baghdad."[3]

In an article entitled "Former Marine Offers Cautionary War Story," Iraq War veteran Jimmy Massey is reported as stating the following regarding an incident at a Baghdad checkpoint in 2003:

> We discharged our weapons into the KIA. There were four occupants in the vehicle. Three were severely wounded and expiring fast. The driver was unscathed. While we were trying to medevac these individuals out,

---

1 Halfa Zangana, January 4, 2007, *The Guardian.*
2 British Broadcasting Corporation, 23 April 2004.
3 Stefan Bos, "Bulgaria Mourns Eighth Fatality in Iraq" 8 March 2005, Voice of America

this young man that was unscathed came up to me and asked, "Why did you do this? Why did you kill my brother? We're not terrorists."[1]

A year before the Operation Iron Triangle killings, the media reported on the shooting death of an Italian agent who was protecting a hostage who had been released, and who was shot by US soldiers:

> An Italian report into the shooting dead of one of its secret agents by US troops in Iraq is expected to differ sharply with a Pentagon investigation when it is published later today. The US *military said its soldiers had followed their rules of engagement* but the Italian report will pick apart US conclusions on the incident [my emphasis]. Secret agent Nicola Calipari was shot dead at a US checkpoint on the approach to Baghdad airport as he shielded Giuliana Sgrena, a hostage whose freedom he had just negotiated, from the gunfire."[2]

A similar incident that allegedly involved ROE is detailed in the *Guardian*:

> The Pentagon has defended the actions of its troops in Iraq after an inquest ruled that ITN journalist Terry Lloyd was unlawfully killed. . . The US department of defense said was an "unfortunate reality that journalists have died in Iraq." It said its *troops had "followed the applicable rules of engagement"* [my emphasis].[3]

A similar report found that "Since the 2003 invasion US forces have killed at least 18 media workers in incidents."[4]

One of the most widely covered incidents of shooting non-combatants involved Blackwater civilian contractors. On September 16, 2006, an Iraqi government report "said 17 people died in the unprovoked shooting and 22 were wounded when Blackwater guards opened fire on civilians." "According to a congressional report, Blackwater has been implicated in nearly 200 shootouts in Iraq since 2005, and its representatives were those who started shooting more than 80 percent of the time."[5] Despite the media attention to Blackwater, no formal charges have been brought against its employees, and the US State Department renewed its contract with this corporation.[6]

Space does not permit more than the small sampling, above, of incidents that are similar to the Operation Iron Triangle killings in that the government referred to ROE as justification for the killings of journalists, civilians, and other non-combatants.

The media dutifully reported these and many other seemingly disparate incidents without disclosing or investigating fully the ROE that was allegedly used. In summary, the public perception, filtered through the informa-

---

1 *Times Union*, Albany, New York, March 9, 2005.
2 *London Guardian* May 2, 2005 "Italian report on Iraq shooting to criticize US."
3 Tara Conian, October 13, 2006 Pentagon Defends US troops, London *Guardian*.
4 *Guardian*, September 12, 2005.
5 "Iraqi families sue Blackwater in US," Associated Press, 29 May 2008.
6 Jeremy Scahill, *Blackwater: The Rise of the World's Most Powerful Army* (New York: Nation Books, 2007).

tion media, of similar incidents frequently invokes ROE as part of the explanation as to why the deaths occurred. But the public does not know what is in the ROE.

In the context of these and other shootings of non-combatants, the seemingly private issues pertaining to the convicted soldiers in the Operation Iron Triangle killings take on a more general, historical, and sociological dimension. The four convicted soldiers, as well as other soldiers on this and other, possibly similar missions, were caught up in a social climate that they did not create, could not control, and could not change. An ROE that is perceived to order the killing of Iraqi males or other non-combatants on sight is highly problematic from a sociological point of view by virtue of the dehumanizing and violent social climate that it creates. Yet this sociological perception seems to be lost on the information media, who address the factual details without bothering to investigate who is responsible for the new ROE as de facto policy, or what the ROE actually state.

Eruptions of Indignation in the Blogosphere

If the "mainstream" and "elite" media who covered the Operation Iron Triangle killings and other ROE-related killings does indeed exhibit some of the fake neutrality that actually protects the power elite in the government, as Riesman, Chomsky, and other sociologists claim, then it is also true that bloggers on the Internet exhibit some of the moral indignation that Riesman thought was becoming extinct in America. Riesman was writing in an era in which the Internet did not exist, of course.

A quick survey of the blogs on the Iron Triangle fiasco demonstrates a clear tendency toward inner-directed indignation aimed at the Army, government, and brigade commander based on gyroscopic principles that a leader is supposed to take responsibility for the actions of his or her soldiers.

For example, a post on the website "Right Truth"[1] expresses home-town support for one of the accused soldiers: "Sgt. Girouard's home town is providing financial and moral support for him, raising money for his legal fees, NPR reports. 'Three other soldiers have struck plea deals. But Girouard says that he and his fellow soldiers were following orders.'" The post continues with the following claims:

> Nowhere else in the media will you find that:
>
> The government's star witness, SPC Bradley Mason, was not even present during the deaths of the Iraqis.
>
> He is receiving immunity for having thousands of child pornography photos on his computer, and
>
> He stated in open court, under oath, that he would like to have sex with a 9-year-old girl in Thailand.

---

1 *http://righttruth.typedpad.com/right_truth/2007/03/staff_sgt_raymo.html*

He went to the Army several times begging to be sent home from Iraq, even claiming that he was crazy.

He had several disciplinary issues, three of which would have been Article 32s had Girouard not intervened on his behalf.

Meanwhile, their second "witness," who later recanted and admitted that the whole story was fabricated, is now missing. As in AWOL. His own attorney has no idea where he is, and neither does the army.

The third "witness," named Graber, claims that Girouard told him to commit a "mercy killing," even though Girouard was inside the building, in the back room at the time that Graber was outside....

The bodies are nowhere to be found, and Graber has full immunity.

The knife ... is also nowhere to be found....

Girouard's attorneys claim the soldiers had rules of engagement from their commanding officer directing them to kill all military-aged men. The officer in question is Col. Michael Steele, famous for the so-called "Black Hawk Down" incident in Somalia.

But Steele has denied stating any such rules of engagement, and a judge says he doesn't have to testify at Girouard's court-martial.

Meanwhile, the convicted soldiers are expected to take the stand to say that Girouard led the planning and cover-up of the killings.

Unlike the mass media, this blog exposed issues that were on the agenda by Clagett's defense team to use in open court, including rigorous cross-examinations of Mason and Graber.

A posting on Townhall.com on January 21, 2007, entitled "Iron Triangle Case Update: Army Knew the Rangers Were Innocent," posted by Kit Jarrell,[1] exhibits similar curdled indignation. Jarrell writes: "Steele told his men to kill all military-age males, and had the Rangers complied to the letter, there would be a lot more dead than there were." Strictly speaking, this is true. Jarrell continues: "The Army ... suddenly pronounced Mason, a well-documented 'problem troop' with several disciplinary issues, a credible witness and started arresting members of the unit in an effort to keep the 'unreleased' disciplinary action against Steele quiet." The tone of this interpretation is angry, but it is factually correct that Steele's letter of reprimand was not released. Jarrell's conclusion is bitter: "Steele is a maggot, a pathetic excuse for a man who is so concerned with his own career and his own image that he was pleading the fifth ... while his own men, one of whom he had worked very closely with, were facing the death penalty for *his* screw-up. Meanwhile, the Army, *knowing* this state of affairs, helped him do it."

Common Dreams posted excerpts from a story published by the *Los Angeles Times*[2] which also touched on explosive issues that were important

---

1 *http://thefrontline.blogtownhall.com/Print.aspx*

2 Borzou Daragahi and Julian E. Barnes, "Officers Allegedly Pushed 'Kill Counts'" *Los Angeles Times* August 3, 2006

at the beginning of the case and then were completely unmentioned at the end. "Many believe the unit's commanders created an atmosphere of excessive violence by encouraging 'kill counts' and possibly issuing an illegal order to shoot Iraqi men." The sworn affidavits show that soldiers confirmed the existence of such kill contests. The article continues: "At a military hearing Wednesday on the killing of the detainees near Samarra, witnesses painted a picture of a brigade that operated under loose rules allowing wanton killing and tolerating violent, anti-Arab racism."

A posting entitled "Black Hawk Down — An American Psycho"[1] on UK Indymedia is especially passionate:

> An American colonel is under investigation for ordering his men to slaughter innocent Iraqis, awarding prizes for the most murders. The investigation coincides with the trial of four of his soldiers charged with such murder. The colonel is an all American hero who had slaughtered foreigners before. Major Mike Steele, was Ranger commander, during the "Black Hawk Down" Battle of Mogadishu massacre. 1500 Somalis died while repulsing a US attempt to kidnap the Somalian foreign minister, compared to a handful of US deaths incurred... He was since promoted to Colonel and given a combat role in Iraq, with predictable consequences. He is being investigated for ordering his men to kill all military-age males whether or not they were armed or in uniform. A lot of right-winger war-mongers and cruise-missile leftists seem to own the movie Black Hawk Down and see it as a gritty and realistic portrayal of modern battle, whereas it is actually the Hollywood glorification of a massacre.

Similarly, a posting by Gary Leupp, Professor of History at Tufts University, on the website, Roundup,[2] offers a fervent analysis of the brigade commander as well as some cultural symbols associated with him:

> Col. Michael Steele is a hero to some for his role ... in Somalia back in 1993.... The 2001 film, "Black Hawk Down" depicts the episode from the imperialist point of view, glorifying Steele (played by Jason Isaacs, best known to any as the evil Lucious Malfoy in "Harry Potter and the Goblet of Fire"). Recently acquiring more glory in Iraq, Steele has boasted of his unit's death count. Last November he declared, "We are absolutely giving the enemy the maximum opportunity to die for his country."... The phrase "all military-age males" surfaced earlier in official commentary on the rape of Fallujah. Lt. Col. Brennan Byrne, who commanded the 5 Marine Battalion in Fallujah in 2004 told the London Guardian that "95% of those" killed by US forces "were military-age males that were killed in the fighting. That's fine, because they'll get whipped up, come out fighting again and get mowed down ... Their only choices are to submit or die." (Submit to the invaders, kids. Or have your — — jihadi heads blown off.).... Polls show a staggering majority of the troops actually believe that Saddam Hussein was involved in the 9-11 attacks. That suggests that their commanders have been telling them a lot that is simply wrong.... Here we have, I submit, a Hollywood movie so much richer than "Black Hawk Down." A courtroom film, with lots of legalistic eloquence and lots of battlefield flashbacks. I'd love to hear Jason Isaacs bark, "Kill all military age men!" Maybe that would arouse

1 *http://www.indymedia.org.uk/en/2006/08/346667.html*
2 *http://hnn.us/roundup/entries/29100.html*

some *moral indignation* [my emphasis] in the audience at the terrorist quality of the war in Iraq.

Indeed, this author exhibits precisely the sort of indignation that Riesman ascribes to inner-directed types from previous generations. The indignation is aimed at both the power elite quality of the military protecting its commanders and at the widespread nature of the policy to kill military-age males, as in Fallujah. However, the fantasy of a film based upon Operation Iron Triangle disappears when one realizes that the Army made sure the commander would not testify. This fantasy film, should it ever be made, will *not* have the quality of the film, "A Few Good Men," in which a fictional military commander proudly boasted on the witness stand that he did, indeed, order a "Code Red," and would do it again. Audiences forget, or perhaps do not know, that a military judge has absolute power to decide on whether or not a military commander, or anyone else, will testify.

Other websites made the connection between the Iron Triangle killings and those in Haditha, which also occurred in the year 2006. "The incident has the potential to become to the Iraq war what the My Lai incident was to Vietnam, an American massacre that severely damages the prestige of US forces and undermines support for the war at home."[1] Similarly, a posting on Antiwar.com on August 9, 2006, entitled "Counting Kills: In committing war crimes in Iraq, were US troops egged on by their commanders?" poses the question: "How is it that the army of a liberal, democratic country, one that prides itself as the champion of liberty worldwide, could possibly descend to the level exemplified by the war crimes committed at Haditha, Samarra, and Abu Ghraib?"

Along these lines, a posting on *Counterpunch*, "Kill all Military Age Men!"[2] reads, in part:

> "Kill all military-age men." Free-fire zone, any 13-year-old boy fair game. Mow the boys down! says the heroic colonel.... No doubt this was the argument fed the four soldiers ... whose case is being heard by a military court in Tikrit."

THE TWO SIDES OF THE "BLACK HAWK DOWN" MEDIA MYTHOLOGY

We have seen that the mainstream media as well as bloggers refer to "Black Hawk Down" as a symbol for apprehending some of the meaning of the Operation Iron Triangle killings. But the meaning of Black Hawk Down is itself ambiguous and carries the double-edged sword of other-directed glamour and camaraderie versus moral indignation at a supposedly failed mission. The distinction between the entertainment and the information

---

1 *http://www.guardian.co.uk/Iraq/Story/o,.835912.00.html*
2 *http://www.counterpunch.org/leupp08052006.html*

media becomes blurred in other-directed society. With regard to the particular case under discussion, and in the prophetic words of Walter Benjamin — who was writing with reference to fascism in the 1940s — "all efforts to render politics aesthetic culminate in one thing: war."[1] He elaborates: "War is beautiful."

The film "Black Hawk Down" was directed by Ridley Scott and released in January of 2002. A blogger captures the general consensus of the advertising slogans as well as reviews:

> Black Hawk is quite simply the best movie of the year and the best war movie I have ever seen.... I really felt this movie, it was tangible to me; the confusion, the fear, the sense of dislocation and horror the soldiers must have faced. At the end I was emotionally and mentally drained.[2]

One can sense what Riesman called the other-directed focus on experience as opposed to meaning in this and other quotes. The synopsis for the film reads as follows, in part:

> This movie had not only the cooperation of the US military, but also the use of weapons, systems and soldiers, some of whom were involved in Somalia. The movie is unique, historic and more so — it demonstrates the heroism that continues to this day, of those Americans who volunteer to serve their country, and to be willing to sacrifice their lives in countries not their own.

Similarly, a synopsis for the deluxe edition 3-disc DVD version of the film reads in part: "From acclaimed director Ridley Scott (Gladiator, Hannibal) and renowned producer Jerry Bruckheimer (Pearl Harbor, Armageddon) comes a griping true story about bravery, camaraderie and the complex reality of war."[3]

In the film, a fictional character named Dominick Pilla imitates a fictional Captain Steele, played by Jason Isaacs:

> "We are on the ten-yard line men, can you count 'em? One, Two, Ten! I need my running backs, hoo-ah!"[4]

Pilla continues:

> "Didn't see you in church on Sunday soldier, you got somethin' better to do? I don't think so; I will make you believe!"

In the movie, Captain Steele catches Pilla imitating him, and the dialogue continues:

> Steele: "Quick word, Specialist."
>
> Dominick Pilla: "Sir."
>
> [Gives "bird" finger to soldiers while walking with Steele]

---

1 Walter Benjamin, "The Work of Art in the Age of Mechanical Reproduction" in Hannah Arendt, ed., *Illuminations* pp. 243-44 (New York: Harcourt, Brace & Co., 1968).

2 *http://www.imdb.com/title/tt0265086/*

3 *http://www.sonypictures.com/homevideo/blackhawkdown/title-navigation-2.html.*

4 *http://www.imdb.com/title/tt0265086/quotes*

Steele: "Tell me, Pilla. You understand why we have a chain of command, don't you?"

Dominick Pilla: "Roger that sir."

Steele: " 'Cause if I ever see you undermining it again, you'll be cleaning latrines with your tongue until you can't taste the difference between shit and French fries. Are we clear?"

Dominick Pilla: "Hoo-ah, sir."

For the purposes of the present discussion, it is significant that the real Steele by the time he was in Iraq was most likely perceived by his soldiers as a quasi-fictional, larger-than-life figure. After all, the soldiers who participated in Operation Iron Triangle were following orders from a commander who had been immortalized in a very popular film, and the film in turn represented some of the most esteemed values in the US army and society as a whole, including courage, camaraderie, and commitment to accomplishing a mission for a noble cause. How could his soldiers seriously conceive disobeying an order that he gave?

But again, the blogs give voice to inner-directed indignation regarding the film's message. In a post on *Slate* entitled "What Black Hawk Down Leaves Out: That Somalia Raid Really Was More a Debacle Than a Victory," Mickey Kaus wrote the following on January 21, 2002:

> For years, the Rangers and Delta Force soldiers who fought the Battle of Mogadishu on October 3, 1993, had a serious beef. Until the publication of Mark Bowden's 1999 book, *Black Hawk Down*, their daylight raid was widely perceived as a failure even in strict military terms. But the Rangers in fact succeeded in snatching and imprisoning the two Somali clan officials they were after. Had you known that? I hadn't. Like everyone else, I mainly remembered seeing the body of a dead American being dragged through the streets.... But would Americans pay to see a film simply about bravery under fire, without a larger, heroic context? As Slate's Inigo Thomas pointed out weeks ago, soldiers can be brave in the service of disastrous policies.[1]

A reviewer for *Pluggedin* writes, "Oct. 3, 1993, has gone down in history as a black day for the United States Army. [The positive aspect of the film is that it shows that] "Americans display incredible courage in rescuing and helping their fellow soldiers." The reviewer also cites negative elements: "The Americans refer to the starving Somalis as 'skinnies.' One young Ranger, eager for battle, says, 'I cam here to kick some a — !'" The review concludes:

> Shortly after this disaster, President Bill Clinton pulled all American forces out of Somalia. The film originally had an epilogue saying that since the US pullout directly led to the terrorist attacks of Sept. 11, since Osama bin Laden cited the Americans' alleged weaknesses and cowardice in Mogadishu as proof that we would not be willing or able to retaliate for those attacks. At the last minute it was removed.... Families will have to think long and hard before choosing to study this chapter in American history at the local Cineplex.[2]

1 http://www.slate.com/?id=2060941

2 http://www.pluggedinonline.co/movies/movies/a0000605.cfm

It is true that at the time it happened, in 1993, the Battle of Mogadishu was labeled as a fiasco; President Clinton pulled US forces out of Somalia shortly afterward; and Osama bin Laden used the incident to mock the United States. More interesting is the fact that the film's producers originally intended to use some of these facts in order to express moral outrage at Clinton. No doubt the reasons for withdrawing the epilogue are similar to the reasons Riesman cites for editors watering down news stories — to avoid offending too many consumers. The film industry is as sensitive as the information media to the issue of avoiding the expression of curdled indignation.

Socialistworker.org ran a post on February 22, 2002, which featured an interview with Brendan Sexton III, one of the actors in the film, who charges that the final version further diluted passionate and indignant portions of the original script:

> When I first read the script to Black Hawk Down, I didn't think it was the greatest thing in the world — far from it. But I thought the script at least raised some very important questions that are missing from the final product.... In certain scenes, US soldiers — before they even entered the now-infamous firefights in Mogadishu — were asking whether the US should be there, how effective the U.S military presence was, and why the US was targeting one specific warlord in Somalia, Gen. Mohammed Farah Aidid. As we moved closer to actually filming the script, the script moved further and further away from the little that existed of its questioning character.[1]

The British Broadcasting Corporation (BBC) also issued a review of the film that shows indignation and criticizes the film's attempt to portray a defeat as a sort of victory:

> As a war film, "Black Hawk Down" is first rate. It's exciting, well paced, and full of lots of action. Director Ridley Scott proves to be at home with the adrenalin rush of modern technological warfare, piling on the firefights, helicopter crashes, and bloody carnage.... In a belated attempt to mould the film to suit the post-September 11 climate, the film makers have added a series of opening and closing titles that desperately try to say something about the Battle of Mogadishu's wider significance, but these simply seem hastily written and ill advised.... [It is] less a film about the American experience in Somalia than a patriotic airbrushing of what was actually America's worst day of combat since Vietnam. The only parallel it really wants us to draw with the contemporary international situation is a facile message about the US of A as an ass-kicking superpower — and that's why it gets top marks for the action; zero marks for the message.[2]

In a review of both the book and the movie, Colonel Jon Campbell offers yet another indignant perspective on the significance of the Battle of Mogadishu:

> Eighteen Americans lost their lives in the process. Somali losses numbered 500–1,000 killed, with total casualties probably running over 5,000. President Clinton decided to terminate the operation and pull Task Force Ranger out quickly. A few months later, all US forces withdrew from Somalia....

---

1 *http://www.socialistworker.org/2002-1/395/395/_08_BrendanSexton.shtml*
2 *http://www.bbc.co.uk/films/2002/01/03/black_hawk_down_2002_review.shtml*

To this day, the country remains an extremely poor, politically bankrupt nation with substantial al Qaeda involvement. The principal issues here lie not at the tactical level but at the strategic. Clearly, removing Aidid or his lieutenants was not well linked to establishing democracy in Somalia. Rather, we would have recognized that nation building would be a long-term process initiated by creating an interim government supported by a national police force defended by our forces operating in the background.... Everyone in the Air Force should either read *Black Hawk Down* or watch the movie version — preferably do both. Each attests to the spirit, professionalism, valor, skill, and nobility of the American fighting forces involved in this conflict. The Somali warlords intended this incident to become a modern-day version of Custer's last stand or the Alamo. But they were denied.[1]

CONCLUSIONS

Riesman's subheading in the portion of *The Lonely Crowd* devoted to the media reads, "The Media as Tutors in Tolerance." We have seen that, taken as a whole, the information and entertainment media's coverage of events pertaining to Operation Iron Triangle does seem to exemplify Riesman's characterization of them. There can be little doubt that the mainstream media "tolerates" the government's rationalizations of a seemingly unlawful ROE and scrupulously avoids a confrontational, morally indignant tone. To criticize the government would not only seem unpatriotic, it might offend audiences, and consequently diminish sales and advertising revenue.

The information media focused its attention on the human drama of the soldiers turning on each other, not on the moral implications of an unlawful ROE. This vacuum in moral indignation is filled by the blogosphere which, taken as a whole, exhibits passionate and forceful moral indignation aimed at the power elite, and a populist support of the soldiers who were betrayed by their commanders as well as their government. In some ways, contemporary, indignant bloggers may be likened to the protesters who took to the streets in the 1960s to protest the Vietnam War, discrimination, and other perceived moral failures. The difference is that in the current millennium, the bloggers express their indignation on the Internet, and not on the streets. Perhaps a tolerant conclusion would be: at least the consumer of information has a choice, between the media elite and the bloggers.

But Riesman pointed out that the overall effect of this apparent freedom to choose the sources of one's information are that the public as a whole turns cynical and apathetic. The media is perceived to be insincere, and the consumer of information fights the feeling that he or she might be "taken in" at any time by developing a passionate commitment to any one point of view. In fact, the American consumer of mass media information tries to avoid being forced to choose between the emotions embodied in the slogan "support our troops," versus the message "support the government" in rela-

---

1 *http://www.airpower.maxwell.af.mil/airchronicles/bookrev/bowden.html*

tion to the Operation Iron Triangle killings or any other similar issue. Even in the film "Black Hawk Down," despite the commander's reassuring words, "Remember, leave no man behind," several groups of soldiers are abandoned. In Riesman's words, "Just as the moralizer romanticizes a government of laws and not of men, the inside-dopester romanticizes a government of men and not of laws" (p. 196). But taking either path subjects one's patriotism to question by the peer group.

I attempt to move beyond this impasse posed by Riesman's conceptual template with the concept of postemotionalism. We have seen that all the media — from the respectable news outlets to the bloggers and also the entertainment media — typically situate the Operation Iron Triangle killings in the context of the Battle of Mogadishu in 1993. This seems "logical" because of COL Steele's involvement as a transition figure in both operations. However, postemotionalism is a general tendency in contemporary social life, such that, for example, the first President Bush sought to avoid conquering Baghdad in order to avoid a "Vietnam quagmire," the Belgrade regime in the 1990s justified their ethnic cleansing as a 600-year-old response to the Battle of Kosovo, the Greek government in the year 2008 continued to invoke Alexander the Great in order to justify its objections to Macedonia's entry into NATO, and so on.

Postemotionalism is an effort to bridge the unbearable cognitive dissonance of being forced to choose between supporting one's government when it acts immorally versus supporting and empathizing with the individual soldiers who carry out unlawful orders. It is not only a matter of support but also interest: contemporary consumers of information are interested in Operation Iron Triangle if it conjures up memories of Mogadishu; in Abu Ghraib if it conjures up emotions related to Saddam Hussein's use of that prison as a torture site, and so on. They are interested in the human, interpersonal aspects of the story, as well as the "government of laws" side. Emotionally-laden echoes from the past, whether or not they are accurate, are an integral part of the human side of the story that other-directed audiences crave. Thus, the unpalatable factual conclusion that the Battle of Mogadishu was a fiasco and a loss is transformed, post emotionally, by "Black Hawk Down," into a story of individual and group courage that simultaneously vindicates government policies. One suspects that if Hollywood ever makes a film about Operation Iron Triangle, the movie will focus on the positive emotions of the soldiers as they strove to vindicate Mogadishu, 9/11, and American honor at the same time they were showing mercy by not killing the women and children on the island and trying to act as a "band of brothers."

What "really" happened during Operation Iron Triangle? Was it "mission accomplished" or a fiasco? It is just as impossible to answer these questions in an entirely satisfactory way in reference to this one mission as it is about the war in Iraq as a whole. The contemporary layperson finds it unbearable to choose between being patriotic versus being interested in, and supportive of, the drama of the individuals who were involved in these missions, at the microscopic or the macroscopic level. The media caters to public opinion and is caught in this cognitive dissonance. Factually, the media reports suggest that a widespread pattern of incidents similar to Operation Iron Triangle have occurred, and such incidents are typically explained in terms of US soldiers following new ROE. The inner-directed moralizer will criticize the unlawful ROE as well as the failure of individual soldiers to disobey an unlawful ROE on the basis of an internalized moral compass. The other-directed inside-dopester will want to know intimate emotional details of what the officers and soldiers thought, felt, and did in trying to carry out the new ROE. Which is more patriotic, to disobey the unlawful ROE or to do one's job and follow ROE handed down by a chain of command?

The truly new (and interesting) aspect of this story that has been missed by the media is that the investigators, lawyers, and others caught up in this drama were as beleaguered as the media and the public by these dilemmas. A careful, scrupulous reading of the sworn affidavits suggests that the investigators were not content to just discover and record the facts as to what happened. They ask questions about how the soldiers felt; how they interacted with each other; how they judged the ROE; and other questions that can be described as other-directed. A few generations ago, such questions would have been unorthodox in a criminal investigation. In the mostly bygone inner-directed era, newspapers boasted the slogan, "all the news that's fit to print," and investigators on television programs such as "Dragnet" were known for their dead-pan expression in asking for "Just the facts, ma'am." Nowadays, no editor or reporter is entirely certain what parts of the news are fit or not fit to print, so they mix interpersonal with factual information. The tremendous popularity of "fake news" such as Jon Stewart's "The Daily Show" and Stephen Colbert's "The Colbert Report" mix factual information with comedy and farce. In a postemotional manner, they blur the distinction between Far Right patriotism and Far Left populism. And military investigators assigned to the Operation Iron Triangle case were interested in far more than bare-bone facts, as subsequent chapters will show.

CHAPTER 5. THE MAY 29 VERSION: PLAYING IT BY EAR

In this chapter we pick up the narrative where the media left off, at the unraveling of the so-called band of brothers. However, the focus will be on showing that the Army investigators were "playing it by ear" on May 29 in deciding whether to pursue the issue of the unlawful new ROE and charge the military commanders or the apparent conspiracy of the soldiers to cover up a situation that may be construed as murder.

The questions posed by the investigators are as interesting as the answers given by the soldiers. Their May 29 sworn statements serve as a transition or bridge between the initial version, which depicts the soldiers in a very matter-of-fact manner following ROE they believed to be lawful and achieving their mission and the June versions which depict cold-blooded crimes that seemingly involve cunning, irresponsibility, and ruthlessness. The contrast among all these versions is stark. Why would soldiers go to all the trouble of slashing each other and making up a false scenario of shooting prisoners who were allegedly hostile toward them when in fact the prisoners showed no hostility? Any meaningful answer to this question necessarily involves an allusion to some degree of cunning. But if some degree of cunning was involved, and if the soldiers really staged the prisoner escape so that they could shoot them, why did some of the soldiers brag about the incident as opposed to keeping their mouths shut? One possible reply is that some (but not all) of them had pangs of conscience, but there is no indication of that in the sworn statements. A more likely reply will include elements of irresponsibility toward themselves, each other, and the unit. But if we settle on irresponsibility as one possible explanation, why did the soldiers show mercy and restraint by not shooting the men when they were using women and babies as shields, yet shoot the same men when they were restrained prisoners? It is truly difficult to arrive at satisfactory answers or explanations.

For example, one of the soldiers, Juston Graber, stated on May 29 that "our ROE was to eliminate all military-aged males on the island." This part of the narrative remains fairly consistent among all the other soldiers interviewed in the first two sets of sworn statements, from May 11 to May 29. He recalled the presence of an Iraqi interpreter on the scene named Harry, and "approximately 5 Iraqi Army soldiers." The mysterious Harry's role during the assault is murky and inconsistent, and some other soldiers stated that he left the island prior to the shootings of the prisoners. The precise number of Iraqi Army soldiers varies dramatically from 1–2 to 4–5, even 6, and no two accounts are consistent about the role of the IA soldiers, what they were doing, when they left the island, or why.

The investigator asked Graber, "Did anyone talk to you about the ROE after the mission?" "Yes, CPT Hart. He reiterated that the ROE for the island was to eliminate all military-aged males due to the intel that was recovered about the island." Why would the ROE be reiterated *after* the mission, as well as *before* the mission? There is tremendous inconsistency among the other soldiers as to who might have "coached" the soldiers after the killings, for what reason, and to what extent.

Graber volunteered that there was a combat photographer present during the mission and that other soldiers had cameras as well. "Who took pictures of the detainees?" a CID agent asked him. "Some of us did, but I'm not sure who, exactly." In general, and using Graber's statement as a rough template with which to compare the other statements, it becomes clear that a wide array of interesting and important factors were de-centered and made peripheral to the story as it emerged in the questions posed by investigators, factors including but not limited to: the interpreter, the Iraqi Army soldiers, the first Iraqi was shot in the window, the weapons that were used, the one prisoner who was not shot, the women, the children, the combat photographer, other amateur photographers and photography among the soldiers, and the role of the commanding officers.

What, then, gradually took center stage in the second version of events? The investigators came to focus on the uncertainty as to who "zip-tied" versus "flexi-cuffed" the prisoners. This seems to be a picayune detail, but centering the attention this way on what some might consider to be peripheral issues is not unusual in trials. (For example, during Lynndie England's trial, an unusual focus was placed on her brief experience at a chicken-processing plant in West Virginia, as if this episode in her life held the key to understanding her behavior at Abu Ghraib.) Graber said that he could not remember who secured the prisoners, and did not know how they escaped or how or why they got shot — and all the other soldiers were just as inconsistent on these facts. Of course, one could argue that the investigators "smelled something fishy" with regard to issues related to the ties that were used to bind the prisoners, and on this basis began to suspect that soldiers were lying about other events. But there are contradictions and inconsistencies on all other aspects of the situation except the ROE. Herein lies the rub: If the ROE were as iron-clad as they seem to have been: to shoot every military age Iraqi on sight — then logically, taking prisoners was a violation of the (unlawful) ROE and killing the prisoners may have seemed "logical" to the soldiers. In focusing on the zip-ties versus flexi-cuffs, the investigators were imposing the traditional ROE onto the narrative, in which taking prisoners is allowable, and strict rules for the treatment of prisoners follow.

Thus, at least two major themes emerge in these sworn affidavits. The first is a centering of the focus on how the prisoners were restrained, and the second is a de-centering of focus on the unlawfulness of the "new ROE" (to shoot on sight), which gradually becomes peripheral to the story, coupled with an implicit centering on the Army's traditional ROE, which made the events seem more like murder and less like obedience to the new ROE.

But even this distinction is too neat and tidy, because the traditional ROE would have made the killings of all four men on the island unlawful, whereas the investigators chose to apply the traditional ROE to only the killing of the three restrained prisoners. This move, in turn, raises the question whether the investigators were ultimately protecting the brigade commander. Ultimately, the major issue remains which ROE — new versus traditional — really applied to the battlefield, in the minds of the soldiers, and in the minds of the investigators as they prepared to press charges?

STATEMENT BY THE MEDIC, MICAH BIVINS

Notice the slight but substantial changes in the story line of what occurred in the statement made by Specialist Micah Bivins, who was the medic in the squad, on 29 May 2006 versus his statement on 11 May:

> After supper chow we were sitting around our humvees when Colonel Steele started making rounds. He would stop and talk to groups of soldiers, shake hands, and just shoot the — — for a little while. Before he left the parking area he gave a pep talk. He told us how proud he is of us and how we are doing a good job. Then he started talking about the mission. He said that a couple of objectives were going to be hot LZs (landing zones). Later my squad had a meeting, and we were told that Apaches were going to light the objectives up. An hour or so later word got around that we didn't have AWT for the objective that we were going to. We were later told that *all military-aged males were to be considered hostile* [all emphases mine]. On 9 May 06, we left for objective Murray. On the first objective we found an empty house and sheep pen. At the second objective we landed maybe 150 to 100 meters a way from a house. Most of the third squad formed a line and started at the house. I was the last person in that line. By the time some of

the squad cleared the house I was told that an Iraqi had been shot. He was brought outside and I started to work on him. He had two bullet wounds to the lower chest. He died about two minutes after the first shots were fired. There were three military-aged males and two adult females. Someone detained the males and stayed to guard them. . . . SSG Girouard told CPL Helton *to provide grazing fire* into the berm on the other side of the second house. He was told to not stop firing until we got to a feeding trench next to the house. We started running down the berm towards the house and rounded a corner of a fence and a military-aged male came out into the open holding a small child in front of his head and chest. Someone took the child from him and gave it to one of the females. The house was cleared and we found an AK 47 and several mags. We moved the detainee back to the first house and started the detainee packets. . . . SPC Graber found a 9 mm pistol in a woman's purse. We finished our search of the house *and started taking pictures* of the weapons and detainees. About this time second squad and LT Wehrheim went to secure the PZ. An UH60 came and took them to the next objective. After they left we were suppose to have an UH60 come back in a few minutes to pick us up. So Sgt. Ryan, Cpl. Helton, SPC Kemp, Sgt. Lemus and the detainee, and myself went into PZ posture. After a few minutes I heard gunshots back at the house, I got up and grabbed my aid bag and ran back to the house. As I rounded the corner I saw the detainees lying on the ground about 20 to 30 feet away from the house. I saw PFC Clagett standing up in the yard by the doorway. He didn't seem to have any obvious life threatening injuries so I went to the detainees. I did a quick assessment and two were dead right there and the third was having agnail breathing. Before I could do anything he had stopped agnail breathing and I called him in dead. About that time I went to check on SPC Hunsaker and PFC Clagett and I saw SPC Hunsaker's arm was bleeding to where I applied a pressure dressing and I cleaned up his wounds on his face. I then went to PFC Clagett and he told me he had been hit so I checked for fractures in his face and found no fractures. I gave him a Tylenol for a headache. After that we started taking pictures of what was left of the detainees and pictures of the wounds. About that time 2nd PLT walked up and SSG Girouard and LT Young had a conversation, but I didn't hear it. Then 2nd PLT took the remaining detainee and KIAs on UH60s. The put all of the KIAs and detainee on the same bird and left. We sat in PZ posture for three to four and a half hours before the next helicopter came for us. We went to a different objective, but I don't remember the name of it. This is all that happened on OBJ Murray that I can recall.

Note the ambiguities that emerge regarding all the major points in the first set of affidavits: to consider every male as hostile is not exactly the same as the order to kill every military-aged male. This is because under the traditional ROE, there are rules spelling out a gradual escalation of force in relation to "hostile" forces. It is not clear who took the photographs or why, or who secured the prisoners. It is not clear who took the baby away from one of the surrendering Iraqis. Finally, one should note that the third prisoner who is described in this statement as dying will be described in the third set of statements as having been shot again, as a "mercy killing."

The investigators attempted to clear up some of these ambiguities. To the question, "Did you hear COL Steele say the ROE was to kill all military-age males on OBJ Murray?" Bivins replied "No." Does this mean that the medic did not hear COL Steele say these particular words or that he did not hear COL Steele give any ROE? The investigator does not pursue this apparent ambiguity. Most of the statements are consistent in indicating that this was the ROE, but some soldiers claimed that COL Steele gave the order while others attributed the order to lower-ranking officers. The interrogation continued:

Q: Who told you what the ROE was, as far as OBJ Murray?

A: I [am] pretty sure it was my squad leader, SSG Bissen. . .

Q: What was the ROE on OBJ Murray?

A: To my knowledge all military-age males were considered hostile.

Q: As to your ROE answer, what does this consideration mean to you?

A: Military-age males were to be shot on sight...

Q: Did *this new ROE* seem strange to you [my emphasis]?

A: Not really. We have seen them before.

Q: What cases or incidents did you have blanket shoot-on-sight authority before?

A: There have been a couple of missions where, if we saw a certain guy, we could take him out.

Q: Did the ROE (such as described above) ever cover an entire objective?

A: No.

The jurisdiction of the new ROE — whether it applied only to this particular mission or more broadly — is brought up briefly but not pursued. It is interesting that the investigator volunteers the interpretation that the ROE under discussion here was "new" but not unlawful.

In any case, Bivins makes it clear that he did not regard it as new. However, the investigator further complicates an already ambiguous interrogation by hinting that the ROE did not cover "an entire objective." The interrogation leaves many questions unanswered, including: Was this ROE, in fact, "new" or was it typical? How broadly (geographically) do ROE typically apply? What are the cognitive "boundaries" of the "mission" on Objective Murray? Did the ROE apply to the first house, the second, the third, and so on? This issue will come up again in other statements, but ultimately it will become peripheral to the narrative.

In the remainder of the sworn statement, Bivins claims that there was no hostile fire or action when the US soldiers landed at the battle site. He did not see the shootings. Bivins answered "I don't know" when he was asked, "Who applied the flexi cuffs to the 3 detainees?" However, he added that "They were not flexi cuffs, they were zip ties." "What was the reaction of the women after the shooting of the 3 detainees?" "It didn't change, they were calm." "What was the reaction of the women after the shooting of the 1st person, the older man?" "They were crying, freaking out." One wonders if this assessment is true, and if it is, why the women reacted so differently to the deaths. Finally, the investigator asked, "Did anyone tell you what to write in your initial statement to LT Wehrheim?" "They didn't say write this, but they did say make it clear Hunsaker and Clagett did this in self-defense." "Who are you referring to as they in the above statement?" "Pretty much everyone there, members of the squad." "Did anyone order you to make a false statement in regards to this incident?" "No."

If Bivins is being truthful, then his answers suggest that the squad was involved in a cover-up, and agreed to a cover story that two of the soldiers involved in the shootings acted out of self-defense.

Statement by LT Justin Wehrheim

Perhaps one of the most important statements in this entire narrative was given by the platoon leader, LT Wehrheim, on 29 May 2006. The lieutenant adds the fresh information that COL Steele was present on the mission for its entire duration, and I re-confirmed this fact with him during a subsequent phone conversation. The lieutenant said:

> We began to conduct rehearsals with our IA [Iraqi Army] counterparts for this mission, Operation Iron Triangle. I was called aside by Choppin' 6 CPT Hart, who told me that the ROE for this mission was that all military-aged males on this objective (objective Murray) were positively identified as being affiliated with Al Qaeda in Iraq and they could therefore be shot/engaged immediately upon identifying them as a military-aged male on objective Murray. We then went to chow with our Iraqi counterparts.... The ROE was reinforced that all military-aged male on objective Murray (the whole island) were positively identified as Al Qaeda in Iraq and could be engaged on sight ... and that all structures were hostile structures. We were also briefed that pre-assault fires had been approved for this objective. I then went back and reinforced this ROE to my platoon. Soon after that, COL Steele came and gave a speech and reinforced that every military-aged male on objective Murray was to be killed....

Note that apparently even the buildings were designated as "hostile structures" ahead of time. It is also worth noting that in the lieutenant's version, the brigade commander's words were that every military-aged male was to be killed. What would the soldiers think about prisoners in this context? The issue of taking prisoners never comes up in the lieutenant's statement.

But he seems to have been concerned from the outset (or perhaps he emphasized the issue in retrospect) about the reaction of the unspecified number of Iraq Army soldiers who would be on the joint mission to this particular ROE, and he continued:

> I talked with my platoon and the IA and told them that there would be dead bodies and discussed any unease they might have. Then everyone was put into rest cycle for the morning.... We learned that the pre-assault fire

> had been cancelled. I then met with CPT Hart and he told me that the ROE
> had not changed when I asked....

Why were the Iraqi soldiers uneasy? LT Wehrheim told me later over the phone that they were so very upset at the killing of the first unarmed man — which was deemed lawful — that he felt compelled to take them with him on the helicopter and away from the scene. Apparently, the Iraqi soldiers could not or would not accept the lawfulness of the new ROE that the lieutenant is discussing here.

> Upon our arrival, there was no one there, either.... I was ensured by CPT Hart that the ROE still applied, to engage all military-aged males on the objective and that these houses to the north were still on the island and were therefore still on objective Murray. COL Steele was present on objective Murray this entire time.

Presumably, the presence of COL Steele during the mission acted as reassurance to the officers and soldiers who were carrying out this new ROE. In any event, one may rule out the possibility that the unlawful ROE itself was invented by the officers and soldiers on the mission. The lieutenant apparently goes to great lengths in the statement and the interview to repeat many times over that he kept asking for and receiving confirmation of the strange new ROE.

> SPC Kemp, my RTO [radio telephone operator], informed me that I had to have an element ready to leave on a helicopter that was arriving in 5 minutes. I had the body in the bag brought to the pick up zone (PZ) and SSG Terrell's squad and the IA and the combat cameraman staged. I left SSG Girouard back to finish the detainee paperwork with his squad.... About 3 to 5 minutes into my flight back to the first objective I overheard on the radio that SSG Girouard's status on the ground had changed from 4 detainees to 3 KIA and 1 detainee. I arrived back at the first objective.... I did not link up there with SSG Girouard's element until about 5 hours later.... I left the ground of this incident from what they said about 1 to 2 minutes before it happened while there were still 4 detainees. I witnessed none of this. I also have no reason to believe anything differently from what I've been shown and told. All ROE on this objective was given and reinforced directly through our Brigade and Company commanders and indirectly by our Battalion commander.

Note that the lieutenant believes that he left four prisoners behind when his helicopter lifted from the ground, but other soldiers believed or claimed that he took one of the prisoners with him. The timing of the incident in relation to his departure is also interesting: within a few short minutes of his leaving the ground, three prisoners were shot and killed. Would things have turned out differently had he stayed on the scene? Why — or why not?

> Q: Was it unusual for your unit ROE to change this drastically?
>
> A: It had been put out a few days prior that a positive identification was enough to engage from then on. However, this was the first time we had been given the circumstances in order to engage. It was definitely a new approach that seemed different from the previous ROE we had been given. Pretty much the other end of the spectrum.

Q: Why do you believe this sudden change occurred?

A: To be in line with the threats and the kind of indirect contact we had taken from the enemy. IEDs [Improvised Explosive Devices], mortars, rockets. The small arms and direct fire had not been a tactic used often since around Jan/Feb, by the enemy. This allowed us to stay in the fight with the enemy's new tactics.

Q: Who is COL Steele?

A: My brigade commander....

Q: Where was COL Steele located on objective Murray?

A: At our initial target house on the south side of the island. I never actually saw him, though.

Q: Do you know if he ever moved from that particular site?

A: He left to go to headquarters after I had returned from the second objective ... I was told, but I did not witness this....

Q: Did you instruct or dictate exactly what was to be put in any sworn statements?

A: No, there were some preformatted parts passed down on the statements that were given to us (grid, names, etc.) left as fill in the blanks. However, on the sworn statements for this incident, I posted the names of the detainees, the grid, and the times of pickups and events on a white board while my guys filled them out, but I in no way directed what they should have as content on their statements. I told them several times to just put whatever they believed to be the truth on their statements when we filled them out.

Q: Who photographed the dead bodies and the mission itself?

A: The combat cameraman and SGT Lemus, for evidence purposes. The pictures were turned in to MAJ Sullivan and then immediately erased by SGT Lemus.

Q: Who is SGT Lemus?

A: SGT Lemus is a team leader in SSG Girouard's squad.

Q: What was the name of the combat cameraman?

A: He was a young black guy from Panama that I believe worked for brigade.

The issue of why the first set of statements seemed scripted is not entirely resolved by this exchange. The issue of how and why and by whom photographs were taken comes in and out of the statements periodically, but is never pursued by the investigators. Why would the photographs be erased? Were all the photographs taken strictly for the purposes of "evidence" — whatever that means — or were there other motives? The investigators seemed more eager to pursue other suspicions:

Q: Why would anyone from your platoon have 3 detainees free at the same time and try to re-flexi-cuff them all at once?

A: Inexperience and the "fog of war" after just shooting someone....

Q: How do you think it is possible for PFC Clagett and SPC Hunsaker to recover so quickly from their attacks to engage the 3 detainees?

A: They were only hit with a punch and a knife blow; both were immediately still relatively conscious....

Q: Did you witness the intentional killing of any detainees or Iraqis which were unlawful or against your ROE?

A: No, I did not.

Q: Did you ever question your superiors about the new ROE?

A: No, I did not.

The phrase *"unlawful or against your ROE"* is loaded with multiple ambiguities and cannot really be answered with a "yes" or "no". Is the platoon leader's ROE the new one or the traditional one? If it is the new one, then all the killings were unlawful, provided the new ROE is unlawful. If the platoon leader was partly following the new ROE (with regard to the man in the window) and partly the traditional ROE (with regard to the killing of the prisoners), then the appropriate answer would have been yes and no, depending on the ROE and death in question.

It seems that the trained investigators became suspicious of the fact that all the soldiers gave nearly identical accounts of what happened — as if the accounts had been rehearsed beforehand. Another set of suspicions apparently arose from the alleged facts of how the prisoners escaped. Finally, the investigators seem to be aware that the new ROE was unlawful. Strictly speaking, it was the duty of the lieutenant and all the soldiers to question and even to disobey the unlawful order.

Here, the investigators still appear to be in the process of making a decisive choice: whether to pursue the unlawfulness of the new ROE by going up the chain of command or to pursue the unlawfulness of the killing of the prisoners vis-à-vis traditional ROE by going down the chain of command. The lieutenant's careful, professional answers were ultimately neutral and probably did not impact this decision one way or another. But the bottom line, as of May 29, is that nothing unlawful happened during the mission, even if questionable things happened.

STATEMENT BY THE SQUAD LEADER, SGT GIROUARD

Because Girouard was the only participant in this drama to later stand trial by military jury, and because he was the squad leader, his sworn statement is very important. In his sworn statement dated 29 May 2006, Girouard asserted bluntly that "the ROE was to kill all military-age males on objective Murray." He continued:

> During the meeting the Company Commander CPT. Hart reinstated the Rules of Engagement, he said it has been confirmed that 20 AIF fighters were on obj. Murray, the informant flew over and did an area recon of the island and confirmed terrorist activity. Kill all military-age males on the island. Everyone understood the ROE. I instructed my team leaders to conduct pre combat checks and pre combat inspections, on our soldiers. Then

I did my final walk through of inspecting my soldiers . . . Then after waiting a while Rock 6 COL Steele gave us a brief, a motivational speech, and reinstated the ROE. He stated for us to kill all military-age males on the island.

One of the new elements in this version of events is that, once the soldiers were on the ground, Girouard claims that "I got a face to face with choppin 36 Lt. Wehrheim and asked him if the ROE was the same and he said yes because the next house was still on the island, so I passed the word to my soldiers the ROE was still to kill all military-age males on the island, they said roger." It seems from this version that the ROE was reinforced verbally several times prior to as well as during the operation. Why would Girouard seek repeated reassurance concerning the ROE? Whatever the answer, the issue becomes increasingly peripheral. In any case, he stated: "Then I positively identified one military-age male in the window and fired at him." He continued:

When I rushed in the 1ˢᵗ door I saw 2 women and 3 military-age males hiding behind them, the 3 military-age males were using the women as shields (an Al Qaeda technique). . . . I pushed the 3 military-age males outside to SPC Graber, PFC Mason, PFC Clagett, I called up DOC Bivens to check out the casualty. DOC said he was dead so I reported it to Choppin 36 LT Wehrheim. I then had SGT Lemus and SPC Hunsaker escort the women to the back of the house and to cover their faces so they wouldn't see the 1 KIA.

Presumably, the three prisoners would have been killed on sight had they not been hiding behind the women. There is nothing unique to the practice of using women as shields; this technique was frequent in the war in Bosnia in the 1990s, and as we have seen, during the Battle of Mogadishu, for example. Girouard then recounted how he ordered his soldiers "to lay down suppressive fire over the top" of a neighboring house, again requested and received approval from LT Wehrheim to apply the ROE, and set fire to the house. Formally, these actions constitute violations of the Geneva Conventions, and similar actions by Serbs against Bosnians were prosecuted at The Hague. There was no evidence of hostile intent coming from the house, and it had women and children inside. "I then saw 1 military-age male step out of the front of the house with a little approximately 2-year-old baby girl holding it in front of his face and in front of his chest, so I could not engage him." The man was taken prisoner, instead of being shot, and Girouard again confirmed his actions with the platoon leader. It is worth noting that in this instance Girouard was showing mercy and disobeying the new ROE, while his behavior was in accordance with the traditional ROE and the Geneva Conventions.

The account touches again on the nagging issue of why the prisoners were restrained with "zip ties" instead of "zip cuffs" (sometimes called flexi-cuffs) and Girouard said he ordered that they be tied with "zip cuffs." Girouard confirms that, at this point, LT Wehrheim had left the island on a Black

Hawk helicopter. The rest of the account of how the prisoners were killed is much the same as the earlier account. The military investigators asked:

Q: What was the mission at Iron Triangle?

A: Go in on the island and kill all military-age males because they were Al Qaeda operatives.

Q: Who gave the order?

A: CPT Hart, LT Wehrheim and COL Steele.

Q: Do you think killing the male in the window was wrong?

A: Negative, because he was a military-age male and that's what I was told to do.

Of course, killing the male in the window was a violation of the Geneva Conventions and the Army's traditional ROE, but clearly the investigators did not linger on this point. No one was ever charged with any crime for killing this male in the window. The investigators continued:

Q: Were you ever given that type of order before?

A: I have been given ROEs similar to that. OIF2 [Operation Iraqi Freedom 2] we were told if any vehicles stop or if anyone gets out of their vehicle between the hours of 2300 and 0400, we were to engage to kill. Because there was curfew and a lot of IED activity on the MSR.

Q: When you engaged the military-age male in the window, did you think at the time you may have been killing a person who was not armed?

A: It did not matter if he was armed or not, he was a military-aged male and we were told to kill all military-aged males.

Q: Why didn't you kill the guy with the baby?

A: I could not properly engage him because as I moved my weapon he moved the baby and put the baby in front, so I could not engage him.

Q: Why didn't you shoot him after the baby was taken away?

A: Because he did not have a weapon, he was detained, and I am human. I did not see the threat anymore. I could have shot him and everyone would have thought that was Hooah, but there was no threat.

Girouard's replies to the investigators do not suggest that he was ruthless. On the contrary, he seems to have displayed mercy as well as behavior in accordance with traditional ROE in this particular instance. An objective assessment of the above exchange would lead to the conclusion that the investigator was asking "trick questions" or was himself confused as to which way to play this situation.

The tricky, and insincere, part is that the new ROE — to kill every military-age male on sight — is unlawful, and one may assume that the investigator knew or at least suspected as much. Thus, had Girouard and the others followed this new ROE, any and all killings of the males on the island, whether they were prisoners or not, whether they were armed or not, would have been "lawful" in relation to this patently unlawful ROE. On the other hand, Girouard is clearly aware of the "old" ROE, which stipulated that an enemy may be engaged only if he shows hostile intent. Girouard had been placed in a lose–lose situation, whereby any answer he gave, and whether or not he killed or did not kill any Iraqi male on the island, his opinion as well as his conduct would be lawful under one standard and unlawful under a different standard. Girouard's reply indicating that he refrained from shooting the unarmed male with the baby out of a sense of humanity pierces through this disingenuous line of questioning. The questions continued:

Q: Why didn't they engage the military-age males in the house?

A: Because they were using the women as shields. I know I could have but they were not a threat and I would have to live with what I had done.

Q: Do you think the guy in the window was a threat?

A: Yes, because it was the first contact with a male and the ROE said to kill military-age males. I don't know if he had anything or not. I didn't take the chance.

Q: What did you expect when you got on the island?

A: I thought we were going into a hot LZ and take a lot of fire. I was seriously thinking there were 20 bad dudes there.

Q: Did you change your mind after going through the objective?

A: Yes, because we didn't take fire, there were women and children there. I didn't know if family was living there or if it was an Al Qaeda cover up. I expected no women and no children. The Intel said 20 AIF [Anti Iraqi Forces] there. But it did not seem right. It seems the women did not like the men. When we completed the mission they did not seem upset the men were dead. They were more concerned with Hunsaker's injuries. I think they were using the women to cook for them and sex. Usually the women scream and call us names. These women were smiling.

Q: Did any of the women communicate this to you?

A: Once we got back in the house they were trying to care for Hunsaker. They said things like I Love You and calm down my love (this was said in Arabic) but I understand phrases.

Q: What were you told about the killing of the three guys who were zip tied?

A: I understand that they were changing the zip ties like I told them. One guy came up with a knife and slashed Hunsaker and one punched Clagett. I should have stayed and supervised but I was told we had to push to the objective. When I picked up my detainee his zip ties were the small ones and they were not strong enough. I told them to change them out. They both said roger, and I handed the stronger zip ties. One of them said that one had already broken. I think they are telling the truth. If it would have happened another way they would have told me and the story has been the same the whole time.

The seemingly peripheral issue of changing the "zip ties" to "zip cuffs" takes on importance as an explanation for why and how the prisoners could have escaped under the scenario presented thus far: that the prisoners were shot trying to escape. In the second version of events, the issue of the zip ties becomes paramount. Presumably, had the prisoners been adequately restrained by the zip cuffs, they would not have escaped and would not have been able to attack Hunsaker, so there would have been no need to kill them. But then, the soldiers would have technically disobeyed the ROE, because they took prisoners. On the other hand, even if the prisoners had been escaping, under traditional ROE, gradual escalation of force would have been required, not the immediate use of deadly force. Girouard's explanation opens up many new questions: why did the soldiers go to battle with both types of restraints, ties and cuffs? The investigator zeroed in on further suspicions:

Q: Have there been problems with the smaller zip ties before?

A: Not before this incident. A week or so later while out on a mission, we picked up some detainee and the small zip ties broke. We told the platoon they broke and sure enough they broke....

Q: What happened to the evidence and the bodies once they made it to the Brigade TAC?

A: I heard the bodies were re-zipped. People are treating us like crap and don't like us. I think it has to do with someone's OER [Officer Evaluation Report]. It's politics. We got the most successful raids and the most enemy kills. We have been in the most fire fights.

Q: Based on what you know now, do you think the ROE for that night was the right thing to do?

A: If I get an ROE from a superior officer I am going to do and believe what he says. Because he is going to have some good Intel and do his homework before he sends us out there to complete a mission.

Q: Do you feel anything you did that night was wrong?

A: No, besides not having the right flexi cuffs.

Q: Were you informed by your soldiers about the flexi cuffs prior to this mission?

A: No, but it was common knowledge, common sense those should not be used. They are too thin, that's why I told them to change them out and I gave them the correct ones to use.

And this is how Girouard's second statement ends. The issue of the zip ties became paramount because it suggested that if the soldiers might be lying about the ties, they might be lying about other things. The bigger issue of the ROE was pushed into the background. The fact that the new ROE was unlawful seems implicitly obvious to both Girouard and the investigator, but neither one seems willing or able to state this fact openly. It is an "open secret" that Girouard was following the new ROE with regard to the man in the window and the traditional ROE in taking three prisoners.

STATEMENT BY BRANDON ANDREW HELTON

The gunner in the squad, Brandon Helton, began his statement in the usual way regarding the ROE: "I saw a man in the window, he was engaged by SG Girouard because of the ROE (every military-age male declared to be hostile on island)." The wording is slightly different, not to kill on sight but to regard any military-age male as "hostile" (as per the old ROE), even if they were not actually hostile, because they were "declared" hostile. Helton confirms that after the first kill, he opened fire on the neighboring house, but one difference is that LT Wehrheim seems to have been involved in this order, not just SSG Girouard: "SSG Girouard and LT Wehrheim met with me and asked me any details of personnel in the house, I responded I didn't see any so they told me to use grazing fire over the house so I began to fire." The rest of the narrative is standard, but he adds: "We then moved all the detainees to the southern most house for pictures, etc." Some soldiers reported that the prisoners were photographed, but others did not. The function of this photography, as well as who took the photos and for what reasons — all this seems unclear. "I heard SSG Girouard yell to SPC Hunsaker and PVT Clagett who were all still located at the house with the detainees to change the flex cuffs because some of the detainees had already broken." He continues:

> At that time I heard pop, pop, pop turned around and the 3 detainees from house 1 were running from the house. The front 2 had 2 blindfolds down the third was in the process of pulling his down. The saw [Squad Assault Weapon] opened up and all 3 detainees fell to the ground. . . . SPC Hunsaker was lying on the ground with a cut across his face and hand and PVT Clagett was kneeling down. I asked them if they were OK. Hunsaker said he needed doc. . . . Doc Bivins said that all three [prisoners] were dead.
>
> Q: Was there a company formation held prior to this mission? If so, who spoke?
>
> A: Kind of we just gathered around and COL Steele spoke and told us that they flew out on a chopper with an informant and the informant said the island was run by Al Qaeda and that SF "Special Forces" went there and a soldier died and they had gotten run out. For us to be safe out there that the whole island was declared hostile, referring to military-age males, and for us to kill them sons of a bitches. COL Steele is our brigade commander.
>
> Q: Who placed the zip ties on the detainees?
>
> A: Not really sure when they first hit the house
>
> Q: Were you aware of the zip ties being weak?
>
> A: I know the ones they gave us before the mission were real small and cheap.
>
> Q: Who photographed the detainees and mission?
>
> A: SGT Lemus and I do not know the name of the combat camera.
>
> Q: Did you ever overhear CPT Hart or anyone else directly tell someone to delete any photographs?
>
> A: No, most definitely not. CPT Hart is as straight lace as they come by the book all the time. And I never heard anyone else say something like that. . . .
>
> Q: Why would a soldier attempt to change the flex cuffs on all 3 detainees at once?
>
> A: No clue.
>
> Q: Approximately how many rounds were fired at the detainees?

A: M-4 probably around 10–12 saw probably 30–40.

Q: Were the detainees inside or outside when they were photographed and during the changed flex cuffs?

A: Outside the house for photos and I believe outside by the doorway for the changing of the cuffs not certain.

Q: Did you witness any unlawful engagement of the enemy during this mission?

A: Negative.

Q: Was it strange for the ROE to be changed as it was?

A: No it changed many times before for certain missions. It matters how bad the area is when identified by an informant.....

Q: Did you physically see who engaged the 3 detainees when they fled?

A: No.

Again, one senses in the investigator's questions a sort of double-edged sword. If the new ROE were lawful, then there would be no need for an investigation — all the killings would have been lawful. But if the new ROE were deemed lawful with regard to the male in the window, but deemed unlawful with regard to the prisoners who were shot, then the investigator enjoys wide latitude in which direction to take, which version of the ROE should become central and which peripheral. The flexi-cuffs become an issue because they suggest that the soldiers are lying about them in order to justify shooting escaping and hostile prisoners, which would be lawful under the old ROE. But under the old ROE, killing the male in the window would have been unlawful. Perhaps the investigators were not sure which ROE they would apply or deem lawful or unlawful with regard to which killings, and this is why their questions consistently cover the ROE without any clear sense of direction and the issue of the flexi-cuffs with a clear sense of suspiciousness.

Statement by William Hunsaker

The second statement by Hunsaker, made on May 29, is a continuation of this cat-and-mouse game with the investigators. Again, "We were given the ROE the day prior to our mission by our brigade commander to eliminate any military-age males on the island." Like the other soldiers, he mentioned the use of "suppressive fire" on the neighboring home and the man with the baby who was captured. Unlike some of the other statements, this one makes mention of the Iraqi soldiers who were on the mission: "Some Iraqi Army also came down with him [LT Wehrheim], but they didn't really do anything except maybe search what we have already searched and try talking to that detainee for whatever reasons I have no idea."

Perhaps Hunsaker was trying to throw suspicion on the Iraqi soldiers collaborating or aiding the prisoners in some way. He returns to this them later in the statement: "I would periodically stop and check on the females because the IA soldier who was told to watch them would leave his post and would wander around and talk to the detainees and come in and out of the house along with two other IA soldiers and were actively being told by myself and a few others to stop talking to the detainees." Hunsaker confirms that the shooting of the prisoners took place after LT Wehrheim left the island on a helicopter, but added that a translator left with the platoon leader. There is no mention of whether the Iraqi soldiers stayed or left the scene. Why would the interpreter be taken away at this tense period of time, when his services would be needed to communicate with the prisoners?

Q: Were the first detainees you found in the first house zip-tied or flexi-cuffed?

A: The detainees were zip-tied and the zip-ties were very thin and colored black.

Q: Who put the zip-ties on them?

A: I don't know.

Q: Who searched them?

A: I don't know.

Q: Did you assume all three detainees were searched?

A: Yes.

Of course, if the detainees had been searched, one would have to account for how one of them obtained a knife with which he allegedly attacked Hunsaker. The investigator asked, "Did you have any reason to believe that any of them had concealed weapons?" Hunsaker replied: "No, because I trusted that they have been already searched and couldn't see how they could have obtained one unless it was given to them." Perhaps Hunsaker was hinting that one of the Iraqi soldiers had given a knife to one of the prisoners. The investigator asked: "Other than finding a knife near his [dead prisoner's] body, can you positively identify that knife as the one he used to attack you?" Hunsaker answered "No." The investigator continued:

Q: When he attacked you with a knife, why didn't you use your M-4 to butt stroke or spear him?

A: The individual attacked with deadly force so I felt it necessary to use deadly force against him to save my life and to protect my comrades.

Q: Why didn't you shoot him as he was attacking you as opposed to shooting him after he was fleeing away, running with his back to you?

A: Because my first instinct was to protect myself with my free hand and reach for my weapon with my other hand, by the time I had taken a step back to grab my weapon he was already running.

Q: So at that point, did you feel he was an immediate threat if he was running away from you with his back to you?

A: I did not know where he was running to, for all I knew he could have been running for a hidden weapon somewhere that we could have missed.

> Q: Why did you shoot the other two detainees?
>
> A: Because they were running with the first one and I didn't know exactly what they had done to PFC Clagett but it was obvious that he had attacked him also.
>
> Q: Did you shoot them because you thought they attacked Clagett?
>
> A: Yes, because from what I saw in that mere second it was obvious that he had done something and so I did what I thought was necessary to protect his life and mine.
>
> Q: You did what you thought was necessary to protect his life and your by shooting them as they were running away and no longer an immediate threat?
>
> A: Like I said I did not know where they were running to.

Clearly, the investigator "smelled something fishy," as the expression goes: the prisoners were shot in the back while they were running away; all were shot and not just the one who allegedly attacked the soldiers; a gradual escalation of force from striking through wounding to finally killing a prisoner was not used, as required by the traditional ROE.

And here we return to the rub that is at the crux of this entire story: Which ROE was being followed at the scene, and which one would the investigators and prosecutors invoke in filing charges?

> Q: If they ran away from you without attacking you first, would you still have shot them?
>
> A: No, I would not have shot them because running away is not a hostile act. If they would have just started running without attacking myself or PFC Clagett they most definitely would not have been shot.

But this reply assumes the validity of the traditional ROE on the battlefield. The investigator seems to be implicitly aware of this tension between the new ROE and the traditional ROE, asking: "If you were not given the order to shoot all military-age males, would you have still shot the three detainees?" Hunsaker replied: "Yes." This is yet another trick question. If the soldiers had not been given the new ROE, shooting the allegedly hostile prisoners would have been justified under the traditional ROE only as a last resort. On the other hand, the new ROE made the lives of the prisoners expendable in any event, whether or not they were prisoners, because the order was to kill all military-age males.

> Q: Would you have shot the detainees if they were not shielded by the women and child?
>
> A: Yes, according to the ROE we were given.

Again, this is a trick question, even if that is not its intention. Under traditional ROE, it would have been unlawful to shoot the men whether or not they were shielded by women and the child because the men were unarmed and showed no hostile intent. Yet the new ROE made killing the men apparently lawful

The investigator also asked specific questions about who shot whom, and how many bullets were fired. It seems suspicious that Hunsaker could not or would not answer some of these questions, given that the bodies of the prisoners were riddled with bullets:

Q: Did you shoot the detainees solely because one of them attacked you?

A: Yes.

Q: At the time you fired the first shot, were you concerned where they were running to?

A: No.

Q: Were the detainees' wrists bound when they were running?

A: No....

Q: Right before you fired your first shot, did you feel any detainees posed an immediate threat?

A: No.

Q: Were any of the detainees facing you at any point when the shots were fired?

A: No.

Q: Why do you think Clagett shot at the detainees?

A: Probably for the same reason I did.

Q: How many shots did you fire?

A: Unknown.

Q: Did you or Clagett fire any sots after the detainees fell to the ground?

A: When we started shooting we kept shooting them until they fell to the ground. And after they hit the ground they were shot a couple of more time before we realized we had to stop.

STATEMENT BY THOMAS A. KEMP

Kemp's sworn statement and answers to subsequent questioning on May 29 yielded some additional precision as well as additional ambiguity on the issues that emerged in the second batch of affidavits. Kemp wrote:

> We were briefed during the op order by our platoon leader, LT Wehrheim that all military-age males on objective Murray, small island in the company sector, were positively identified by high level informants to be members of al Qaeda, Iraq and that we were clear to engage on sight. Upon our arrival at Remagen the same ROE was also briefed or reinforced by CPT Hart. Later, the brigade commander, COL Steele briefed the same ROE to us while we were in formation prior to leaving for the mission. When we got to the island we cleared the first group of houses but we did not find anything. We then regrouped and air assaulted to a second group of buildings on the island. When we got to the second group of houses, a military-age male was spotted in a window in a house and he was engaged by the elements clearing the house.... LT Wehrheim and elements from our platoon were going to be air assaulting to another objective after they dropped off the bag (guy shot in the first house).... While I was at the pick zone I heard a burst of gun shots, but I am not sure how many. I heard the saw and

some M4 fire. I turned around and saw all three detainees fall. Then I ran over to the house where they were located and saw they were all dead.

The soldiers claim consistently that the new ROE was verbally repeated to them multiple times; that the platoon leader left the battlefield immediately prior to the shooting of the prisoners; and that all three prisoners died almost immediately.

Q: Who removed the blindfolds and flexi-cuffs?

A: I don't think they had blindfolds on but they did have flexi-cuffs on during the pictures.

Q: When were they blindfolded?

A: I didn't blindfold them and I am not sure when they were.

Q: Were they blindfolded prior to you and SS Girouard moving to the pickup zone?

A: I believe they were but I am not sure.

Q: When you returned to where they were shot were they blindfolded and flexi-cuffed?

A: Their blindfolds were on partially but all the flexi-cuffs were broken.

We have already read that some soldiers testified that the prisoners were flexi-cuffed when their bodies were taken away, but Kemp states clearly that the restraints on all of them were cut or broken. The mystery of photographing the prisoners emerges again, but is not pursued. Why would prisoners be photographed on the battlefield? The investigator continues:

Q: How did the flexi-cuffs get off the detainee?

A: Clagett and Hunsaker were cutting the flexi-cuffs off so they can change them out.

Q: So, one was already broke and then they cut the other two off, just in case they broke?

A: Yeah, I think so.

Q: What is the procedure for placing flexi-cuffs on detainees?

A: You would get the detainee in a controllable position and then you have one person guard and the other put the flexi-cuffs on.

Q: Are you saying you were told no one was guarding the detainees and the detainee was not in a controllable position when they cut two of the detainees' cuffs off and one detainee's cuffs were already broken?

A: They did not elaborate....

Q: So, six guys left with one detainee. Two guys stayed behind with three detainees and one of those detainees' cuff was already broken.

A: Yes.

Indeed, many aspects of the situation seem suspicious: six soldiers left the scene with one prisoner, who was taken away on a helicopter along with a dead man in a body bag; only two soldiers were left to guard three prisoners. Why weren't all four prisoners taken away from the battlefield? In this particular account, where the Iraqi army soldiers were goes unmentioned.

Q: What happened to Hunsaker?

A: He said he had been cut by a knife by one of the detainees.

Q: Where is the knife?

A: I think I may have left it on the objective or it may have got lost in the shuffle.

Q: Whose knife was it?

A: It did not look like it belonged to any of us (Americans)....

Q: Was the objective to kill all military-aged males on the island?

A: Yes.

Q: How did the Iraqi Army soldiers react to the incident?

A: They were visibly angry when the first guy got shot but I really didn't pay attention to their reaction when the other guys were shot.

Q: So why were they flexi-cuffed?

A: I think it was more out of habit. They did not have a clear line of sight to engage the target.

Q: So if they would have had a clear line they would have shot them anyway?

A: Yes.

Q: Is it possible they may have thought they should just kill them because that was the objective?

A: Anything is possible, but I don't think they would have done that.

It would be disclosed later that the Iraqi Army soldiers were not even on the island when the prisoners were shot — they were whisked away on the helicopter along with the platoon leader. In fact, they may have been taken away precisely because they were so angry that the man in the window had been shot. The double-edged sword of the ROE emerges again: Some of the soldiers may have concluded, and evidence would later reveal they did conclude, that the prisoners should be killed because it was already their destiny to die because of the ROE.

But it was the issue surrounding the flexi-cuffs that would be the undoing of the soldiers in trying to cover up this fact. In trying to follow the new ROE, the soldiers concocted a story based on traditional ROE (the prisoners had to be unrestrained and hostile in order to warrant firing upon them), and the two different story lines based upon two widely divergent ROE did not mesh.

STATEMENT BY LEONEL LEMUS

Many discrepancies emerged from the versions of events given by Lemus versus that told by other soldiers. Lemus claimed that there were "about 4–5 Iraqi Army soldiers" present, whereas other soldiers said there were 2–3 or failed to mention them at all. How many Iraqi Army soldiers were there? The Iraqi translator named "Harry" is mentioned again and that a combat photographer named Teddy Wade was present. Lemus was at considerable distance from the house when the prisoners were shot but said that he saw the prisoners run and fall to the ground. They fell with "about 2 seconds in between" them. When he ran to the scene, he saw "the male farthest left was about 10 feet from the male to his right," the second prisoner was "about 20 feet away from the house," and the third prisoner was "about 12 feet from the house." Some of the other accounts posited that the bodies were stacked on top of each other. Lemus also distinguished that the prisoners had been zip-tied but not flexi-cuffed. Toward the end of the interview, the investigator asked:

> Q: Did the killing of the three fleeing detainees coincide with the guideline of the Rules of Engagement?
>
> A: Yes they were because they stressed to us that the males on the island were in an al Qaeda cell and have had significant engagement with other US forces in that area.

The tricky part of this trick question is the prefix "the" before the words ROE. Was the investigator referring to the new ROE or the traditional ROE? The soldier's reply is somewhat "correct" only in relation to the traditional ROE (provided other conditions are met, such as gradual escalation of force), but inconclusive if he was answering in relation to the new ROE. The new ROE apparently said nothing about taking prisoners, so was Lemus claiming that it was permissible to kill prisoners because the order was to kill all military-age males on the island? The investigator continued,

> Q: Are you authorized to shoot at an enemy who was previously searched, detained and decided to flee?
>
> A: Proper escalation of force was used when the detainee became hostile and armed himself with a weapon and wounded one soldier and struck another.
>
> Q: Is there anything you want to add to this statement?
>
> A: Our actions on OBJ Murray were in accordance to the ROE briefed to us prior to our mission and moments before our air assault was conducted.

The first reply is correct in relation to the traditional ROE, but the second reply remains inconclusive: the overall point seems to be again that the soldiers may have interpreted the new ROE as a license to kill regardless of circumstances.

STATEMENT BY KEVIN RYAN

Discrepancies also emerged in Ryan's sworn affidavit. In his statement, he wrote, "The ROE for objective Murray was to kill any military-aged male that was not actively surrendering." But when asked by the investigator, "What exactly was the ROE?" Ryan replied, "On objective Murray the ROE was to kill any military-aged male we came into contact with." The two replies differ on the issue of surrendering prisoners. Which version is correct?

Like some other soldiers, Ryan mentioned, "we started detainee packets and picture taking" after the Iraqis were taken prisoner. The purpose of the photography never seems to emerge in the statements, and it is not clear who took the photos.

> Q: Who gave you the ROE for objective Murray?
>
> A: COL Steele had come by the night before and talked to Charlie Company about the mission at hand and he mentioned the ROE for obj. Murray. This was also enforced by our company commander CPT Hart....
>
> Q: Were you or your squad engaged with enemy fire?
>
> A: Not on objective Murray. I do not think we were ever engaged on Operation Iron Triangle.

By the standards of the traditional ROE, all the killings on this mission were unlawful because the enemy showed no hostile intent. The investigators consistently touch on this issue, and just as consistently assume that the unlawful, new ROE applied to the man in the window. "Who were the 2 IA [Iraqi Army] soldiers?" "I do not know any names or ranks." The number of Iraqi soldiers is never consistent, and they seemed practically invisible to the American soldiers. "Who took pictures?" the investigator asked. "Doc Bivins and CPL Helton" — the identities of the photographers varies greatly across the statements. "With what camera?" Ryan replied, "I think it was SGT Lemus's camera."

One learns from other statements that an unnamed combat photographer was also present. According to Ryan, after the prisoners were shot, their bodies were "about 20 to 30 meters north of the house, at least 2 of them were on top of each other." Other soldiers described the scene differently in terms of location and without the bodies being on top of one another.

> Q: What was the process of writing your statement after the mission?
>
> A: When we returned to Ramagen, we were all called into a room. Information such as grids and detainee names were written on a board for reference. We now proceeded to write statements separately.
>
> Q: Who wrote the information on the board?
>
> A: SPC Kemp.
>
> Q: Were you told what to write on your statement?
>
> A: No.

Ryan states that Kemp put the information on the board, but the platoon leader, LT Wehrheim, said that he wrote the information. Who is telling the truth? If some of the information was scripted, in that it was written on the board, how much of the other information might have been scripted verbally?

STATEMENT BY BRADLEY MASON

Mason's statement and replies to the investigator's questions gave a slightly different perspective on what transpired during the assault. Mason wrote:

> On May 8, 2006 we were given the ROE to kill all military-age males on OBJ Murray. Given by the brigade commander we headed to the first hour of the Obj. SSG Girouard, SGT Lemus, myself and I believe one other individual fired at a male in the window in accordance with the ROE that was given the day before. We continued around the house to the front. As we entered the house we found three other males hiding behind two women so we detained them and took them outside and brought the man that we shot in the window outside so that the Doc Bivins could help him. By the time I had searched the three males and had turned back around the fourth male had died from a sucking chest wound. After that I went around the house with the women. The rest of third squad along with Gun 6 went to the second house where a man comes out of the house with a baby in front of him so that he would not get shoot [sic]. They brought him to the first house so the total count of detainees was 4. 3 from the first house and 1 from the second house. I don't remember what time it was by then. LT and second squad had took off with the KIA leaving third squad Gun 6 and the RTO at the OBJ. I was in the back of the house with the women and SSG Girouard and the women when I heard oh shit and gun fire following. SSG Girouard and I ran around the house to find out what happened he told me that they had noticed one of the flex cuffs were broke s they started to change out the flex cuffs as they were changing the flex cuffs on one of the detainees swung around with a knife and swung at SPC Husker and slit his arm. And one of the other detainees swung around and hit PFC Clagett in the eye. I looked in the door and saw that SPC Husker was ok so I went around to the other side of the house and went back in the room with the women and stand there till we left.

> Q: Did you type the above narrative?

> A: Yes

> Q: What is your position in the squad?

> A: SAW [Squad Assault Weapon] gunner.

> Q: Could COL Still be spelled Steel?

> A: I don't know how to spell his name.

As an aside, the reader should note that, in fact, the brigade commander's name is spelled "Steele." Mason's repeated misspellings and difficulty with punctuation, coupled with the fact that the narrative is well written as a whole, suggests that this military unit relied more upon oral than written transmission of information, from ROEs to people's names. Why the investigator also misspelled Steele's name is curious.

> Q: Had you ever been told to kill all military age men as an ROE before?

> A: Before this incident, no.

> Q: Did you question the above order?

> A: Not to them. I kept it to myself.

Q: Prior to this operation, what was the ROE?

A: To detain any suspicious males unless they posted a threat to you, then you should kill them.

Under strict interpretation of the Army's guidelines, Mason and other soldiers who questioned the order had a duty to disobey it as unlawful. However, in practice, following this guideline would entail mutiny, which is also a crime. And strictly speaking, it is not true that under traditional ROE prisoners who pose a threat should be immediately killed — a gradual escalation of force is required. The more important point, in trying to understand what soldiers felt and were thinking, is that apparently Mason did not feel comfortable with the new ROE, but he also did not fully understand the traditional ROE.

Q: Based on what you saw, did you encounter any hostile action while on OBJ Murray?

A: No.

Q: Did you see the 3 detainees get shot?

A: No.

Q: How did you learn what happened to the 3 detainees that got shot?

A: PFC Clagett.

Q: Did anyone else tell you what happened to the 3 detainees?

A: I heard it from SPC Hunsaker when we got back.

The investigator's questions regarding the lack of hostile action as the soldiers approached the island suggest that he is invoking the traditional ROE, in which all the killings would have been unlawful. But that would include the man in the window, who is not mentioned, whose killing seems to be lawful under the new ROE. The investigator also established that the basic narrative of how the three prisoners were shot came exclusively from two soldiers, and that there were no independent witnesses. The investigator changed tack:

Q: What happened to the fourth detainee?

A: He got taken in.

Q: Was he ever with the other detainees?

A: I believe he was, but I did not see it.

Q: Was he taken away before or after the 3 detainees were shot?

A: After.

Q: How was he transported?

A: By helicopter.

The other soldiers seem to be unanimous in claiming that the fourth prisoner — who was unharmed — was taken away before the other three prisoners were shot. In general, the question of why only one prisoner was taken away from the island, alive, will remain a mystery forever. Toward the end of the interview, the investigator finally shows his hand and for the first time betrays his suspicions about what occurred:

Q: Did you see SPC Hunsaker self-inflict his cuts to his face or arm?

A: No.

Q: Did Hunsaker tell you he self-inflicted the injuries as stated above?

A: No.

Q: Did you see any injury to PFC Clagett?

A: I saw the right side of his face near the eye had been hit, cause it was swollen not bruised.

Q: Did you hear from anyone, another account of this incident, contrary to what has been reported?

A: No.

Q: Did anyone coach you during your initial statement given to the platoon leader?

A: It was written on the board the names of the detainees who were shot, the location and the times.

Q: Did anyone direct you to write in a certain way?

A: No.

Q: Did anyone direct you to write a certain fact or bit of information of which you were uncertain to its truthfulness?

A: No.

STATEMENT BY COREY CLAGETT

Clagett makes a notable departure in his second statement having to do with the addition of a narrative about one of the Iraqi soldiers, which seems to throw suspicion on them:

I saw the detainees lying on their stomachs facing outside the house. SGT Lemus and SPC Graber and myself went to check out the river to see if anyone had been hiding over there. We didn't see anything so when we were coming back I saw an IA guy kneeling by the detainee's lower body, the guy further to the right, and I told him to get the — — away "Yella" so he looked at me and left....

Q: Who briefed you on the ROE for obj. Murray?

A: Captain Hart and LT Wehrheim.

Q: Was your squad engaged with enemy fire?

A: No....

Q: During the second objective on Murray, who shot who and why?

A: SSG Girouard, SGT Lemus, SPC Hunsaker shot and because I was told they saw him in the window and shot cause ROE kill any military-aged male cause the whole island was a threat.

Q: What did they see?

A: They saw a military-aged male in window....

Q: Where did the knife come from?

A: I don't know. We suspect that IA guy.

Again, the death of the man in the window seems unproblematic. Clagett tries to throw suspicion on the Iraqi Army soldiers. To the important question, "What happened to the detainee from the second home?" Clagett replied, "2nd platoon took him." One of the unsolved mysteries in this case will remain how one prisoner survived.

STATEMENT BY JUSTON GRABER

Q: Who briefed you on the ROE?

A: 1LT Wehrheim, and SSG Girouard.

Q: Did you hear CPT Hart or COL Steele brief the ROE for objective Murray?

A: No....

Q: Did anyone talk to you about the ROE after the mission?

A: Yes, CPT Hart. He re-elaborated that the ROE for the island (obj. Murray) was to eliminate all military-aged males due to the intel that was recovered about the island.

This is a departure from the consistent statements by others that both Hart and Steele verbally gave the ROE prior to the mission. Why would CPT Hart be involved in verbally presenting the ROE *after* the mission?

Q: Who took pictures of the detainees?

A: Some of us did, but I'm not sure who exactly...

Q: Where is the fourth detainee?

A: The Battalion holding area for detainees. Not sure on exact location.

Q: Were the 4 bodies transported at the same time?

A: No, the 1st body left with the platoon leader, and the last 3 were taken with 2nd platoon.

Some of the other statements suggest that all 4 bodies were taken from the scene at the same time. The photography issue is never resolved — who took the photographs, how many, and for what reasons?

CONCLUSIONS

One senses in the investigator's questions the attitude that is labeled "We know everything" a standard interrogation technique used by the Army. This is a deceptive and insincere attitude, of course, designed to intimidate soldiers.

In reality, the investigators seem to be undecided as to the direction they could or would take, against the commanders or against the soldiers. One gets the feeling that the investigators sense that all the soldiers are lying, or covering up for the ones that are lying, about how the prisoners allegedly attacked Hunsaker and Clagett, and escaped. There are simply too many inconsistencies in all the accounts when it comes to the details of the alleged attack on the soldiers and their alleged right to kill them in self-defense, as asserted in the first set of sworn statements. This part of the investigation comes across as standard operating procedure on the part of the investigators.

The more subtle dynamic that emerges from the statements, questions, and answers is that the unlawfulness of the new ROE is gradually pushed into the background and periphery of the narrative, while the traditional ROE slowly but surely becomes the center of the story. This shift might also be comprehensible as a normal, standard operating procedure had the soldiers in the unit invented the new ROE while the traditional ROE was operative. In that case, one would have a right to conclude that the soldiers were guilty of murder as well as ruthlessness, cunning, cowardice, and other vices. But the soldiers insist that they were trying to follow the new ROE, and give hints that versions of this new ROE were applied in other situations at other times. And we have seen from the documents by COL Steele and CPT Hart that the new ROE apparently existed, at least that they were given verbally. There are no inconsistencies in their account on this score, so that it is difficult to suspect that they are lying. Moreover, the investigators do not try to break or trick them regarding their accounts of the new ROE.

The ultimate proof that the new ROE was real is that the killing of the old man in the window went unpunished, uninvestigated, and was not prosecuted. Not a single soldier was charged with the killing of the man in the window. Had the new ROE been a lie, as the "escape" of the prisoners was a lie, then the prosecutors could have brought charges under the traditional ROE for all the killings: the man in the window and the three prisoners. Instead, the killing of the man in the window becomes peripheral, and the investigators and prosecutors shift their focus on the killing of the prisoners vis-à-vis traditional ROE.

This is a disconcerting solution to the dilemmas and inconsistencies presented thus far. Its consequences are that the unlawfulness of the new ROE would never be exposed or questioned; the soldiers who would be accused of murdering the prisoners but not the man in the window would become scapegoats for whoever promulgated an unlawful policy; and the question of which rules of engagement really applied on the battlefield would not be confronted or resolved.

Chapter 6. The Third Version of Events: Conspiracy, Cunning, and Cold-Blooded Murder

One of the most intriguing statements made on June 15 is that of First Sergeant Eric Geressy, who admitted the following:

> I made the statement that I do not know why we have 3 detainees or why do we have any enemy alive. I said something to this effect. I cannot remember the exact words.

LT Wehrheim sighed over the phone when I asked him to verify whether Geressy had made this statement. Wehrheim confirmed that Geressy said it over the radio, and added that several soldiers heard it. He added further that anybody with an FM radio could have picked it up and heard the statement. Wehrheim speculated that Geressy was probably being sarcastic. Geressy's own explanation is that he "was wondering why they did not kill the enemy during the contact."

Indeed, the entire platoon seemed to be wondering the same thing. Clagett told me that news of Geressy's comment "spread like wildfire" through the platoon. Soldiers were still discussing it two to three days following the killings. In its own way, Geressy's public statement is logical: If the ROE ordered the soldiers to kill all military-aged males on sight, why were some taken prisoner? This question is as important as the question why the prisoners were killed — in fact, the two questions may be related to each other.

Other soldiers would wonder why Iraqi males on the island shouldn't be killed, whether or not they were taken prisoner. Does it matter whether the original order, which was given verbally, was to kill the enemy versus "kill or capture" the enemy? None of the May 11 statements used the phrase "kill or capture." The May 11 narratives are consistent and clear that the order was to kill the enemy on sight. The May 29 statements are also consistent on this point. Apparently, some memories changed on June the 15.

Geressy explained: "At no point did I ever try to put any idea into those Soldiers heads to execute or do any harm to the detainees. The Soldiers were briefed thoroughly on the ROE and the intent of the mission to Kill or Capture the enemy. They were all trained on the Safe Guarding of detainees."

An investigator asked him, "Do you believe that the command climate would have influenced the detainees to be killed?"

Geressy replied: "No I do not think so. We have a very aggressive unit with a very aggressive Commander. But there is a big difference between killing the enemy and executing a prisoner. Everyone knows this."

Is it true that "everyone" on this mission knew this difference? This crucial difference only makes sense in relation to the traditional ROE, not in relation to the new ROE.

STATEMENT BY ERIC GERESSY ON 15 JUNE 2006

Q: Was there a time while on Iron Triangle that you made a statement in relation to the alive detainees?

A: Yes after the initial radio reports from PFC Kemp I made the statement I do not know why we have 3 detainees or why do we have any enemy alive. I said something to this effect. I cannot remember the exact words. I made this remark because the initial report I was given on the radio was they had one enemy KIA. We had bad communications ... and I had a hard time hearing PFC Kemp ... So when PFC Kemp got back to me that they had one enemy KIA then 3 captured I was wondering why they did not kill the enemy during contact. I then instructed PFC Kemp to get the detainees ready for movement and that we would get aircraft to them to get them back to our Company CP at Objective Murray ... I then handed the radio off to CPT Sienko and went and informed SGT Kilb the THT Team Leader that we would have 4 detainees arriving at our location and to be ready to screen them. At no point did I ever try to put any idea into those Soldiers heads to execute or do any harm to the detainees. The soldiers were briefed thoroughly on the *ROE and the intent of the mission to Kill or Capture the enemy* [my emphasis]. They were all trained on the Safe Guarding of detainees and like I said I instructed them to get the detainees ready to be moved to our location for screening.

This is perhaps on of the most significant passages in this entire narrative. Note that Geressy distinguishes between the ROE and the "intent" of the mission, even though he claims they were one and the same, to kill *or* capture the enemy. On the contrary, we have seen thus far that the ROE has been described solely to kill the enemy, with no mention of the possibility of capture. The context for Geressy's explanation is defensive, an understandable reaction to the possible charge that his remark, which was broadcast far and wide over the radio, might have triggered the murder of the prisoners. Such cause and effect explanations are always difficult to prove, and shall not even be considered in the present analysis.

0086-06-CID469-75447

SWORN STATEMENT

LOCATION: Tikrit CID Office
Contingency Operating Base (COB) Speicher
Tikrit, Iraq, APO AE 09393

DATE: 15 June 2006   **TIME:** 1800 hrs

NAME: GERESSY, Eric Joseph   SSN: ███████   **GRADE/STATUS:** 1SG/AD

ORGANIZATION OR ADDRESS: C Company 3/187th Infantry, FOB Brassfield-Mora, APO AE 09393

I, Eric J. GERESSY, **WANT TO MAKE THE FOLLOWING STATEMENT UNDER OATH:**
This Statement is a Clarification to some questions that CID had about my statement I made on 14 June 2006.

Q: SA MCCORMICK
A: 1SG GERESSY
Q: Was there a time while on Iron Triangle that you made a statement in relation to the alive detainees?
A: Yes after the initial radio reports from PFC Kemp I made the statement I do not know why we have 3 detainees or why do we have any enemy alive. I said something to this effect I cannot remember the exact words. I made this remark because the initial report I was given on the radio was they had one enemy KIA. We had bad communications even with the COM 201 antenna set up and I had a hard time hearing PFC Kemp. It took me several attempts to get a grid to their location of the contact. So after their report of one enemy KIA I assumed they were in direct fire contact firefight with the enemy. So when PFC Kemp got back to me that they had one enemy KIA then 3 captured I was wondering why they did not kill the enemy during the contact. I then instructed PFC Kemp to get the detainees ready for movement and that we would get Aircraft to them to get them back to our Company CP at Objective Murray so we could have THT who was with us at the CP screen the detainees. I then handed the radio off to CPT Sienko and went and informed SGT Kilb the THT Team Leader that we would have 4 detainees arriving at our location and to be ready to screen them. At no point did I ever try to put any idea into those Soldiers heads to execute or do any harm to the detainees. The Soldiers were briefed thoroughly on the ROE and the intent of the mission to Kill or Capture the enemy. They were all trained on the Safe Guarding of detainees and like I said I instructed them to get the detainees ready to be moved to our location for screening.
Q: Do you believe any rational person would interpret what you said to mean kill the detained personnel?

INITIALS OF PERSON MAKING STATEMENT _CBL_

PAGE 1 OF __4__ PAGES

DA FORM 2823 (*Computer Generated*)

EXHIBIT_____

FOR OFFICIAL USE ONLY - LAW ENFORCEMENT SENSITIVE

Sample of a portion of the sworn statement by Eric J. Geressy.

What seems far more significant is that if Geressy was thinking out loud that the prisoners should already have been dead, many other soldiers might have been thinking the same thing, albeit not out loud. The investigator continued:

> Q: Do you believe any rational person would interpret what you said to mean kill the detained personnel?
>
> A: Absolutely not, I would never have thought anyone in our Company would be capable of such a thing under any circumstances.

It is intriguing that the investigator asked Geressy whether what he said could have been interpreted as a license to kill, when clearly the real issue is whether the new ROE could have been interpreted as a blanket license to kill, including prisoners.

Placed in the context of the new ROE, to kill every military-age male on the island, the murders of the prisoners do not seem any more or less "rational" than the killing of the unarmed man in the window. A bit later in the interview, the investigator asked:

> Q: During your interview, you mentioned that SPC Hunsaker and PFC Clagett made spontaneous statements on the morning of 15 June 06; can you clarify these statements?
>
> A: Yes SPC Hunsaker said to SFC Newman that can someone call his mother because I am going to jail and PFC Clagett said to SFC Bruce can I see my Squad Leader SSG Girouard....
>
> Q: Did you advise SGT Lemus to obtain legal counsel?
>
> A: Yes I did. I advised SGT Lemus to call TDS to advise him on his rights. I was concerned about his camera being taken away.... After I received the information about what went on with SSG Girouard's squad during Operation Iron Triangle, I felt like an idiot for defending them. I feel very sorry for this....
>
> Q: Did you see what pictures or videos were on the camera?
>
> A: No I did not.
>
> Q: Do you have any second hand knowledge of what was on the camera?
>
> A: No I do not.

What, exactly, was on this camera? How many other cameras were used to take photos or videos during this mission, by whom, and for what purpose? These issues simply disappeared from the narrative. Given the fact that the abuse at Abu Ghraib would not have been as believable as it was due to the photographs that were leaked, this is a significant issue.

STATEMENT BY JUSTON GRABER

On June 15, 2006, Graber gave a completely different account of what happened to the prisoners and implicated most of the squad in the conspiracy to commit murder:

> At the time before the conversation in the house, I was walking on the right side of the house going between checks of the detainees and the women

when SPC Hunsaker approached me to tell me he wanted to kill the detainees, because he suspected them of being AIF due to how they hid behind the women when we entered the houses to clear it. SSG Girouard then got 3rd squad in the house to tell us what was up. He said that Hunsaker and Clagett were going to kill the detainees and the story was going to be that the detainees broke the flexi-cuffs and made an attempt to flee. He gave everyone in the room a choice whether or not they wanted to be involved. The people in the room included SPC Hunsaker, myself, PFC Clagett, SGT Lemus. I cannot remember if PFC Mason was in the room at the time, but found out later he did not want to be part in it. I did not want a part in it, nor did SGT Lemus. PFC Mason was pulling security on the females, SGT Lemus and myself were at the LZ/PZ pulling security, getting ready and prepared to lift off when the blackhawks would arrive. I then heard the gun shots, ad sprinted t the house, behind the house I linked up with SSG Girouard and we ran around the left side to the front of the house where the 3 detainees layed on the ground, 2 dead, 1 still gasping for air about every 10 seconds. We yelled for Doc Bivins to aid Hunsaker, and the WIA. Doc said then he couldn't do anything for the WIA. SSG Girouard's instructions were to put him out of his misery. I felt that it was the humane thing to do, and complied with my squad leader's order. During a patrol at a later date, probably a few days after Iron Triangle, I asked SSG Girouard and PFC Clagett what exactly went down that day. They told me that Hunsaker punched Clagett first, then when he wasn't expecting it, SSG Girouard punched him. Then SSG Girouard scratched Hunsaker's face with the shank found in the house. I believe it was after they shot the 3 men was when SSG Girouard cut SPC Hunsaker's arm. Another day I was talking with PFC Clagett in his room about the incident when he old me how he and Hunsaker cut the cuffs off. Then PFC Clagett said he told the men, "Yalla," which means, "go," and "hurry," in Arabic. He told me they were going slow so he yelled it again, one guy turned back and saw him raise his weapon to make them hurry and go faster which was when Hunsaker mistook Clagett's gesture for them to run faster for his ready to engage so he engaged first, then Clagett. We had a squad meeting outside our pad where SSG Girouard stated to us that if one of us spoke up, that he would find whoever snitched and kill them. I don't remember who exactly was there besides all of 3rd squad being SSG Girouard, SGT Lemus, SPC Moor, SPC Hunsaker, myself, PFC Mason, and PFC Clagett. He may or may not have meant it, but I blocked it out. I saw it as a joke. Sometimes it's hard to read SSG Girouard. Sometimes he does things that don't make sense, but when confronted, it is always in the best interest of his guys. He has always looked out for me and his squad. I may be wrong, but I believe there has to be a reasonable explanation for Hunsaker's and Clagett's actions on that day.

Q: Who do you believe came up with the idea to shoot the three detainees?

A: I believe that Hunsaker and SSG Girouard came up with it and PFC Clagett just followed along.

Q: Why do you believe this?

A: Because of what SPC Hunsaker said before the meeting in the house as stated before. I believe SSG Girouard's involvement with the plan because possibly he felt he had to.

Q: Do you recall Clagett saying anything during the meeting?

A: No, I do not.

Q: What about SG Lemus? Did he say anything?

A: As he was walking out he stated he did not want to do it. I followed and said "me either."

Q: How long was the conversation in the house?

A: About 3 minutes.

Q: Did anyone specifically state they were going to cut the cuffs?

A: Yes, SSG Girouard and PFC Clagett....

Q: When you left the meeting at the house, did you believe Girouard, Hunsaker and Clagett intended to kill the detainees?

A: No, I thought they were just talking smack. I didn't expect Hunsaker or SSG Girouard to actually go through with what they did that day. I've gotten to know the 2 guys really well....

Q: How did you feel when you saw this [the crime scene]? What emotions?

A: I was surprised to see Hunsaker lying on the ground with his arm lacerated and bleeding. Nothing was said about anyone getting cut or hurt in the initial meeting in the house....

Q: How long was it before Bivens arrived?

A: It took him about a minute to get there from the LZ/PZ. After we called for him, SSG Girouard and I both yelled, "Medic."

Q: What did you do while you were waiting on Bivens?

A: I was in awe and shock watching one WIA puke up blood and die before Bivens arrived.

Q: Regarding the detainee that Bivens said he could not help, what exactly did Girouard say?

A: His exact words were, "Go ahead and put him out of his misery."....

Q: Did you believe Girouard was saying to shoot the detainee?

A: Yes, I believe it was just a suggestion.

Q: Did you believe Girouard was ordering you personally to shoot the detainee?

A: He did not say it in a manner of which if I didn't comply I would be punished, but it was in a manner in which it was what he wanted to get done.

Q: What did you do?

A: I brought my rifle to the ready, without aiming because I felt I couldn't miss at point-blank range. I missed. I looked and about an inch or two from his head, to the right of him was a hole in the ground. I took a sight picture for the next shot which was directly under his eye....

Q: When you shot at the detainee what were you trying to do?

A: To prevent him from further suffering.

Q: Did you intend to kill him when you shot him?

A: Yes.

Q: Did you feel that Girouard's statement to "put him out of his misery" was a lawful order?

A: Yes, I felt it was the right thing to do.

Of course, Girouard's order was unlawful vis-à-vis traditional ROE. Graber went on to say that Girouard, Bivens, Hunsaker and Clagett were all present when he shot the wounded prisoner. He also said that prior to the killings, the prisoners were "separated about 10 feet, north of the house, 15 feet apart from one another, belly down, chin touching on the ground, flexicuffed and blindfolded."

> Q: Were you entirely truthful in your previous statements?
>
> A: Not entirely. Everything is true except for the fact that I didn't fess up with the truth. My reasons were that I wanted to keep loyalty to my squad. I truly did not want to believe the "truth" and what my squad members (SSG Girouard, PFC Clagett) had told me. I also did not witness anyone from my squad get punched or stabbed. I did not see the detainees run, stab, or punch anyone either.
>
> Q: Were there any efforts by anyone else in the chain of command to conceal what really happened?
>
> A: No.
>
> Q: After you found out what really happened, did you tell anyone else about it?
>
> A: Yes, I confided in SPC Lopez and SGT Newman.

Later in the interview, the investigator asked Graber how he had been treated in the interview, and Graber replied, "Well." "Have you been given food, drink, and breaks to use the latrine?" "Yes." This exchange is interesting in that the defense was prepared to argue at the trial that Graber's confession had been "coerced" by the investigators. Perhaps the investigators anticipated this defense, or it had already been raised, and either way they sought to document that the interview was normative.

STATEMENT BY LEONEL LEMUS

> Q: Did you omit and provide false information in your first sworn statement to CID?
>
> A: Yes.
>
> Q: Provide details of what you omitted and the false information.
>
> A: After giving us sitrep to choppin' 6, *chopin' 7 said over F.M. that the detainees should have been killed* [my emphasis]. About ten minutes or so, SSG Girouard called our squad into the room of the 1st building ad said he wanted to change the zip-ties on the detainees, but his hand gestures and body language seemed to say something else. I took it as something else was going to happen so I walked toward the door....
>
> Q: Clarify your previous answer.
>
> A: SSG Girouard gave a situation report to CPT Hart on our ASIP radio. He informed him of our 4 detainees and 1 KIA. 1SG Geressy transmitted over the radio that those detainees should have been killed. As I waited to get word if helicopters were enroute to transfer the detainees, I sat in the house and took my helmet off so I could cool down. So after about 10 minutes of sitting down, I got up and looked in each room. Every room was

empty except the first room where SPC Graber, SSG Girouard, myself, PFC Mason, and PFC Clagett were in. SSG Girouard called for SPC Hunsaker to come into the room. PFC Mason went and got him. As we all stood there, SSG Girouard said to bring it in close. In a low toned voice he said, "We are going to change the zip-ties..." and glanced at the detainees, who were outside. He mentioned that 1SG Geressy transmitted over the radio that the detainees should have been killed. So, again he said we needed to change the zip-ties, as he looked at the detainees. SSG Girouard talked with his hands and his body language was to say that these detainees were going to get rotated up. I didn't like that idea so I walked towards the door. He looked around at every one and asked if anyone else had an issue or a problem. Nobody said anything so he told SPC Hunsaker, PFC Mason, and PFC Clagett to stay there while he gave me instructions. He told me to grab SGT Ryan and CPL Helton with 1 detainee and have them sit at the LZ. As SPC Kemp, SPC Kemp, SPC Bivins and SPC Graber and I pulled security. As we sat there I asked the 1 detainee if he was an "ali-baba" which means "thief" or "bad guy" in Arabic. The detainee did not respond. I told SGT Ryan that I was smoked and turned towards the detainee. Right then I heard "oh shit" and saw 2 detainees running away. They all got shot and fell so I called SSG Girouard on my ICOM to see what happened...no answer...I made my way to the house only to see 3 bodies, which were the detainees, and SSG Girouard. I asked him what happened, but he couldn't answer. He just looked at the bodies and had this frozen look on his face. I asked where my guys were and he stuttered that they were in the building getting first aid from SPC Bivins. A week later, while we sat at combat outpost 2 in Samarra, I over heard all the talk about what had really happened from PFC Clagett and possibly SPC Graber. I heard half of what they said, but PFC Clagett mentioned to people in his truck that SSG Girouard had punched pretty hard.... I told my team, SPC Graber and PFC Clagett that there is no need to brag because nobody wants to hear that kind of stuff.

Q: While in the house, did you specifically hear Girouard state that he was going to cut the detainee's zip-ties and shoot them?

A: After he pulled in close, yes he did.

Q: Did he specify who was going to do the shooting?

A: Not while I was in the room. He told PFC Mason, PFC Clagett, and SPC Hunsaker to stand-fast....

Q: Did you hear a single shot moments later after you heard and saw the detainees get shot?

A: No I didn't hear a single shot.

The narrative now shifts between the small-group conspiracy to kill the prisoners and the radio transmission from Geressy which questioned why the prisoners had not been killed. Which ROE, new or traditional, pertains to these two competing "centers" of the narrative, the conspiracy versus the radio transmission? In both competing narratives, the new ROE seems to apply, albeit clumsily, because it did not clearly address the issue of prisoners. In other words, all the soldiers seem to have been focused on the order to kill all military-age males on sight. But in both narratives the traditional ROE applies just as well because both the first sergeant's transmission and the conspiracy violate the standard ways that the Army is supposed to approach hostile forces and prisoners. It only adds to the confusion to recall that the Iraqis showed no hostility toward the soldiers, and the prisoners are routinely called "detainees," which places them in a no-man's land between the two competing ROEs. Prisoners have rights under traditional ROE and the Geneva Conventions, but what are the rights of "detainees?"

> Q: Why didn't you attempt to stop Girouard, Hunsaker, and Clagett from killing the detainees?
>
> A: Afraid of being called a pussy.
>
> Q: Why didn't you immediately inform your platoon leader or anyone else, on the radio?
>
> A: Peer pressure and I have to be loyal to the squad.
>
> Q: Do you feel what Girouard, Hunsaker and Clagett did was wrong?
>
> A: Yes it was wrong.
>
> Q: Do you know what they did is a violation and is punishable under the UCMJ [Uniform Code of Military Justice]?
>
> A: Yes.

Of course, the investigator is correct that the soldiers violated the UCMJ. But the new ROE was also a violation of the UCMJ as well as the Geneva Conventions. From this point on, the interview becomes cloudy again in relation to the obligations imposed by the two competing ROEs.

It is helpful to compare this exchange between the investigator and soldier with fictitious conversations in Joseph Heller's novel, *Catch-22*. The main character, Captain Yossarian, frequently complains that he is guilty of dereliction of duty if he refuses to fly the unlawful missions given to him, but guilty of war crimes if he does fly them. Lemus and the other soldiers in the present narrative are repeatedly caught in similar instances of Catch-22.

> Q: Do you know that you are obligated as a soldier to report any crime you witness?
>
> A: Yes.
>
> Q: Do you know by withholding that information, you have violated the UCMJ?
>
> A: Yes.
>
> Q: In your previous statement on 29 May 06, you stated that the killing of the three fleeing detainees coincided with the guidelines of your rules of engagement. Did you falsely state that?
>
> A: Our rules of engagement state that once the enemy has been taken prisoner he is a noncombatant. Therefore unarmed detainees should not be killed....
>
> Q: Prior to being in the house with Girouard and the other squad members, did anyone plan or conspire to kill any detainees or anyone considered noncombative.
>
> A: No, this was not planned.

Which ROE is being used as a referent for these questions and answers, the new or traditional ROE? The investigator's question does *not* refer to "the" rules of engagement (traditional), but "your" rules of engagement. All this begs the question, which version of the ROE were the soldiers owning as "their" ROE? And why were these Iraqi men considered the "enemy," given that they showed no hostility to the soldiers? The only reasonable reply is that the Iraqis were designated as hostile and designated as the enemy prior to the mission. It is also interesting that while the investigator sees a conspiracy, in the legal sense of the term, in this narrative Lemus replies that the murders were *not* planned. From his perspective, the situation comes across more like the soldiers were confused by the two competing ROEs and the first sergeant's widely broadcast question as to why the prisoners were still alive.

> Q: Are there any photographs taken with your camera of the shooting of the detainees?
>
> A: No, MAJ Sullivan of the 320 F.A. has the pictures. No pictures of the actual shooting were taken.

Throughout this narrative, the issue of the photographs comes and goes, but one never learns the details of who took photos of what for what purpose.

> Q: What was Clagett's demeanor while Girouard was talking about the plan?
>
> A: His reaction was normal. It was later on that I took notice how he was feeling ill. Three days later he told me he couldn't stop thinking about it. As if it bothered him. He then asked me about my previous deployment and how I dealt with seeing dead bodies and shooting the enemy. I told him it was alright that he felt like that. He was really stressed because when he slept the few hours he did, he dreamed about it over and over.

I am able to corroborate that Clagett told me over the phone that he could not sleep for months after the shooting incident and had to be put on anti-depressants and other medications in order to cope. As with the so-called rotten apples at Abu Ghraib who were traumatized by the abuse they inflicted, it seems that committing heinous crimes is traumatic for the victimizer and victim alike.

> Q: What was 1SG Geressy's comment over radio verbatim?
>
> A: His words were, "They should have been killed."
>
> Q: Who is "they" that he was referring to?
>
> A: He was talking about the male detainees.

This is an important clarification, as it highlights that the women on the island were also non-combative prisoners, even if they were not restrained. The fact that Lemus and the other soldiers understood the referent, "they," as meaning the male prisoners, shows that in their minds they were concentrating on the ROE to kill all military-age Iraqi *males*.

> Q: Has Girouard ever threatened your or anyone else's lives if they spoke of the circumstances of how the detainees were killed?
>
> A: ...He said to be loyal and not to go bragging or spreading rumor about the objective. He said to act like grown men and be quiet professionals. After that he said if he found out who told anyone anything about it, he would find that person after he got out of jail and kill him or her. I laughed about it and most of the squad smiled and blew it off.
>
> Q: Is there a competition in your unit of who gets to kill the most Iraqis?
>
> A: No, but there is an HVT list of who we have caught and who is still on the loose. The HVT list is a list of high valued targets throughout Samarra. We simply update it as "caught" or "killed" and mark him or her off the list.

Strictly speaking, an HVT list is more like an FBI list of "most wanted" persons, but not a traditional military strategy. Even in the case of the FBI or other police departments, "most wanted" persons are supposed to be captured, not killed on sight, because they are presumed to be innocent until proven guilty under the Constitution. In the pastiche blurring of military and police roles in the war in Iraq, it seems that designated "bad guys" on the HVT list are presumed to be guilty, and it does not matter if they are killed or captured. The information media has saturated the airwaves and Internet with such killings or captures throughout the war in Iraq, making it seem to be a widespread, de facto policy. However, whether this policy is lawful or not has never been seriously discussed in the media.

STATEMENTS BY BRADLEY MASON

Mason's statement of 15 June is markedly different from his previous statement and also from some of the statements made by other soldiers on this date. The most important discrepancy seems to be the implication, made by the investigator, that the three prisoners were killed inside the house, and then their bodies were dragged outside. The investigator repeats the same questions many times throughout the interview. According to Mason, "They told me the plan was SPC Hunsaker and PFC Clagett were going to kill the 3 detainees from the first house." Mason added: "I told him [Girouard] again that I was not down with what they were doing [and] about that time we heard oh shit then gunfire, SSG Girouard ran around front and hit Clagett and cut Hunsaker on the arm." Mason's version is that Girouard did the punching and cutting of his comrades *after* the shooting, and was not present during the killing of the prisoners. However, Mason claimed that he did not witness any of the details other than the meeting and conversation with Girouard. Mason said: "I lied on my last statement for fear of my life and my family's life."

> Q: Were you present when the detainees were shot and killed?
>
> A: No, I was with the women on the other side of the house.

Q: Are you aware the detainees were killed inside the house?

A: Not until I got here and you told me.

Q: Did you assist in pulling the bodies from the house?

A: No I stayed with the women til we left for the LZ.

It is not clear whether the prisoners were actually killed in the house, or whether the investigator is lying as part of an interrogation tactic, or whether some other process was at work during the interview. We still don't know the answer to the question: Were the prisoners killed inside or outside the house?

Q: Approximately how many times were you threatened by SSG Girouard, SPC Hunsaker, and PFC Clagett?

A: About 5 or 6 times.

Q: What exactly was said when you were threatened?

A: They told me if I told anyone that they would kill me....

Q: Did they discuss this plan before the mission?

A: No....

Q: Was there ever a mercy killing?

A: No. I did not hear any shots nor did SSG Girouard tell anyone to kill him....

Q: Did anyone tell you that SPC Graber shot one of the detainees?

A: No. However, shots were fired after the 3 detainees were killed.

This is yet another discrepancy — other soldiers described an alleged "mercy killing" of a wounded prisoner, but Mason denies this.

Q: Where were you when you heard the two shots?

A: In the house still with the women.

Again, it is not clear why the investigator is apparently planting information. Mason never said he heard two shots, only that he heard shots. The defense attorneys were prepared for a vigorous cross-examination of Mason because they felt that his statements were the most inconsistent with regard to the versions given by other soldiers, but also because they felt that the prosecution was going to rely upon his statements more than any of the others. In addition, the defense was going to raise questions about the investigators allegedly "planting" ideas in the heads of the soldiers, particularly Mason, as to what really happened. Of course, none of these issues could be explored because Clagett's trial was cancelled.

Q: Did you believe them when you were threatened?

A: Yes.

Q: Do you believe they will carry out their threats?

A: Yes

Q: Are you afraid now?

A: Yes, because I know the judge is going to read out this statement and call me up to testify. And because I know SSG Girouard, SPC Hunsaker and PFC Clagett and I know that they would kill me if the find out that I snitched on them...

Q: Do you have anything else to add to this statement?

A: If I get killed tell my family and girl I love them and blame the judge that used this in the court and called me up as a witness.

It seems that Mason was very much afraid of the threats made by some of his comrades. On the other hand, his fear is out of sync with some of the other statements in which soldiers treated the threats as if they were a joke of sorts.

In addition to the 15 June statement, the investigators interviewed Mason again on 19 June 2006 regarding the issues of alleged photography and lost videotapes.

Q: Have you seen any of the tapes?

A: I don't know about these ones. I have seen some of his, SSG Girouard's, tapes.

Q: Who else took videos or pictures while on Operation Iron Triangle?

A: SGT Lemus but CID already has his camera....

Q: Has anyone spoken to you about the video taken on Operation Iron Triangle?

A: Not till I got here to CID....

Q: Are any of these videos or photos or text concerning Operation Iron Triangle on your computer?

A: I know I don't have text or videos. But I don't know about photos. I have let just about everyone in my platoon use my computer to transfer pics. But as far as I know, no.

Issues surrounding photographs and videotapes are reminiscent of the Abu Ghraib scandal, but no clear assessment can be made on the basis of the scattered questions about photography in the sworn affidavits.

Statement by David Neuman on 19 June 2006

Q: What did Graber tell you about what happened during Operation Iron Triangle?

A: SPC Graber confided in me, from what I remember, that on 3rd squad's objective after the original shots were fired, they were clearing the objective and SPC Graber moving through the area came upon a wounded national. He shot the national and continued with the objective.

Q: Did Graber tell you that Girouard, Hunsaker, and Clagett conspired to cut zip-ties of three detainees, tell them to run, and shoot them?

A: No, he did not.

Q: Did anyone else tell you that?

A: No, nobody ever said anything like that.

Q: Did you hear that?

A: No, never any hear-say.

Q: Did Graber tell you of Hunsaker and Clagett shot three detainees after cutting their zip-ties and making them run?

A: No, because I never heard about the soldiers cutting the ties. It was told to me that the IA [Iraqi army] had given the detainees a knife and they cut the cuffs off themselves.

Q: Did Graber or anyone else tell you Girouard punched Clagett and cut Hunsaker to cover up the killing of three detainees, but stating they shot them in self-defense?

A: No, nothing was said like that to me.

Note that Neuman refers to the prisoner who was shot as a "national," not as a detainee. There is no discussion of the ROE. In contrast to the several other soldiers who had allegedly heard rumors or some versions of what happened during the mission, Neuman claims he heard or knew very little, if anything.

STATEMENT BY MARCUS SANDOVAL ON 15 JUNE 2006

Sandoval's version of events is again different from other statements taken in June. He begins his statement as follows:

> After the mission Iron Triangle, SGT Lemus looked worried and sad so I came up to him and told him what was going on. I was then told by him that the mission was stupid and that the guys in his squad were stupid. I asked why, and then he took me aside in a low voice he told me what had gone on in their objective. He tells me that his squad plans out a mission that one would cut himself and the other would get punched so it would make it seem that they had gotten hurt by the detainees. SGT Lemus then tells me that the guys that were in one the plan were SSG Girouard, SPC Hunsaker, and PFC Clagett and the rest of the guys did not want any part in it. Then he says that SSG Girouard tells them that whatever happened in the mission nothing to be told to anyone.... I think to myself that was why when I was on the objective ... SSG Girouard had trouble sending up the information about the detainees of the count of how many detainees they had and how many KIA they had.

In the question and answer portion of the interview, Sandoval said he did not know when the plan to kill the prisoners was made, who cut Hunsaker, who punched Clagett, or who cut the cuffs on the prisoners. Several competing versions of answers to these questions emerge in the June statements: that Girouard cut Hunsaker, that Hunsaker cut himself, that Clagett cut Hunsaker, and that a prisoner cut Hunsaker. Some of the soldiers deny that the plan was made before the mission, but Sandoval claims in his statement that it was, but then tells the investigator that he does not know when the plan was made. The portion of the interview on the radio transmissions does not square with Geressy's account or the platoon leader's confirmation that Girouard did radio in that they had 4 prisoners and 1 KIA. And of course one is left wondering why one prisoner was allowed to live, and whether the 1

KIA was killed as described unanimously by the soldiers, given that the June version of events seems contradictory to all details of the events.

Statement by William Christy on 19 June

Christy's statement begins as a carbon copy of the statements made on 11 May:

> "We were told to clear the island and that all males were confirmed to be insurgents."

But in the interview, he begins to offer more diverse interpretations in what was ordered, done, and why.

> Q: What were the standing orders regarding military-aged males on the island?
>
> A: Shoot all military-aged males unless they were actively surrendering.

The ROE now become "standing orders." The phrase, "unless they were actively surrendering," is a departure from the earliest statements in which there is no mention of the surrender option. Christy answers further that he was present on the island during the entire operation, that the platoon leader was present when the prisoners were taken, and that the soldiers did not encounter any hostile fire. Christy confirms that he did not witness any of the killings, but heard of them second-hand from others.

> Q: Did any of the individuals relate to you who shot the detainees?
>
> A: I never asked who had shot them....
>
> Q: Do you know if anyone else was around who would have seen what happened?
>
> A: No, I'm not sure....
>
> Q: Did you hear anything regarding SPC Graber shooting anyone?
>
> A: No.
>
> Q: Did you ever see the detainees?
>
> A: No....
>
> Q: Have you ever heard any of these individuals exclaim any disdain for the Iraqi people?
>
> A: No, there did not seem to be any personal problems or dislike for the Iraqi people.
>
> Q: Have you ever heard any of those soldiers talk about contests regarding who can achieve the most kills?
>
> A: No.

Chapter 7. Explaining the Imperfect Crimes at Operation Iron Triangle

Popular books, television programs, and films often play off the theme of the perfect crime which is supposed to leave no clue, no trace of who committed the crime or why. Audiences gain relief when their favorite fictional characters, from Sherlock Holmes to Perry Mason, and more recently Adrian Monk, among others, resolve what was supposed to have been an impenetrable puzzle. Some readers will be tempted to breathe a sigh of relief given that, despite the complexity of the material presented so far in this book, and the many contradictions in the ROE and what soldiers said, believed, and did, in the end four soldiers were convicted (although only one was actually tried). It appears that the military investigators solved what could have been the perfect crime — three prisoners shot and killed in cold blood — if only the band of brothers had been able to keep their cover story intact afterwards.

But wait! This conclusion still fails to account for the killing of the man in the window. Actually, the most elegant and parsimonious explanation is the truthful one: four, not three, men were killed on a mission in which soldiers followed an unlawful ROE. The commanders as well as the soldiers should be punished for these crimes. By ignoring the new ROE that led to the killing of the man in the window, and convicting four soldiers on the basis of a traditional ROE that had been superseded by a new, unlawful ROE, it is the government that pulled off what might be called "the perfect crime."

In a book by that title, the French sociologist Jean Baudrillard shocks readers with his provocative claim that in postmodern society, reality has been murdered, and no one knows who killed truth or why.

It hardly matters whether one labels contemporary society as postmodern, postemotional, other-directed, or with any other tag that denotes a radical break with a less cynical, historical past. In Baudrillard's words, "Were it not for appearances, the world would be a perfect crime, that is, a crime without a criminal, without a victim and without a motive."[1]

I began this book with the overall framework that I would be analyzing the "fake sincerity" in the narrative, on the part of the soldiers as well as the investigators and the government. It is true that the military investigators unraveled the "fake sincerity" of the soldiers, but in the process they established another layer of "fake sincerity" with regard to the government's motives. By convicting four soldiers for the murder of three prisoners, the government subtly yet effectively covered up the murder of the man in the window under the new and unlawful ROE.

A similar approach was taken in the Abu Ghraib trials, wherein all the blame for the abuse that was committed at the prison was shifted onto seven so-called "rotten apples." Yet government reports and scores of studies showed that the convicted soldiers were following a de facto policy that had "migrated" from Guantanamo Bay via Major General Geoffrey Miller's infamous visit to Abu Ghraib in August of 2003. The abuse was too widespread across too many US-run prisons scattered over the globe to be the result of something that was dreamed up by a handful of soldiers. Even so, despite the logic of the common sense conclusion that all the blame cannot lie with the individual soldiers, most laypersons and professionals alike have accepted the bad-apple theory.

Similarly, with regard to the Operation Iron Triangle killings, evidence presented so far shows that the new, unlawful ROE was not really new and was more widespread than its usage than we might suppose. Yet, following the convictions of four soldiers, all media and scholarly interest in the case was dropped.

I shall explore in the final chapter some of the possible reasons why blame is typically shifted downward and rarely up the chain of command. In this chapter, I intend to analyze common psychological and sociological explanations for the crimes that occurred. The purpose is to show that in the play of appearances and "fake sincerity" that have become commonplace in contemporary social life, even social scientific explanations unwittingly participate in covering up the perfect crime. The bottom line is that ROE are a matter of public policy, so that ultimately all of us are responsible for what happened during Operation Iron Triangle. This is the uncomfortable conclusion that is covered up by resorting to pseudo-psychological and for-

---

1 Jean Baudrillard, *The Perfect Crime* (London: Verso, 2008, p. 1)

mal psychological theories of "rotten apples" doing bad things and therefore being solely responsible.

The Charges Against Clagett

Clagett was not charged with the murder of the man in the window. Instead, he was charged solely with regard to conspiracy, premeditation, and murder of the three prisoners. The exact wording of the charge sheet, imposed on 15 June 2006, includes the following violations of the UCMJ:

> Article 80, "attempt with premeditation to murder a male detainee of apparent Middle-Eastern descent whose name is unknown by means of shooting him with a firearm."

> Article 81, "conspire with Corporal William B. Hunsaker and Staff Sergeant Raymond L. Girouard to commit an offense under the Uniform Code of Military Justice, to wit: premeditated murder of three male detainees of apparent Middle-Eastern descent whose names are unknown... and in order to effect the object of the conspiracy, the said Private First Class Corey R. Clagett, Specialist William B. Hunsaker and Staff Sergeant Raymond L. Girouard staged the murder scene so as to appear that the aforementioned three detainees of apparent Middle-Eastern descent whose names are unknown attacked the said Private First Class Corey R. Clagett and Specialist William B. Hunsaker during an escape attempt."

> Article 91, "by saying to [superior]... 'My lawyer will — — you up' or words to that effect, by saying to him, 'I don't give a — — about rank'..." and "by saying to [superior] ... 'I can do anything in this facility and can't be charged with it,' or words to that effect."

> Article 118, "with premeditation, murder a male detainee of apparent Middle-Eastern descent whose name is unknown by means of shooting him with a firearm."

> Article 134, "wrongfully communicate to Private First Class Bradley L. Mason a threat, to wit, 'Staff Sergeant Girouard will not have to kill you because I will kill you if you say anything' or words to that effect," and "wrongfully endeavor to influence the testimony of Private First Class Bradley L. Mason, as a witness in the investigation into the shooting of three male detainees of apparent Middle-Eastern descent whose names are unknown..."

Legally and formally, the killing of the man in the window under the new, unlawful ROE was not treated as a crime.

The Psychiatric Reports

As an expert witness in the Abu Ghraib trials, I was required to analyze the psychiatric reports on the so-called "rotten apples" — which is the term that the government applied to the soldiers who were later convicted for abuses committed at Abu Ghraib.

Based on these reports, it seems that not one of them was a "rotten apple." In formal psychological language, a "rotten apple" is a person with a "character disorder," and especially an "anti-social personality disorder," and such persons are presumed not to have a conscience. In the Harman trial, I was asked to testify that Harman's psychiatric tests did not show any sadistic or other traits that would explain her smiling during the abuse as the result of character disorder or sadism. Most likely, she was smiling because she was anxious, and in any case, as scores of sociologists have shown, contemporary Americans are smilers in photos. The reader can verify this for his or herself by comparing photos of serious-looking, non-smiling grandparents and great-grandparents with contemporary photos of most people smiling in family photos — as well as magazine covers. The prosecution did not attempt to rebut my testimony, and the prosecution did not call a single psychological or psychiatric expert to try to prove the so-called rotten apples were really rotten as part of sworn testimony in the courtroom. The evidence simply wasn't there. But dropping the talking point "rotten apples" in news conferences was enough to get the other-directed media to spread this prejudice worldwide.

What about PFC Corey Clagett, one of the four convicted soldiers in the Operation Iron Triangle killings? Was he a "rotten apple"? It is important to note that LCDR Karen A. Karadimov, the military psychiatrist who evaluated PFC Clagett, concludes her evaluation report as follows: "Patient *does not display* any anti-social personality traits such as conformity to norms, cunning, impulsivity, aggressiveness, disregard for others, irresponsibility, or lack of remorse." Experts in psychology know that these words were chosen carefully by the psychiatrist. These are the key symptoms of anti-social personality disorder, which is the poster-child for what laypersons call a "rotten apple." She concluded that Clagett did not have these traits.

Several conclusions follow from this evaluation. The conclusions are internally consistent with the rest of her report and also consistent with the overall position of psychology on understanding disorders and their relationship to legal issues. I will not delve into all details of these understandings but will get to the point that is most important: Karadimov's evaluation effectively suggests that Clagett's participation in the crimes committed during Operation Iron Triangle was not the result of character traits that are typically associated with crimes like the one portrayed here by the prosecuting attorneys, namely, a ruthless, cold-blooded, crime involving cunning and lack of conscience.

Each and every one of the character traits that the military psychiatrist rules out with regard to PFC Clagett is implicit or explicit in the June descriptions of the crime on the part of the investigators. At least two points are important in this regard. The first is that the prosecution knew that if the case ever went to trial, the psychiatrist could have been asked to present her views as part of her testimony for the defense, and furthermore, an expert witness could have used her findings to further weaken the prosecution's argument that the killings were the result of an anti-social character disorder. Second, one may speculate that the prosecution was eager to get the soldiers to turn on each other through plea bargains rather than go through four separate trials.

Suppose, for the sake of argument, that the social construction of reality of the crimes as alleged by investigators in the June sworn statements is accepted as more or less true. Let us suppose that the alleged decision to execute the prisoners was made impulsively (for the sake of excitement) and violated the traditional procedures (norms) for treating prisoners. A great deal of cunning would have been required to pull off the crimes in such a sneaky way that other soldiers and the Army would not realize what had happened. The crime would have required reckless disregard for the prisoners but also for fellow soldiers, Army values, and the mission. Because such a crime was unnecessary, given the existing new ROE, it would have required tremendous aggression as well as lack of responsibility on the part of the soldiers toward the mission and Army values. Finally, the soldiers would be required to lack a conscience or remorse in order to carry out the crime in this manner. But, to repeat, the Army psychiatrist had minimized the possibility that any of these negative and disturbing character traits were part of Clagett's personality.

Logically, it is still possible that one or more of the others involved in the crimes as they are described by the prosecution suffers from a personality disorder or possesses enough of the constellation of these negative character traits to give these crimes their typical signature. I was not given access to the psychiatric reports of the other soldiers in the squad. Nevertheless, it is a telling sign that except for the prosecution's star witness against the other soldiers (Mason), the grueling interrogations did not turn up any abnormalities in the squad's behavior that would have suggested the presence of "rotten apples."

For the prosecution's social construction of reality to hold up (in the eyes of social scientists), their construction has to show consistency, with regard to the accused's personality structure, the psychiatrist's evaluation, other evaluations made by psychologists and social workers, and other behaviors by Clagett and his fellow soldiers. Moreover, in the rest of her report, Karadimov shows that Clagett was undergoing a severe depression with melancholic features (weeping, openly expressed emotion) following the incident. Anti-social types do not typically exhibit sadness or other emotions related to remorse — but Clagett did. His behavior is inconsistent with the prosecution's depiction of the crime but is consistent with the psychiatrist's evaluation. Finally, a different social worker evaluated Clagett later in time, and her report is consistent with the psychiatrist's evaluation. Thus, the psychiatrist's report is consistent internally with the rest of her evaluation, externally with a second professional's evaluation, and externally with scholarly works on psychological disorders.

There is no reason to doubt that Clagett was one of the ones who pulled the trigger and shot prisoners during Operation Iron Triangle. The doubt pertains to the prosecutor's depiction of the crime as cold blooded and ruthless.

Psychological Analysis of Cover-Up and Manipulation

There can be little doubt that the June sworn statements suggest that some of the soldiers lied or otherwise gave inconsistent, manipulative versions of what happened. However, it is important to note that lying in order to avoid getting into trouble is not what psychologist generally mean when they refer to deceit, cunning, and manipulation with regard to traits of Personality Disorder (PD).

According to the American Psychiatric Association's Diagnostic and Statistical Manual-IV (DSM-IV), individuals "with Antisocial Personality Disorder are manipulative to gain profit, power, or some other material gratification" (p. 705). The material gratification may also include excitement and fun. It is difficult to conclude, based on the sworn affidavits, that any of the soldiers engaged in the cover up for the sake of profit, power, fun, or gratification. They seem to have been motivated by peer pressure, loyalty to each other, confusion, and fear of getting caught.

Writing on manipulation and cunning from a psychological perspective, Nina Brown describes these issues this way: Those with personality disorders "simply feel that it's okay to lie, cheat, mislead, or manipulate since they must be served, enhanced, and preserved, and others should be happy to do whatever is needed" (p. 35). But this is not the attitude that any of the soldiers display in the sworn statements and interrogations.

Again, a constellation of negative traits is implied in the specific sort of deceit and manipulation that is characteristic of what laypersons regard as cold-blooded crimes: the deceit is typically related to grandiosity, lack of empathy for others, habitual abuse of others (including pets and animals), feelings of entitlement, and other negative traits. But the soldiers in this incident showed empathy and mercy for the women and children, as well as for the men who were using the women and children as shields. Far from exhibiting grandiosity and entitlement, they were clearly showing subservience to an ROE that some of them admitted they thought was questionable. Lying in order to avoid getting into trouble is fundamentally different from the motivations of "rotten apples" to lie.

INTERNAL CONSISTENCY IN THE PSYCHIATRIST'S REPORT

According to the psychiatrist, Clagett has a "desire to care for" his mother and he has a "good nature." Moreover, she writes that "patient has relied on the Army as his primary family and support system and feels betrayed yet again by another 'family system'." I learned from speaking with Clagett that he was emotionally and physically abandoned by both his father and mother and was raised by his grandparents. A psychological conclusion that is consistent with the psychiatrist's report is that Clagett has "abandonment issues" and would most likely avoid doing anything that would harm his relationship with his most important "family" and support system — the Army. In effect, the Army had become a substitute for his family. Moreover, his "good nature" and desire to care for others are inconsistent with the prosecution's depictions of the crime.

The psychiatrist writes that Clagett "really desires to trust and connect with people." He is "sensitive and vulnerable." "He often cried in his tent/cell to release tension." He exhibited "major depressive symptoms with melancholic features." "Patient is very cooperative in his treatment plan." Each and every one of these observations is consistent with the psychiatrist's overall report and supports her conclusion that he does not have any traits of Anti-Social Personality Disorder. Anti-socials typically do not show genuine, consistent, or long-lasting emotions.

Each and every one of these observations is also inconsistent with the descriptions of the accused in the June statements. None of this information raises doubts that he pulled the trigger. But the inconsistencies between the psychiatrist's report and the prosecution's version of the motives for the killings in the June statements do raise doubts whether *some* of the soldiers who decided to testify for the prosecution in exchange for immunity or reduced sentences — in other words, who were motivated by fear — were telling the truth about the motives of their comrades. Because Clagett's case never went to trial, and witnesses could not be cross-examined, these questions will never be resolved completely.

The psychiatrist has also diagnosed PFC Clagett with ADHD (Attention Deficit Hyperactivity Disorder) and notes that he had already been diagnosed with ADHD in high school. She lists his symptoms of ADHD including "poor concentration," "fidgeting," and being "challenged by the organizational demands that require him to work on his legal case." She also recommends that he resumes treatment, including medication, for ADHD. She seems to imply that he was not on medication for ADHD at the time of the incident in question.

The ADHD dimension lends further, consistent support for the professional judgment that Clagett was unsuited to commit the crimes in the manner in which they are described. Given that he has ADHD, he would most likely have had problems concentrating on the alleged conspiracy and on the "organizational demands" of the conspiracy and its attendant behaviors (cunning, deceit, cover-up, etc., as these terms are understood by psychologists). In other words, the fact that he does not have anti-social personality disorder and the fact that he does have ADHD combine to make it highly unlikely that he had the psychological "wiring" in place to commit the crimes as they are described. It seems highly unlikely that he could have masterminded the alleged conspiracy (as understood by psychologists). Because of his ADHD, it is highly improbable that he could have concentrated, in a combat zone, on the "organizational demands" of any conspiracy contrived by someone else.

The JAG officer with whom I spoke, CPT Matt Landseth, explained to me that ROE are explained to soldiers repeatedly. This claim was supported by LT Justin Wehrheim during a telephone conversation on 6 January 2007. From a psychological perspective, it is consistent that a person with ADHD could have comprehended an ROE or any other order or directive that is stated repeatedly. It is common advice in psychology books that children and adults with ADHD need repetitive restatements of commands and directives in order to comprehend them and comply.

Based on these facts, a psychologist may conclude that Clagett understood the ROE — which was to kill every military-age male on sight. By the same psychological reasoning, Clagett, because of his ADHD, would have been unable to participate fully in any "conspiracy" (in a psychological sense) unless the conspiracy was of long duration and was repeatedly and consistently laid out for him. There is no evidence that the alleged conspiracy to kill the prisoners was planned prior to the few moments before the killings occurred. In fact, investigators asked several soldiers whether they knew or thought the alleged conspiracy was planned ahead of time — specifically, before the mission started — and all the answers by the soldiers were consistently negative.

Consistency With and Within the Social Worker's Report

The social worker's report, made at a different point in time, is consistent with the psychiatrist's report and it is also internally consistent. PFC Clagett is still judged to be suffering primarily from a Major Depressive Episode, as not having a personality disorder, and as suffering from ADHD. In line with the psychiatrist, the social worker writes, "SPC Clagett has invested much emotional support in the Army. This accounts for the depression symptoms as he feels that the Army abandoned him." The theme of abandonment issues is consistent across the two reports.

The social worker writes that "SPC Clagett's personality is that of a follower." It is important to consider an alternative social construction of reality such that his being a "follower" might have induced him to go along with the others passively in the alleged conspiracy and its attendant behaviors.

Being a "follower" is not a diagnosis from the DSM-IV, but I have seen this phrase used by experts in psychology at courts-martial. Specifically, both Sabrina Harman and Lynndie England were described by expert witnesses in psychology at their trials as "followers." The typical way that psychological professionals interpret being a "follower" in tandem with abandonment issues is as follows: The patient's tendency to follow will not overstep boundaries that would lead to abandonment. There are firm limits to his being a follower, and these involve not doing anything that would lead to abandonment of him by the Army. There exists the disturbing possibility that he "went along" with an unlawful ROE precisely because of his loyalty to the Army, his unit, and his comrades. But this is not so unusual. The cover of Riesman's book, *The Lonely Crowd*, features a herd of sheep, and part of his overall argument is that other-directed Americans are increasingly becoming apathetic "followers." Clagett is not unique.

It is possible that his being a "follower," in tandem with his ADHD, would have set the stage for him to be unable to resist going along with others in an act which caught him off guard — for which he did not have the repeated directives to do or not do something. But given all the other descriptions of the accused by the psychiatrist and social workers, it follows that, had he acted in a way that is inconsistent with his habitual behavior, he would have felt profound guilt and remorse. Depression (especially with melancholic features) is commonly understood by psychologists as indicating severe self-reproach.

PSYCHOLOGICAL ANALYSIS OF THE SWORN STATEMENTS THAT ARE INCONSISTENT WITH THE INITIAL VERSION OF EVENTS

The reader has probably noticed that the soldiers in the sworn statements made in June 2006 display no overt, self-conscious signs of guilt. This is significant because for the prosecutors' social construction to hold up consistently (namely that some soldiers came forth in June and betrayed their comrades due to pangs of conscience), the soldiers would have to show some signs of remorse, guilt, and other related emotions vis-à-vis the alleged murder, conspiracy, and subsequent cover up. But they display no signs of and make no statements that might suggest remorse or guilt.

Psychiatrists and psychologists still uphold Sigmund Freud's observation that the superego is the seat of conscience in the individual, and its primary function is that of guilt. The chief way that guilt is expressed psychologically is through depression. Clagett is the only one in the sworn affidavits who is described by his comrades as having signs of depression, including sleeplessness.

While the soldiers in the June statements do not display signs of guilt or remorse, they do display and make several statements indicative of extreme fear. One must pursue the question: What is making some of these soldiers appear to be so very afraid? Not one of the soldiers exhibits any fear of combat. Persons who feel genuine guilt often welcome punishment, or accept it with equanimity, as a way to relieve themselves of the guilt. But fear typically suggests that something or someone external to the person is causing the person to experience a "fight or flee" response, which results in extreme fear.

For example, Mason states in his sworn statement dated 15 June 2006 that he did not tell the truth the first time "because my life was threatened." It seems plausible, at first blush, that he was afraid because Girouard, Hunsaker and Clagett "told me that they would kill me if I told anyone." But he adds quickly: "SSG Girouard's uncle is in the mob and I know they don't just kill you but they kill your whole family. I am sorry I did not come forward the first time and caused all this frustration . . . please don't ask me to come to the witness stand for this still in fear of mine and my family's lifes." If, in fact, SSG Girouard is linked in some way to the Mafia or made threats concerning the Mafia, or pretended to be linked to the Mafia in some way, then Mason's fears might seem plausible. But if there is no foundation or linkage to the Mafia, then Mason's fears come across as so extreme as to be delusional. Does Girouard have links to the Mafia? Whether he does or not, in fact, have links to the Mafia, did he threaten the others with being killed by the Mafia? The important point is that the Army's star witness, Mason, exhibits extreme fear, but the grounds for his fear were not explored during cross-examination because Clagett's trial was cancelled.

Furthermore, Mason answered "no" to the question whether he heard when or how the three accused soldiers would kill him if he cooperated with the investigation. Finally, it comes across as unusual that Mason ends his statement as follows: "If I get killed tell my family and girl I love them and I blame the judge that used this in the court and called me up as a witness." In summary, these statements, and the sworn statement overall, indicate no feelings of guilt but they do indicate extreme fear. Wouldn't the judge and the Army be able to protect a witness from retribution if the grounds for the fear were credible? Why didn't the investigator reassure Mason on this point during the interview?

Mason further alleges that the prisoners were killed in the house, but this claim is contradicted by numerous other soldiers who saw the prisoners running outside the house. For example, Thomas Kemp states, "I turned around and saw all three detainees fall"; and Kemp was outside the house. All the other soldiers also stated that they saw the prisoners run and fall due to gunfire outside the house.

Another contradiction in the June construction of reality (conspiracy with its attendant behaviors) is that some soldiers flatly deny its chief elements. For example, David Neuman was asked, "Did Graber tell you that Girouard, Hunsaker and Clagett conspired to cut zip-ties of three detainees tell them to run, and shoot them?" "No he did not." "Did anyone else tell you that?" "No, nobody ever said anything like that." "Did you hear of that?" "No, never any hear-say." Again, while I am not alluding to the legal definitions of conspiracy, I will note that to the layperson, descriptions of this sort fall under the domain of something other than conspiracy.

The social construction of reality that the "truth" about the conspiracy first broke on or about 15 June 2006 in a spontaneous manner is contradicted by questions from investigators that suggest suspicion earlier than this date. For example, an investigator asked Kemp on 29 May 2006, "So if they would have had a clear line they would have shot them anyway?" "Yes." "Is it possible they may have thought they should just kill them because that was the objective?" "Anything is possible but I don't think they would have done that." These questions and answers raise the issues of command climate and whether soldiers were trained properly in traditional ROE pertaining to the treatment of prisoners, which will be addressed later.

On 15 June 2006, Eric J. Geressy stated that he had indeed "made the statement I do not know why we have 3 detainees or why do we have any enemy alive," and adds: "At no point did I ever try to put any idea into those Soldiers heads to execute or do any harm to the detainees." Apparently, Geressy made this statement over the radio, and according to LT Wehrheim this statement could have been heard by several soldiers. A psychologist would inquire as to how fast news of Geressy's statement spread through the squad. A sociologist would inquire into the command climate that would have set the stage for Geressy to ask this question on the radio, regardless of what his personal motives were (which may have been benign, such as sarcasm).

In response to the question whether the command climate would have "influenced the prisoners to be killed," Geressy answered: "No I do not think so. We have a very aggressive unit with a very aggressive Commander. But there is a big difference between killing the enemy and executing a prisoner. Everyone knows this." It is probably true that the average soldier knows the difference between killing the enemy and killing a prisoner. However, the particular details of the Operation Iron Triangle killings call into question how the average soldier would discern the difference between a *bona fide* prisoner under traditional ROE and an Al Qaeda terrorist under the new

ROE? It is not OK to kill a prisoner. But according to the new ROE, it is OK, and it is required, to kill all the military-aged males on the island because they are presumed to be terrorists. This profound confusion as to what is permitted and not permitted, and the impossibility of making out the difference between "prisoner" and "terrorist," would establish extreme cognitive dissonance for all the soldiers on the mission.

Some of the statements by soldiers, analyzed in previous chapters, who were not involved in the shooting, suggest that the cognitive dissonance was pervasive. The issue and influence of a dysfunctional command climate cannot be ruled out.

Micah Bivins was asked by an investigator: "Did this new ROE seem strange to you?" "Not really we have seen them before." "What cases or incidents did you have blanket authority to shoot on sight authority before?" "There have been a couple of missions where if we saw a certain guy we could take him out." "Did the ROE (such as describe above) ever cover an entire objective?" "No." This is an important exchange, because it suggests (1) the new ROE on this mission was not really "new" to some of the soldiers; (2) killing a specific individual at a specific target was considered acceptable but killing many individuals in an "entire objective" was perceived to be new and problematic.

Psychologically, this would have contributed to cognitive dissonance for the soldiers on this mission. What is permitted and what is prohibited? The psychological effects of cognitive dissonance include feeling disoriented and showing impaired judgment.

In summary, and based on all the sworn statements, it seems that soldiers exhibit many negative and dysfunctional psychological as well as sociological elements: fear, confusion, inconsistency, cognitive dissonance, inappropriate remarks, inappropriate emotions, and an overall sense of a chaotic, arbitrary, and capricious mission. The soldiers met absolutely no hostility on the objective, yet were ordered repeatedly to carry out the "new" ROE. The fact that soldiers in the platoon and squad other than those involved directly in the killings made the statements quoted above, and others similar to them, suggests a dysfunctional social climate. There is no way for an objective person to conclude from these sworn statements, and others like them, that this was an average and routine mission. Too many soldiers confessed that they had doubts about the new ROE. On the other hand, some soldiers also confessed that this was not the first time that the new ROE had been implemented.

We come back again to the fundamental ambiguity that characterizes this mission, and perhaps many other missions in Iraq. There is a strong suggestion that the social climate was dysfunctional because it forced soldiers to do their jobs under two versions of ROE that were, in the words of one soldier, "on the opposite end of the spectrum" from each other. One was to shoot if the enemy shows hostility, and the other was to shoot on sight. Without condoning the crimes that were committed, a reasonable person will most likely empathize with the ordinary soldier for being forced by the Army into such a profoundly uncomfortable and morally perilous position.

SOCIOLOGICAL ANALYSIS OF THE SOCIAL CLIMATE

To make a firm professional determination as to the impact of command and social climate on the crimes at issue, I would have had to have access to the written ROE, operational orders, Standard Operating Procedures and other data. Nevertheless, it is clear from the sworn statements that profound contradictions exist in how the new versus the traditional ROE and other rules were perceived and interpreted by soldiers.

These contradictions and inconsistencies in themselves suggest that the question of "poisoned social climate" — a term used by M.G. Fay in his report on Abu Ghraib to characterize the overall situation that led to the abuse — ought to be pursued in seeking an explanation for the killings during Operation Iron Triangle. As with the abuse at Abu Ghraib, if the crimes were not the result of a "few rotten apples," then logically, the abuse and, in this case, killings were the result of a poisoned social climate.

For example, the sworn statements reveal the fact that "someone" wrote on a chalkboard the standard version of what the soldiers would state, including the phrase "kill all military-age males" as a summary of the new ROE. A few statements contradict this otherwise consistent version with the claim that COL Steele actually said "kill those sons-of-a-bitches," or words to that effect. Both Clagett and LT Wehrheim told me over the phone that, in his pep talk, Colonel Steele actually used the precise phrase sons-of-a-bitches. If true, this discrepancy can be rationalized with the claim that the brigade commander was giving a motivational speech. Nevertheless, use of the phrase "sons-of-bitches" can be interpreted sociologically as dehumanizing the perceived enemy — including prisoners — and setting the stage for reckless behavior.

Moreover, some of the sworn statements suggest that some soldiers understood the ROE as "kill or capture." There is a big difference, normatively speaking, between an order to kill all the enemy with whom one comes into contact versus an order to kill or capture. First, the kill or capture version leaves open the crucial question as to who would be the decision-maker or authority in choosing between these two options. Is the soldier the decision maker or someone higher up in the chain of command? Second, the option to capture — regardless of how it was decided whether to kill or capture —

leaves open the sociological question of what sort of force (escalating versus immediate use of deadly force) was authorized to control prisoners.

The many conflicting, contradictory sworn statements regarding these two issues suggest that the squad and platoon were confused as to how to interpret the new versus traditional ROE in these regards. Confusion as to social norms (social agreements as to what is expected) — of what sociologists refer to as a state of anomie — is a definite indicator of social chaos and a definite contributor to deviant (non-normative, unlawful) behavior.

Let us return to Geressy's comment that was broadcast over the radio questioning why any prisoners were taken in the first place and why they were not immediately killed. From a sociological perspective, Geressy's private motives in making this comment are not important. Sociologically it is more important to understand the social climate that led Geressy to make this remark, and the social consequences of the remark.

One of the most fundamental findings in sociology is that people act differently in groups and crowds than they do as individuals. A poisoned social climate would have enabled Geressy to make this disturbing comment precisely because it was not perceived to be inappropriate or non-normative, given the confusion cited above. And the consequences of the remark — which was broadcast over the radio and was heard by other soldiers — are amplified in a group setting. Crowds are highly suggestible and act on impulses very quickly unless those impulses are restrained by an authority figure. In this regard, it is significant that 5 to 10 minutes after LT Wehrheim — the most important authority figure in the immediate area of battle — left the scene, the crimes were carried out. Sociologically speaking, this suggests that a collective predisposition to kill the prisoners spread like a contagion in the group, and as soon as it could find expression (when the restraint of a gyroscopic authority figure was absent), the murderous impulse toward the prisoners was acted out.

Had the murderous impulse in the group not already pre-existed, LT Wehrheim's absence would have made no difference in the normative performance of the group. But soon after he left, the crimes occurred. Moreover, the crimes did not occur while he was present at the scene of battle. The murderous impulse was expressed by several soldiers other than the four accused soldiers, which suggests that the predisposition was widespread and involved at least the entire platoon.

By predisposition, sociologists do not mean conspiracy (which is conscious and usually a response to paranoia). Rather, group predispositions are typically unconscious or lie beneath fully-aware conscious decisions, and they are spread through a group by a contagion-like effect. Sociologists typically make the analogy between a sociological contagion and a biological contagion that spreads quickly through an organism and is passed from one organism to another.

Common examples of the contagion effect are the "wave" in the audience during basketball, football, and other sports events. When someone starts a "wave," typically most people in the stadium follow and participate, without a true conscious, rational decision as to do the wave or not. The predisposition to follow the wave is unconsciously present in the audience members prior to the game, and the tendency to follow is heightened by being in a crowd. Another example is that the Golden Gate Bridge in San Francisco is frequently cited as a "contagious" site for committing suicide. Careful studies have documented that many people who jump off the Golden Gate Bridge did not visit the bridge with a conscious aim of committing suicide, but once they are there, a group "impulse" contaminates them. Many studies have shown that there are specific trees, hooks, other bridges, and other sites that are used repeatedly for suicide. Suicide also frequently spreads like contagion in high schools and dormitories, so that the suicide of one individual is followed in quick succession by other suicides. In these and other cases of social contagion, the concept of conspiracy is irrelevant: individuals do not conspire to do the wave or commit suicide. Rather, they bring to the group setting a latent predisposition which is exacerbated by the group setting or symbolic meaning of the setting, and they act out the predisposition as if they were infected by a germ or virus.

The group contagion concept rules out conscious conspiracy, and it also rules out the "obedience to authority" paradigm. LT Wehrheim apparently did not order anyone to kill the prisoners. On the contrary, he was enforcing the traditional ROE with regard to the prisoners. However, the new ROE was also planted in the minds of the soldiers — this is why the man in the window was killed on sight. The confluence of this ambiguous and confusing perception as to what was normatively accepted — the new versus the traditional ROE — with the radio broadcast by Geressy, and also with the fact that the outraged Iraqi soldiers were whisked away from the battle scene, along with the departure of the authority figure, along with the perception that the company had the highest kill ratio in the brigade; allusions to "kill contests," allusions to rewards for kills, allusions to an aggressive brigade commander — these and other factors suggest a poisoned social climate and the contagion effect of the order to kill every military-age male on the island, whether or not they were prisoners.

Did everyone on the mission hold a similar and consistent construction of reality regarding the enemy and how to treat or even take prisoners? The most compelling evidence that the reply is negative comes from the descriptions of the roles of the Iraqi soldiers on the mission. The Iraqi soldiers are described as being visibly angry and otherwise upset at the killing of the elderly man who showed his head in the window. They are described as being suspected of slipping a knife to the prisoners. In general, one gets the impression that the American soldiers were suspicious of the Iraqi soldiers and that the Iraqi soldiers were upset with the Americans. LT Wehrheim told me over the phone that the chief Iraqi soldier told him they would take prisoners from that point onward, and that this mission was the first time that the American soldiers had worked with these particular Iraqi soldiers. Why wasn't this important piece of information included in the sworn statements? If it is true that the Iraqi Army soldiers were so upset at the killing of the man in the window that they demanded other males on the island be taken prisoner — indeed, that the Iraqi soldiers would take prisoners — then the entire plot of the narrative changes. The Iraqi soldiers were whisked away after making this demand, and then, and only then, were three prisoners shot and killed.

It is a firm sociological finding that military units are more functional when they have trained together repeatedly. Even though the Iraqi soldiers were apparently briefed in the same new ROE as the American soldiers were, clearly the two groups of soldiers held widely divergent interpretations of the mission and the ROE. This joint operation between US and Iraqi soldiers does not come across as functional, normative, or routine. This is yet another indicator of a possibly dysfunctional social climate.

This was Clagett's first time on a mission in this particular squad, and it was the first time he had killed someone. This mission was apparently the first time that this particular ROE was used with regard to an entire objective. This was the first time on a mission that these particular Iraqi soldiers were used. The Iraqi soldiers were held in suspicion so they were whisked away from the scene by helicopter minutes before the killings occurred. None of these observations suggest a coherent, functional unit with clear goals.

Were the soldiers trained in the Geneva Conventions? What was the extent of their training? What happened to the other prisoners once they were taken away from the battlefield? Were there soldiers from the Military Police to guard the prisoners, or were the prisoners guarded by soldiers who would have felt hostility toward them? What were the Standard Operating Procedures for the treatment of prisoners? What were the procedures, training, and directives in the capture and screening, of prisoners? How was the new ROE interpreted once the social status of an individual deemed to be a legitimate target to be killed was transformed into the social status of a prisoner? What was the training in the Laws of Land Warfare for the soldiers? Was the International Committee of the Red Cross given access to the prisoners, and at what locations? These and related issues are not addressed in the sworn statements. Yet these issues form an important backdrop for understanding the killings that occurred.

And most of these issues apply to other recent sites of US abuse and war crimes such as Abu Ghraib, where ROE were similarly interpreted to be "loose," Standard Operating Procedures frequently changed and were confusing, Military Police functions blurred into Military Intelligence functions, and in general social chaos was more prevalent than social order.

THE INADEQUACY OF MAJOR PSYCHOLOGICAL AND SOCIOLOGICAL THEORIES FOR EXPLAINING WAR CRIMES

A cursory glance at the literature in psychology and sociology in their roughly one-hundred-year history since their inception in the late 1890s and the early 1900s reveals the peculiar fact that both disciplines have been relatively silent on the subject of war crimes even though they have engaged in a far-ranging discourse on other subject matters. For example, it is peculiar that Harvard sociologist Talcott Parsons ruled the discipline from the publication of his 1937 book, *The Structure of Social Action*, to the 1950s. The time period between 1937 and the 1950s witnessed the Holocaust and scores of other war crimes, but Parsons was silent on these topics and his theory has been applied toward explaining ordinary crimes but not war crimes. His successor at Harvard, David Riesman, manages to avoid the topics of fascism and genocide in *The Lonely Crowd*. Similarly, psychologists have made great contributions in understanding the criminal mind, but hardly any in understanding the mind and milieu of the war criminal.

A possible exception to this rule is Erich Fromm's *Anatomy of Human Destructiveness*, but this book focuses on the sadistic and disordered personalities of Hitler and Stalin, not the reasons why or how their societies went along with them. More recently, Philip Zimbardo has revived the "obedience to authority" paradigm, but this explanation is overly simplistic when it comes to explaining war crimes committed during World War II or more recently, My Lai, Abu Ghraib, and Operation Iron Triangle among others. War crimes always involve tension and ambiguity between lawful versus unlawful authority, or as in Operation Iron Triangle, new versus traditional ROE. It is not obedience to authority in general that is the explanatory factor, but cognitive dissonance and chaos in deciding between lawful versus unlawful authority. Again, there is nothing unique about obedience to authority: it is so commonplace that no society could function without it (children obeying parents, citizens obeying police forces, subordinates obeying superiors at work, etc.). But a perceived discrepancy between lawful and unlawful authority is profoundly disturbing, disorienting, and invalidating to most persons.

For reasons stated above, it is tempting to analyze the abuse at Abu Ghraib and the killings during Operation Iron Triangle in terms of Parsonian understandings of dysfunctional or anomic social systems. But here again, the facts do not fit the theoretical constructs adequately. Parsons (1937) conceptualizes anomie as a "war of all against all" and his disciple, Robert K. Merton (1957), sees it as a condition of "normlessness." However, in fact, there were plenty of norms at Abu Ghraib and during Operation Iron Triangle (memorandums, written as well as verbal orders); however, they were out of sync with traditional, accepted Army procedures that were in place prior to the global "war on terror."

Both Parsons and Merton cite Emile Durkheim's concept of anomie as their inspiration. But as noted previously, Durkheim defined anomie as a societal condition of *dereglement* or derangement.[1] Literally, a deranged social milieu feels "crazy" to its participants: it is "a rule that is lack of rule." An unlawful order is precisely such a "rule" that promotes "lack of rule."

The soldiers from Abu Ghraib testified openly during trials that they thought Abu Ghraib was "bizarroworld" or a "crazy place," because they were ordered to do things that made no sense to them and that violated their training, such as forcing naked Iraqi men to wear panties on their heads. Similarly, we have seen in the sworn statements that the soldiers at Operation Iron Triangle thought the new ROE were "strange" and out of sync with their traditional training. In sum, a century of theorizing by Parsons, Merton, and their followers have followed a fake version of Durkheim's apt observation that anomie is "derangement" (a crazy social situation) transformed into the unhelpful idea of "normlessness."

Similarly, it seems tempting to turn to Erving Goffman's famous analysis of "total institutions" as a template for comprehending the abuse at Abu Ghraib as well as the killings during Operation Iron Triangle. Perhaps it is still true to some extent that the modern United States Army is a total institution in Goffman's sense, in that it controls most aspects of a soldier's appearance, personality, and life, and makes him or her almost completely dependent upon the Army as a sort of surrogate parent. But testimony during courts-martial at Ft. Hood revealed that Abu Ghraib was not a total institution. The Taguba report (a 2004 investigation into complaints of Military Police wrongdoing at Abu Ghraib) revealed that all aspects of military discipline and performance at Abu Ghraib were functioning below Army standards; testimony revealed that soldiers did not know which commander was in charge or to which chain of command they belonged; government reports and testimony revealed that Abu Ghraib was run by a chaotic mix of organizations that included the CIA (Central Intelligence Agency), civilian

---

1 Emile Durkheim, *Le suicide* (Paris: Presses Universitaires de France, [1897] 1983, p. 287).

contractors, Iraqi police and OGA (other government agencies) such that the Army was not really in charge; and one learned from soldiers that the boundaries of Abu Ghraib were so porous that civilian Iraqi vendors openly sold cameras, snacks, and other consumables on the premises of this Army base/prison with minimal if any supervision. The very reason that soldiers were able to purchase and use cameras on the premises of Abu Ghraib is that it was a porous, non-total institution.

Similarly, sworn statements in the Operation Iron Triangle killings suggest that the image of the Army as a total institution is a simulacrum. Iraqi soldiers were involved in what appeared to be a joint operation, but there was friction between the American and Iraqi soldiers. There were all sorts of mysterious photographers and photography during the mission, and it is not clear what happened to the photos or the photographers or the extent to which the photography was performed for official versus touristic purposes. The new ROE was unlawful and out of sync with traditional ROE. For these and other reasons, one may reject Goffman's concept of total institution as a viable theoretical framework for comprehending the killings during Operation Iron Triangle. The Army unit that performed the mission at Samarra was chaotic, porous, confused, and unlike a "total" institution.

Similarly, Philip Zimbardo draws upon the obedience-to-authority paradigm in social psychology and his famous Stanford Prison Experiment to explain the abuse at Abu Ghraib on the basis of "good" people turning "evil" as the result of "situational" factors. There are many problems with this explanation. In his experiment, Zimbardo was the sole authority figure and his orders to the students who pretended to be guards and prisoners were unequivocal. But facts and reports concerning Abu Ghraib suggest the opposite of what Zimbardo intends: an egregious lack of authority and leadership at Abu Ghraib contributed to social disorganization and social chaos, which in turn set the stage for abuse at Abu Ghraib. Similarly, during Operation Iron Triangle, the authority of the new ROE was in open conflict with the authority of the traditional ROE. Moreover, one may question the assumption that Harman or Clagett or any of the other defendants involved in Abu Ghraib or Operation Iron Triangle became "evil," even if some of them committed acts that some (but not all) segments of American society would label evil. Clinical psychologists generally hold to the assumption that ordinary people can do things that can be labeled good or bad, but no one is inherently good or evil. In any case, there is no evidence to suggest that Clagett or the other three convicted soldiers in the Operation Iron Triangle case were evil, even if what they did was evil.

The widely popular post-structuralist mode of analysis represented by Michel Foucault's cultural analysis in *Discipline and Punish*[1] also misses the mark. Foucault's overall argument is that in modern versus traditional punishment, the "soul" is controlled and punished more than the body. He holds that as societies become increasingly modern, punishment becomes more humane in contrast to medieval, cruel punishments of the past. Moreover, he holds that the ancient method of convicting criminals was by extracting a confession through torture whereas modern penal techniques rely upon evidence and surveillance. But clearly, at Abu Ghraib, the "souls" as well as the bodies of prisoners were abused, with no way to discern a modern trend toward lenience or humanity in punishment. In fact, the punishments at Abu Ghraib were apparently simultaneously modern (using the latest psychological theories on breaking down prisoners) and medieval (chaining prisoners in extremely painful "stress positions").

Similarly, the treatment of prisoners deemed to be terrorists hardly qualifies as modern, humane, or in conformity with the Geneva Conventions. One of the central issues in this analysis is that new ROE presume that the targets of modern extraction methods are "bad guys," without any notion that everyone is innocent until proven guilty, and that such persons may be killed on sight rather than be arrested. In this sense, the new ROE qualify as medieval.

Another irony is that the military investigators relied upon the ancient method of extracting confessions from the accused soldiers and not upon modern techniques of gathering evidence. The bodies of the victims, the knife used in the assault, and other evidence mysteriously disappeared. An investigator's fidelity should be to the facts, not any particular theory.

Finally, Anthony Giddens has criticized Parsons severely vis-à-vis the notion of human agency, and argues that Parsons made the human agent into a "dope." Nevertheless, it seems that the soldiers at Abu Ghraib and Operation Iron Triangle were more like Parsons's "dopes" than Giddens's knowledgeable agents with regard to understanding the reasons for the abuse they committed or the orders they were given. Suppose that soldiers questioned every single ROE or order that struck them as unlawful. Giddens might applaud such exercises in human agency, and Zimbardo openly calls for such heroism among soldiers. But these images of agency and heroism presuppose a fake sincerity concerning the functions of the military. Soldiers are taught to trust their superiors and to obey orders, and in real life disobedience is a crime.

In the following chapter, we shall take up the issue of the soldier's duty to disobey an unlawful order. Even more important is the fact that theorists

---

1 Michel Foucault, *Discipline and Punish: The Birth of the Prison* (New York: Vintage, 1975).

and lawyers alike fail to hold the officers who give the unlawful orders accountable, and they place all the burden on the soldier who obeys. Society cannot and does not expect the constant threat of mutiny if soldiers feel that a given order is unlawful.

Chapter 8. The Doctrine of Command Responsibility as an Exercise in Fake Sincerity

The complexity of the case of the Operation Iron Triangle killings and the convictions that resulted from some (but not all) of the killings lies in the implementation of the new, unlawful ROE in conjunction with the traditional ROE. If it is true that the convicted soldiers were guilty of not following the traditional ROE when they killed three prisoners, who is guilty for ordering the new ROE which resulted in their killing the elderly man in the window? This is the central question in this study, and it cannot be answered clearly or adequately.

On the one hand, there is the doctrine of command responsibility, which holds that a commanding officer is responsible for the outcome of an unlawful order, through omission or commission or both, even if the commander did not actually pull the trigger. On the other hand, the US military, at least since the Vietnam War, has held firmly that it is the duty of the soldier to disobey an unlawful order. In most publicized cases of war crimes including and since the Vietnam War, soldiers have been court-martialed and found guilty of committing war crimes but the commanding officers who issued the unlawful orders were typically not prosecuted. In the exceptional cases where they have been prosecuted — such as LT Calley's superiors at My Lai — the doctrine of command responsibility was not applied, and the commanders were found not guilty.

The complexity of this case, involving new versus traditional ROE, is compounded by the antagonism between new and traditional standards of responsibility (hold the soldier responsible for failure to disobey an unlawful order, versus hold the commander responsible for issuing the unlawful order). The transition from traditional, inner-directed, gyroscopic standards of warfare to new ROE accompanies an equally significant, seismic transition from traditional, inner-directed, gyroscopic standards of command responsibility to laying all the blame on the low-ranking soldier for obeying an unlawful order.

This sea change in military standards and law is part of the general transition from inner- to other-directedness in society, from rigid standards of honor regarding the duties and responsibilities of officers to flexible standards of shifting responsibility to where it will stick.

Consider again the Battle of Mogadishu in 1993 in relation to Operation Iron Triangle in 2006. Both missions involved an "extraction force," which Senator Hart suggested is the new paradigm for military operations. Both missions involved reliance upon an informant who gave incorrect information. The "intelligence" was faulty (like the "intelligence" that was presented to the United Nations and to the American public as the reason for waging war against Saddam Hussein in the first place). In both missions, prisoners were taken. But in the movie version of Mogadishu, it seems that prisoners were not executed, whereas in Operation Iron Triangle they were. The key difference is that in *Black Hawk Down*, which purports to be historically accurate, soldiers are reminded by their superior officers, and they remind each other repeatedly, that they should fire only if they are fired upon — in other words, traditional ROE were implemented. In one scene, General Garrison tells his men, right before they leave for the mission: "Don't fire unless you're fired upon." In another scene, the exchange goes like this:

> Grimes: Why aren't you shooting?
>
> Waddell: We're not being shot at yet.
>
> Grimes: How can you tell?
>
> Waddell: A hiss means it's close. A snap means... [A bullet whizzes close by.]
>
> Waddell: Now they're shooting at us! [They begin returning fire.]

In stark contrast, the ROE in Operation Iron Triangle was to kill every military-age male on sight. The soldiers on this mission encountered no resistance or hostility at all. The brigade commander denied for the media that he issued this new ROE. However, all the soldiers and officers on the mission who made statements swore that he did issue the new ROE. Furthermore, the brigade commander did not testify and was not cross-examined at any hearing or trial related to the crimes committed during Operation Iron Triangle. It is difficult to avoid the suspicion that the Army covered and hushed up public debate on the new ROE by coercing soldiers into plea bargains and by making sure that there was no need to have the brigade commander testify due to the testimony of soldiers who had accepted plea bargains against each other.

FRAMING THE ISSUE OF COMMAND RESPONSIBILITY

Every culture relies upon a frame of reference that is used to apprehend events ranging from natural disasters to wars and acceptable modes of leisure. Like a picture frame, a cultural frame excludes elements from discourse at the same time that it includes other elements. And some of these elements are contradictory. In part because of publicity given to the Abu Ghraib abuses and shootings of non-combatants similar to the killings during Operation Iron Triangle, the image of the United States has been framed by some in the international community as that of the country that "liberated" Iraq and at the same time as the country that became Iraq's brutal "occupier." The notorious prison that Hussein used to inflict torture, Abu Ghraib, served as a symbol of Arab oppression for Americans who framed themselves as liberators but later became a symbol of American abuse and torture. One could multiply these with similar examples of how the popular consciousness changes the focus and frame of reference by which we perceive events and their significance.

James Loewen's book *Lies My Teacher Told Me: Everything Your American History Textbook Got Wrong* exposes how facts about US history change in meaning when one questions one's assumptions and frames of reference in approaching these facts. Throughout this book, I have approached the meanings of ROE and the doctrine of command responsibility in a similar way, with the implied subtext, "Lies My Government Told Me." While it remains beyond the scope of this analysis to review every or even most instances of ROE and use of the doctrine of command responsibility, the most important point, for this discussion, is that the existence of the new ROE seems to be invisible in American public consciousness, and the doctrine of command responsibility remains largely unknown.

The conceptualization of cultural frames of reference is very significant when addressing issues pertaining to law, crime, and justice. How and why do societies frame some acts as crimes in general and crimes of war in particular, yet exclude other similar acts from such frames of reference? An implicit answer seems to be that war crimes involve ROE or public policy and are not just crimes committed by individuals for personal motives.

How does the collective consciousness come to regard the outcome of trials as restoring justice versus engaging in scapegoating? The notion of "war crime" was not formally and legally conceptualized until the twentieth century and especially the end of World War II. Although massacres and mass killings are to be found throughout history, it is only in the post-Nuremberg era that genocide, persecution, and other war crimes came to be defined and delineated from other crimes *per se.*[1]

The central meaning of the relatively new conceptual frame regarding war crimes is that this sort of crime is typically depicted as being intentional, rational, planned from the top of a hierarchical organization, and widespread.[2] In other words, war crimes imply the existence of established policy in conjunction with an organized bureaucracy and well-developed, modernist, state functions. This collective, cognitive shift — the ability to conceive of war crimes in a frame of reference that goes beyond the old adage that all wars are brutal — involves a fundamental ambiguity or ambivalence from the outset in conceptualizing war crimes as well as crimes committed during wars. It involves the forced conjunction of radically "split" categories: that which is regarded highly (the many manifestations of modernism embodied in bureaucracy and the idea of the chain of command) and that which is despicable (the passion and chaos of crime).

The inherent contradiction in depicting war crimes as intentional, rational, planned, and widespread is that modern Western societies value highly the notions of agency, rationality, planning, and organization. Part of the shock of the Holocaust remains the fact that genocide was carried out in a cold, calculated, organized and almost business-like manner. It is as if the West's most esteemed virtues came to be twisted into the most abhorrent vices. Additionally, contemporary Western societies seem to insist that international war crimes must be delineated, conceptually, from crimes that are spontaneous and limited in scope, which is to say, distinguished from ordinary crimes of passion committed by a few corrupt individuals.

Nevertheless, it seems that regardless of how logically academics and jurists conceptualize war crimes in theory, an event or set of events comes to be regarded as criminal only when these events offend what Emile Durkheim called the collective consciousness. The so-called world community responded in widely divergent ways to war crimes in the former Yugoslavia, Rwanda, Cambodia, Sierra Leone, and Abu Ghraib, among other sites. Reactions of the collective consciousness are emotional, unplanned, unscripted, and disorganized. In Durkheim's view, this is because they are based upon spontaneous "collective effervescence." To be offended is to give in to passion. When one is discussing international war crimes, one needs to analyze which collective consciousness is offended, by which aspects of a given situation, at what time, and why. It seems that Durkheim's concept of "collective consciousness" is very similar to Riesman's idea of the "jury of one's peers" as society. In this sense, all courtroom trials are simultaneously tri-

---

1 Roy Gutman and David Rieff, *Crimes of War* (New York: Norton, 1999).

  2 Zygmunt Bauman, *Modernity and the Holocaust* (Ithaca, NY: Cornell University Press, 1990).

als in the court of public opinion. However, neither Durkheim nor Riesman could have foreseen the power of the contemporary media in shaping public opinion, or worse, its collusion with governments and corporations. On the other hand, analysts of the media, from Baudrillard to Chomsky, completely overlook the power of society as a separate "jury of one's peers." There exists a gaping chasm in contemporary social theorizing concerning the roles of the media versus society at large as the "jury of one's peers." My own, brief, stance on this dilemma is that the information media in contemporary American society comes close to usurping society's role as the "jury of one's peers." However, the Internet offers one of several possible outlets (such as the blogosphere) for the dissemination and expression of views that pertain more genuinely to the collective consciousness.

One also needs to consider whether a true global, international collective consciousness exists or can exist. Can the international community maintain a consistent frame of reference with respect to war crimes? And how can American society exhibit inner-directed indignation at unlawful ROE issued as public policy in its name if it is becoming more other-directed, and therefore less prone to moral outrage?

Durkheim pronounced in 1893 that an act — no matter how heinous — that is not punished by the collective consciousness is not a crime. Conversely, a punitive reaction by a collective consciousness transforms an event into a crime. To put it another way, cultures vary greatly in their responses to collective abuse, ranging from Pol Pot's regime, America's extermination of Native Americans, and the Balkans to the Holocaust. The fact that the international community will respond to certain events and thereby transform them into crime is universal, but the threshold for the kind of acts that will provoke this strong reaction is not universal. Yet the very concept of international war crimes seems to presuppose a universal standard for what is deemed criminal. In fact, as already noted, the world community responds in a politicized and inconsistent manner to war crimes — as defined by the Geneva Conventions — depending upon various factors and cultural frames of reference. For various reasons, a sufficient critical mass of the international community responded with passionate revulsion at the war crimes in Yugoslavia and Rwanda sufficient to establish international tribunals. Yet other incidents of apparent disregard for the Geneva Conventions failed to offend the international community's collective conscience strongly enough to react punitively against the policy-makers, including the killings committed during Operation Iron Triangle, as well as abuse at Abu Ghraib, in Afghanistan and Guantanamo. Punishing the low-ranking soldiers involved in a violation of the Geneva Conventions is not the same as punishing the policy-makers and commanders who give unlawful orders and established those unlawful policies in the first place.

In practice, the ways that the United States and the international community frame and react to violations of the Geneva Conventions are dramatically different. At the International Tribunal at The Hague, judges have found culpable leaders in the chain of command who may not have pulled the trigger, who may not have known that crimes were committed low in the chain of command and who did not directly order crimes and abuse, but who laid out a *policy* that led to abuse and crime or who failed to prevent criminal and abusive acts.[1]

Moreover, in all of the cases where the defendant was found guilty by the Tribunals for Yugoslavia and Rwanda, the Tribunal's judgments asserted that none of the guilty parties necessarily had to be "an architect or the prime mover" of the established persecution in order to be deemed guilty of war crimes. Instead, the principle established by the Tribunals is that the guilty war commander could have known or *should* have known, and therefore prevented, the criminal actions of subordinates.

The Tribunal's precedents have been reversed at the courts martial pertaining to violations of the Geneva Conventions committed by American soldiers. The United States chose to prosecute primarily low-ranking soldiers and not prosecute officers high in the chain of command, in addition to accepting the excuse offered by many officers that they did not know or did not order the crimes committed by their subordinates, without raising the issue that they should have known, and either way are legally culpable under international law.

No one engaged in discussions of alleged war crimes committed by Americans, or other Westerners such as Britons, seriously believes that an American or a Briton will be put on trial for war crimes at The Hague in the near future. Instead, the United States has put forth the argument that it will monitor and try US military lawbreakers under its UCMJ. However, the UCMJ and the entire system of military courts in the United States is entirely dependent upon commanders to convene trial proceedings. It is enormously difficult to expect military commanders to instigate criminal proceedings against their colleagues, namely, other commanders.

Some journalists as well as human rights groups claim to have uncovered evidence that leaders high in the "chain of command" either knew or should have known and should have taken steps to prevent alleged abuses and war crimes committed by US troops in Iraq, including Abu Ghraib and Guan-

---

1 Pierre Hazan, *Justice in a Time of War* (College Station, TX: Texas A&M University Press, 2004).

tanamo.[1] The ICRC (International Committee of the Red Cross), in particular, has labeled the abuses at Abu Ghraib and elsewhere as "routine," hence systematic, not as isolated incidents. We have reviewed media reports of killings throughout Iraq that are similar to the Operation Iron Triangle killings and that were based on similar new ROE.

A plethora of US government reports on abuses committed by US soldiers arrived at the general conclusion that abuse has occurred, but a wealth of competing and contradictory interpretations are offered regarding who knew or ordered what sort of abuse or torture in the chain of command. The general conclusion reached by all the US Government reports is that the abuse was not ordered by anyone high in the chain of command; but at the same time policies that led to the abuse are linked to the White House.

Again, the important point is not who ordered a particular war crime but who established the general policy that led to the war crime. The mainstream discourse on this explosive subject has so far avoided completely the subject of putting on trial Americans who are high in the chain of command and who should have known and should have taken steps to prevent the abuse even if they did not order the abuse. It is primarily in the less reputable blogosphere that inner-directed indignants call for the impeachment or war crimes trials of the President and Vice-President of the United States.

Because the possibility of truly applying the doctrine of command responsibility to US politicians and military commanders seems to be out of the question, the Abu Ghraib torture scandal, the Operation Iron Triangle killings, and other sites where the Geneva Conventions have been violated have been framed consistently by the US government and the mainstream media as a set of events that involved a small group of disorganized and unprofessional soldiers whom they labeled as morally corrupt. The dominant frame of reference in the United States, namely, American Exceptionalism (the widespread belief that Americans are morally superior to other peoples)[2] cannot tolerate the cognitive dissonance that arises when an American (as the idealized representative of highly superior values) engages in war crimes — unless he or she was acting outside the American frame of reference.

At the same time, some journalists and some organizations such as Human Rights Watch frame the abuses and war crimes committed by the US military in Iraq as a set of events that flowed from a general "climate" of disregard for the Geneva Conventions that was established at the highest levels of the United States military and political chain of command and

---

1 Seymour Hersh, *Chain of Command: The Road From 9/11 to Abu Ghraib* (New York: Harper Collins, 2004).

2 Seymour M. Lipset, *American Exceptionalism: A Double-Edged Sword.* (New York: Norton, 1997).

that trickled down to the soldiers on the ground.[1] The perspective taken in the present study supposes that it is not a matter of choosing between top-down versus bottom-up explanations, but integrating both perspectives and finding a middle ground between them. Specifically, some soldiers low in the chain of command clearly committed crimes, but officers high in the chain of command should have known and should have taken steps to prevent the crimes because of the unlawful policies they were implementing.

THE GHOSTS OF VIETNAM

As I have stated at the outset and throughout this book, if the story told in "Black Hawk Down" serves as an important contrast to the killings of Operation Iron Triangle, the killings at Son Thang and My Lai, Vietnam are close parallels. More important, the convictions in the year 1970 of low-ranking soldiers but no officers for the war crimes committed at Son Thang, or the Marine Corps My Lai, mirror the outcome of the Operation Iron Triangle convictions. It truly seems as if the US military is bound to a Freud-like "compulsion to repeat" mistakes of the past both with regard to implementing unlawful ROE and punishing low-ranking soldiers but not commanding officers.

Gary Solis, the author of *Son Thang: An American War Crime*, who is a former Marine Corps prosecutor and judge, writes of "killer teams" in Vietnam that were not unlike the extraction teams at Operation Iron Triangle or elsewhere in Iraq. He writes:

> "Killer teams" do not appear in the training syllabus of any Marine Corps instructional program or school. They are unmentioned in any official account of the Vietnam War, except in relation to the Son Thang incident.... Asked to define the term, Lieutenant Ambort described a killer team as a four- or five-man patrol, intended, he said, "to search out, locate, and destroy the enemy" (p. 29).

On the one hand, Solis makes it seem as if these killer teams were unique to this particular Marine Corps unit, and on the other, he makes comparisons to the My Lai massacre and to the general policy of killing noncombatants in Vietnam. We see a similar tension in depictions of the Operation Iron Triangle killings: the unlawful ROE are described as "new" and "strange" in the sworn affidavits, as if they were unique, yet evidence exists that similar ROE were and continue to be used in Iraq. Solis continues, using words about the Son Thang mission that, with slight modification, could apply to the mission on Operation Iron Triangle:

> Was a killer team's mission the one of "hit and run," or reconnaissance? Was it to search, or just to kill whoever was encountered after nightfall?

---

1 See "The Civil Liberties and Civil Rights Record of Attorney General Nominee Alberto Gonzales" American Civil Liberties Union (2005); "Memorandum for Alberto R. Gonzales, Counsel to the President" US Department of Justice, August 1, 2002

> The killer team's mission was unclear to those who undertook it.... The only common understanding was that they were to kill the enemy. The problem was in defining who was "the enemy" (p. 30).

What about ROE during the Vietnam War? Solis offers the uncomfortable appraisal that "the effectiveness of Vietnam ROEs has often been questioned, both by historians and by those who had to implement them" (p. 97). Perhaps twenty years from now, historians will write something similar about ROE used in the war in Iraq. Alongside the traditional, formal ROE in Vietnam, which apparently was not uniformly or effectively followed, there existed the informal "Mere Gook Rule." Solis writes:

> "Gooks are gooks," a pretrial witness unabashedly declared.... "The rule in Viet-Nam was the M.G.R. — the 'mere gook rule': that it was no crime to kill or torture or rob or maim a Vietnamese because he was a mere gook." Telford Taylor confirms this in *Nuremberg and Vietnam*: "The trouble is no one sees the Vietnamese people. They're not people. Therefore it doesn't matter what you do to them" (p. 103).

One learns from Solis that the UCMJ, "a largely civilian-written reform and consolidation of the eighteenth-century codes, became law in 1950" (p. 75). Moreover, one learns that the UCMJ incorporates the Geneva Conventions so that there is no need, from the US government's point of view, to hand over soldiers to international tribunals to be tried specifically for violations of the Geneva Conventions. According to Solis:

> When US military personnel are accused of crimes amounting to violations of the law of war, UCMJ Article 18 incorporates such war crimes into military law.... "The military court, by punishing the acts, executes international law even if it applies ... its own military law. The legal basis of the trial is international law, which *establishes the individual responsibility* of the person committing the act of illegitimate warfare" [my emphasis]. The fact that the Son Thang courts martial would, in international law, be trying war crimes, went unnoticed by those involved. The murder of noncombatants, whether enemy nationals or co-belligerents, is a war crime under a variety of international agreements, as well as under international case law (p. 108).

Note that the UCMJ incorporates the Geneva Conventions as a matter of individual responsibility, but not also as a matter of command responsibility. I have raised this issue with military lawyers at Ft. Hood, Texas, who retorted that the UCMJ incorporates the doctrine of command responsibility elsewhere. But the important point is that no matter how one argues that international conventions are incorporated into the UCMJ, the predictable outcome is that officers generally get reprimanded while low-ranking soldiers go to prison for incidents that involve breaches of the Geneva Conventions. This was true at courts martial pertaining to Son-Thang, My Lai, Abu Ghraib, Operation Iron Triangle, and scores of other trials.

Solis emphasizes that military judges typically reject the "obedience to authority" defense, e.g., that a soldier committed a war crime (or any crime) because he or she was following orders. Perhaps it is for this reason that Zimbardo's testimony on behalf of the Abu Ghraib defendant Ivan Frederick fell on deaf ears. The military judge at Ft. Hood, Texas, COL William Pohl, ruled that soldiers should have disobeyed the "obviously" unlawful orders to abuse prisoners. Solis makes a similar argument, which is not surprising given that he is a former military judge:

> Such ruminations belittle battlefield war crimes, which are usually naked criminal acts by anyone's definition. There was no Vietnam-era murder prosecution for having mistaken a civilian for a combatant. Instead, at My Lai, Calley demanded of one of his soldiers, "Why haven't you wasted them yet?" In another case, an Army captain commanded, "Take [the prisoner] down the hill and shoot him." "Kill all the bitches," Herrod shouted. Given those circumstances does a soldier require a class on Geneva Conventions to recognize the illegality of the order? Can possible disciplinary action for not obeying such commands excuse the obeying of them? Recognizing the illegality of such orders requires neither superior intelligence nor academic accomplishment. There are improper orders of less clear illegality, no doubt, subtle in their wrongfulness, requiring a fine moral discernment to avoid criminality in their execution. But they are rare on the battlefield (p. 270).

This argument is not compelling, and it serves more as an illustration of how military judges and military law in general approaches these topics. At the Abu Ghraib trials, COL Pohl practically parroted these lines at various junctures. But is it really true that unlawful orders are always obvious, and that the need for fine discernment of the difference between lawful and unlawful orders is "rare" on the battlefield?

The careful reader will find in the quote from Calley an echo of Geressy's remark on May 9, 2006 during Operation Iron Triangle, wherein he wondered out loud and over the radio why the prisoners hadn't been killed yet. Perhaps such orders seem obviously unlawful to military judges because they revere "the law" as an abstraction and assume that the individual soldier's main concern in disobeying an unlawful order is disciplinary action. But, in fact, "the law" on the battlefield is a matter of *policy*, not abstraction. ROE embody "the law" for the soldier and the entire chain of command, going all the way up to the President of the United States, and as expressing the will of the people of the United States. To disobey an order on the battlefield is not like disobeying "the law" when, for instance, one runs a red light. Soldiers are weighed down by concerns of entrusting their lives to other soldiers, by codes of honor and loyalty, peer pressure, and wanting to succeed in the mission. Disobeying an unlawful order, though glamorized as heroic by many authors, would, in the soldier's mind, amount to an act of mutiny and would disrupt the functioning of the unit. This is not meant to condone obedience to unlawful orders, only to emphasize that such disobedience is not as easy as on the battlefield as some judges and authors seem to think.

In the heat of battle, the Army does not want moral heroes who question orders, but does want obedient soldiers who trust their commanders and the lawfulness of the orders they carry out.

Moreover, why would a low-ranking soldier necessarily carry the heavier burden of determining that an order is unlawful and should be disobeyed when officers all the way up the chain of command — through which the unlawful ROE traveled down to the soldier — signed off on the unlawful order, and the officers also failed to disobey the unlawful order. The UCMJ crime of "dereliction of duty" applies to officers and soldiers alike. What the military judges are really saying is that officers, who are better educated, better paid, and enjoy more privileges and the life of the "leisure class" (from Veblen) relative to the low-ranking soldiers, have less responsibility than the ordinary soldiers in discerning or even giving unlawful orders. Given America's proclaimed value of equality under the law, this line of reasoning is disconcerting because it privileges the power elite (from Mills) within the military.

Consider the contrast to Solis's orthodox point of view in Luther C. West's perspective on the same issue, in his book, *They Call It Justice*. West, who also worked as a military lawyer, and attended Calley's court martial, notes that the judge instructed the jury that they must "determine in light of all the surrounding circumstances, whether the order ... is one which a man of ordinary sense and understanding would know to be unlawful."[1] West writes, concerning Judge Kennedy's instructions to the jury:

> While Kennedy was careful to list many circumstances for the court martial jury to consider, he *omitted* two circumstances that would have borne quite heavily upon the jury's determination in this regard — and might well have even changed the nature of Medina's alleged order to wipe out the inhabitants of My Lai from a clearly illegal order, as Kennedy instructed it was, to a clearly *legal* order. The omitted circumstances, circumstances that were proven in the Calley trial and circumstances that were undisputed by the government, were (1) that the village of My Lai 4 at the time of the massacre was located in a *free fire zone*, and (2) that the mission in which My Lai was destroyed was a *search and destroy mission* (terms conjured up by the American government to sanction wholesale, indiscriminate killing of Vietnamese people in total contradiction to the rules of land warfare). In short, while Lieutenant Calley and his men might as reasonable men know that a specific order to kill women and children and babies in Trenton, New Jersey, was an illegal order, and that if they obeyed it they did so at their peril, transplant the scene to Vietnam in the year 1968, into a village located in the midst of a free fire zone during a search and destroy mission, and the legality of the order becomes less clear (p. 177).

I agree with West that "the concepts of free fire zones and search and destroy missions were in contradiction to the laws of land warfare" (p. 179).

---

1 Luther C. West, *They Call It Justice: Command Influence in the Court-Martial System* (New York: Viking, 1977, p. 175).

Similarly, the wording of the new ROE in Iraq contradicts the traditional ROE, and the ordinary soldier would not have been able to discern that the new ROE was "obviously" unlawful. In addition, Calley's commander, Captain Ernest Medina, was court-martialed and acquitted. The details of his defense and acquittal are worth quoting at length:

> F. Lee Bailey, Medina's chief counsel, was terse and to the point in his opening statement to the jury. He asserted that Captain Medina remained on the outskirts of My Lai while his men made the assault, and that when he discovered what was going on later in the day, ordered the massacre terminated.... Bailey asserted that Medina did not order, observe, or encourage the massacre and that he did not observe any dead bodies until after he ordered the cease-fire.... Bailey was concerned, however, with a possible prosecution theory that could convict his client despite the failure of the government to link him personally to the killings that took place at My Lai. The theory feared most by Bailey was the Yamashita ruling of the United States Supreme Court in 1946, wherein the Supreme Court affirmed Japanese General Yamashita's death sentence on the basis that he failed to prevent troops under his command from killing innocent Filipino civilians toward the close of World War II. Yamashita's defense was identical to Medina's (namely, "I didn't know my troops were killing civilians").... Yet General Yamashita was hanged because he had in fact "failed to control his troops." As General Douglas MacArthur stated, "responsibility lies with command." But Bailey was outraged with the notion that the Yamashita ruling might be applied in Medina's case. "I don't think that what is done to a Jap hanged in the heat of vengeance after World War II can be done to an American on an imputed theory of responsibility," he asserted. Colonel Howard [the military judge] was quick to soothe Mr. Bailey's fears. He assured him that Captain Medina could be held criminally responsible for the My Lai massacre only if it was proven that he personally participated in the massacre or that he had knowledge of it and did nothing to stop it. (Otherwise, the Yamashita ruling might be applied against any number of Americans, including no less than the sacrosanct chief of staff of the United States Army, General Westmoreland himself. Bailey's fears were perhaps more pretended than real. Judge Howard would hardly have remained on the "bench" throughout the close of the day had he ruled that the Yamashita principle applied to American officers who were on trial for genocide) (pp. 185-6).

But according to the inner-directed standards of command responsibility, Medina was culpable for the crime of omission in failing to stop the carnage, and General Westmoreland was responsible for the policy of search-and-destroy missions, even if he did not order it specifically and directly. This fact makes no difference given the fact that American military judges and society as a whole refuse to invoke this doctrine, on the basis of precedents established by the United States Supreme Court or The Hague.

In the final analysis, these issues and arguments come down to emotional allegiances and cultural frames of reference, not impersonal logic. As stated previously, the international tribunals at The Hague hold military and civilian leaders more accountable than low-ranking soldiers in the commission of war crimes, while the US military justice system does the opposite. It is not likely that this state of affairs will change any time in the near future because cultural habits of feeling and thought are exceedingly difficult to change.

And this focus exclusively on the low-ranking soldier's individual responsibility for obeying an unlawful order denies the public the opportunity to examine or understand American policies and ROE in the first place. Commanding officers and civilian leaders in the United States military rarely or ever testify in trials that involve violations of the Geneva Conventions. By contrast, European proceedings at The Hague are televised on time delay over the Internet and over television, and have involved testimony from presidents, vice-presidents, generals, and other high-ranking civilian and military officials.

A FORGOTTEN PRECEDENT

Discussions regarding the doctrine of command responsibility tend to focus on foreign examples such as the Yamashita case, which involved a Japanese general in World War II who was held guilty by a United States military commission for the atrocities committed by his subordinates even though he did not directly order the acts. As mentioned previously, rulings by the International Tribunal in The Hague regarding Yugoslavia have also applied the doctrine of command responsibility.

However, the clearest court martial case in United States history in which this standard was applied (without using the term "doctrine of command responsibility") was the trial of Henry Wirz, commander of the infamous Andersonville Prison in Georgia in the year 1864. Historians estimate that this Confederate prison held up to 41,000 Union prisoners of war, of which over 12,000 died from abuse, murder, starvation, and disease. Wirz was found guilty and sentenced to death for his responsibility in these war crimes.

The military commission held Wirz responsible for acts of omission as well as commission in the war crimes committed against prisoners of war at Andersonville, but what is not widely known is that it also charged and found guilty his co-conspirators leading all the way up the chain of command to Jefferson Davis, President of the Confederate States. Long before the existence of the Geneva Conventions, ROE, and the legal enactment of the doctrine of command responsibility, rules of war and this doctrine embodied in different words were applied by inner-directed lawyers, judges, and public. Notice the wording of the court's findings in his case:

> Of the specifications to charge I, "guilty," after amending said specifications to read as follows: In this, that he, said Henry Wirz, *did combine, confederate, and conspire with them, the said Jefferson Davis,* James A. Sedon, Howell Cobb, John H. Winder, Richard R. Winder, Isaiah H. White, W.S. Winder, W. Shelby Reed, R.R. Stevenson, S.P. Moore, __ Kerr, late hospital steward at Andersonville, James Duncan, Wesley W. Turner, Benjamin Harris,

and others whose names are unknown, citizens of the United States aforesaid, and who were then engaged in armed rebellion against the United States, maliciously, traitorously, and in *violation of the laws of war* [my emphasis], to impair and injure the health and to destroy the lives, by subjecting to torture and great suffering, by confining in unhealthy and unwholesome quarters, by exposing to the inclemency of winter and to the dews and burning suns of summer, by compelling the use of impure water, and by furnishing insufficient and unwholesome food, of large numbers of Federal prisoners, to wit, the number of about forty-five thousand soldiers in the military service of the United States of America, held as prisoners of war at Andersonville, in the state of Georgia, within the lines of the so-called Confederate States....And the court do therefore sentence him, the said Henry Wirz, to be hanged by the neck till he be dead, at such time and place as the President of the United States may direct, two-thirds of the members of the court concurring herein.[1]

Even though the conviction of Jefferson Davis and others, combined, confederated, and in conspiracy with Wirz, was mostly symbolic, it sent an unequivocal message that Wirz's superiors were as responsible, at least through acts of omission, as he was for the malicious acts of his subordinates. The conviction even went so far as to find guilty "others whose names are unknown." Case law in the year 1864 was not as extensive as it is at present, and legal precedents and rules were not nearly as codified and complex as they are nowadays. Nevertheless, and long before the ever-changing, highly complex legal landscape emerged in the United States, post-Civil War society managed to express moral outrage for the evils that were committed at Andersonville, and held accountable everyone above Wirz in his chain of command.

To be sure, contemporary society is unlikely to emulate such an act of moral indignation, and especially it will not convict "others whose names are unknown" who are responsible for unlawful ROE. But the contrast in the outcome of the Operation Iron Triangle and Abu Ghraib convictions versus the Andersonville Prison convictions is instructive for precisely this reason.

POSTEMOTIONAL SCAPEGOATING

We have seen that the world's first professor of sociology, Emile Durkheim, seems more convincing than his successors that anomie is not just "normlessness" but is a "rule that is lack of rule," which produces genuine social "derangement" in social functioning, which in turn leads to equally grievous and long-lasting negative consequences. In this case, the killings committed during Operation Iron Triangle and other similar killings based on new ROE, along with the abuse at Abu Ghraib, Guantanamo, and elsewhere, have undermined America's stated intentions of bringing "our way of life" to Iraq. On the contrary, the long litany of such well-publicized unlaw-

---

1 General N.P. Chipman, *The Andersonville Prison Trial: The Trial of Captain Henry Wirz* (Birmingham, Alabama: Notable Trials Library, 1990).

ful actions may have contributed to post emotional repetitions of the image of the "ugly American" from the Vietnam era.

Contemporary assumptions (such as those of Parsons and the functionalists) that social systems automatically self-correct seem to be off the mark. If Durkheim's classical perspective is more correct, then one should take seriously his proposed program for repairing anomic social systems. This means that the American collective consciousness has to be informed and involved in the policies that are established in its name. But how can this information reach the American "jury of one's peers" given that the media and the government are in collusion to squelch such knowledge? Nevertheless, and according to the inner-directed standards that established the American republic, only lawful Rules of Engagement that are approved by "the people" and that are in sync with the Geneva Conventions and other lawful standards should be used by the military.

This last point holds immediate consequences for the United States Army and US society. Like the My Lai and Son Thang courts martial, the Abu Ghraib courts martial and convictions for the crimes committed during Operation Iron Triangle were supposed to repair the damage to the fabric of society caused by the abuse, and restore justice. But if Durkheim is correct, the fact that the Army chose to shift all the blame onto a handful of low-ranking soldiers may not appease the collective conscience in the long run. In fact, Durkheim introduced the concept of "scapegoating" to account for such instances of miscarriage of justice, in which the "sins" of a larger social group are displaced onto a few individuals, animals, or even objects. In the case at hand, the sworn affidavits suggest that the responsibility of this nation's society as a whole and many of its institutions for the implementation of unlawful ROE were displaced onto a handful of low-ranking soldiers. Presumably, the soldiers were responsible for failing to disobey an unlawful ROE (although this is not clear), but their superiors and society as a whole should be held responsible for the existence and implementation of the new ROE in the first place.

By "scapegoating," I do not mean that the convicted soldiers were blameless or that they were not guilty of the crimes for which they were convicted. Rather, Durkheim's concept of scapegoating suggests that the low-ranking soldiers who are typically convicted for following unlawful policies established by the government in the name of the people are scapegoats for much greater pain and rage, most recently stemming from the event that has come to be known as 9/11. Iraqis who were abused at Abu Ghraib, Samarra, and elsewhere were themselves the scapegoats for America's pain and rage in response to terrorism. Durkheim writes:

> When society undergoes suffering, it feels the need to find someone whom it can hold responsible for its sickness, on whom it can avenge its mis-

fortunes, and those against whom opinion already discriminates are natu-rally designated for this role. These are the pariahs who serve as expiatory victims.[1]

Thus, scapegoating is operating on two levels: against Iraq in general and against low-ranking US soldiers who carry out the scapegoating against Iraqis.

By now it is accepted that Iraq had nothing to do with 9/11. As of this writing Osama bin Laden, who has supposedly claimed responsibility for that calamitous event (the relevant video is widely believed to be fake), is still at large. Why, then, did the United States attack Iraq? A rational reply is difficult to find, but the irrational motive of scapegoating, displacing anger onto a weak enemy, is easy to discern. Similarly, regarding Operation Iron Triangle, no credible evidence has linked the low-ranking soldiers to creat-ing the unlawful ROE out of thin air or on their own in some malicious act of criminality. On the contrary, credible evidence does exist that the unlaw-ful ROE was issued and reinforced by numerous officers in their chain of command. But low-ranking soldiers, in this and other war crimes that were committed, are far more vulnerable and easier to convict than commissioned officers. Durkheim elaborates:

> When the pain reaches such a pitch, it becomes suffused with a kind of anger and exasperation. One feels the need to break or destroy something. One attacks oneself or others. One strikes, wounds, or burns oneself, or one attacks someone else, in order to strike, wound, or burn him.... The reason is a felt need to find a victim at all costs on whom the collective sorrow and anger can be discharged. This victim will naturally be sought outside, for an outsider is a subject *minoris resistentaie*, since he is not protected by the fellow-feeling that attaches to a relative or a neighbor, nothing about him blocks and neutralizes the bad and destructive feelings aroused by the death.[2]

The historical context for Durkheim's claims is the Dreyfus Affair, in which Durkheim participated on behalf of Dreyfus. It was an event that shook French society to its core. But the Operation Iron Triangle murders are not likely to become anything more than a footnote in history. The ghosts of Vietnam haunt the American military in Iraq, and may continue to haunt future wars and missions, until the compulsion to repeat the past is broken.

CONCLUSIONS

Relative to the perceived inner-directed, gyroscopic standards of World War II and the Nuremberg era, most of the actors in the drama that has been dissected in this book did not perform their jobs in accordance with these traditional, normative standards. Senator Hart's conceptualization of "new"

---

1 In Steven Lukes, *Emile Durkheim and His Sociology* (New York: Harper, 1985, p. 345).
2 Emile Durkheim, *The Elementary Forms of the Religious Life*, (New York: Free Press [1912] 1965, p. 404).

warfare based upon the "extraction" and elimination of pre-tagged "bad guys" is a violation of Article 3 of the Geneva Conventions.[1] The same is true for the "new" ROE issued by the Brigade Commander. All the killings on the mission were unlawful, including the Iraqi man in the window. The investigators and prosecutors went through the motions of doing their jobs, but they failed to prosecute the commanders who issued the unlawful ROE. The platoon commander failed to challenge his commanders for issuing the unlawful ROE. All the soldiers on the mission kept their doubts to themselves, and should have disobeyed the unlawful ROE. All this is easy to conclude with the assumption that soldiers are supposed to behave in an inner-directed manner. Had this crime occurred in the context that a traditional ROE had been issued, and the soldiers deliberately shot and killed an unarmed man and three prisoners — the crime would have seemed heinous indeed and the punishment just.

But American society has changed into a predominantly other-directed one that cannot adequately distinguish "fake sincerity" from "real" sincerity. The US military commanders rationalized the ROE on the basis of informants' reports and many insurgent attacks — but such excuses fell on deaf ears among the judges at The Hague when it came to rationalizing similar ROE and behaviors by Serbs soldiers who carried out the policies of Slobodan Milosevic. The US investigators and prosecutors went after the soldiers on the basis of a traditional ROE that had been superseded by the new, unlawful ROE. As such, their actions are disingenuous, and the conviction of the soldiers rings hollow. The events during Operation Iron Triangle, and their legal aftermath, fail to engage one's faith that justice has been achieved, because of the fake and false premises in the mission as well as the convictions that ensued. The new, unlawful ROE were treated as lawful, while the traditional, lawful ROE were used to convict the low-ranking soldiers but were not in use during the military mission — all this chicanery before, during, and after the mission constitutes fake sincerity and constitutes a well-orchestrated series of empty gestures. The doctrine of command responsibility for the unlawful ROE came up in the questions that were posed by the investigators as they "played it by ear," but they abandoned this important issue. It is unrealistic to expect Army commanders to police themselves.

Moreover, the event at Operation Iron Triangle and its aftermath are like a hologram of the entire post-9/11 drama by the US military. Iraq was not guilty of any role in 9/11, and the justifications proffered for the war against

---

1 Even the "new penology" or police model used in the so-called "war on crime" is problematic, quite apart from its uses by the military. For an excellent discussion, see Leonidas K. Cheliotis, "How Iron is the Iron Cage of New Penology? The Role of Human Agency in the Implementation of Criminal Justice Policy," *Punishment & Society*, Vol. 8(3):313-340, 2008.

Ihave been exposed by numerous authors as phony. Iraq may have become a haven for terrorists and Al Qaeda after the US invasion, but it was not one before. President Bush's "mission accomplished" slogan with regard to the war in Iraq has since been shown to be as hollow as Captain Hart's conclusion that Operation Iron Triangle was a "mission accomplished." The military commissions at Guantanamo Bay were struck down as unlawful by the United States Supreme Court, and then re-instated anyway by a Republican-led Congress. Three times the Supreme Court ruled against the Bush Administration with regard to unlawful policies and procedures at Guantanamo and the War on Terror in general, and the Bush Administration ignored, circumvented, or otherwise failed to comply with the Supreme Court's rulings each time. These court cases, too, came across as exercises in fake sincerity. What is the purpose of the Supreme Court, or the Constitution and the Geneva Conventions, if these social institutions are not obeyed? Ironically, those who protested the unlawful US government policies at Gitmo were arrested in front of the Supreme Court building and later imprisoned for their attempt to exercise their First Amendment rights through peaceful demonstration.[1] The subsequent 9/11 trials that began in the Summer of 2008 came across as a postemotional and insincere imitation of Nuremberg trials, because the defendants at Guantanamo had been tortured while the Nazi defendants were not, and because the US followed far more procedures that evidenced a fair trail for the Nazis than it did for the prisoners at Gitmo. In any case, the summer trials of alleged terrorists were quickly deconstructed as an insincere ploy to garner votes for Republicans in the general election in November. The abuse at Abu Ghraib became possible after unlawful techniques from Guantanamo "migrated" via General Geoffrey Miller's infamous visit in August of 2003. The US military at Abu Ghraib was put in the fake position of torturing prisoners to obtain information that they did not have — the government's own estimates are that 90% of the inmates were not hostile to the United States, and had no information to give. The "enhanced interrogation techniques" (a euphemism for torture) were unlawful in any case.

In *Boumediene v. Bush*, the US Supreme Court ruled on June 12, 2008 that prisoners at Guantanamo Bay "have the constitutional right to habeas corpus."[2] Writing for the majority, Justice Anthony Kennedy wrote: "The laws and Constitution are designed to survive, and remain in force, in extraordinary times." Justice Kennedy was expressing what Riesman called inner-directed standards, which are not supposed to change drastically in

---

1 Frida Berrigan, "Jailed for Protesting Gitmo: 35 Convicted for Demonstrations Outside Supreme Court," AlterNet, 30 May 2008, http://www.alternet.org/rights/86810?page=entire
2 http://www.supremecourtus.gov/opinions/07pdf/06-1145.pdf

one's lifetime, but are supposed to connect successive generations in relation to long-standing values and principles. In this particular case, the Supreme Court was harking back to principles that were valued by the framers of the US Constitution and further back to the framers of the Magna Carta. Far from being a limited ruling on the rights of prisoners at Guantanamo, this Supreme Court decision, like the two historic decisions that preceded it and defied the Bush Administration (*Rasul v. Bush* in 2004 and *Hamdan v. Rumsfeld* in 2006), invoked broad issues pertaining to the Geneva Conventions, the US Constitution, and other laws and policies vis-à-vis the current War on Terror. As I have argued throughout this book, seemingly disparate events and issues such as Operation Iron Triangle, the torture at Gitmo, the abuse at Abu Ghraib, and the new ROE are all interconnected. Indeed, the full texts of the Supreme Court's decisions range far and wide in issues they invoke in justifying their judgments, from the Magna Carta through the Yamashita case to Andersonville Prison and the hearings at Gitmo. The dissenting justices warned that this latest decision could cost American lives and could endanger security. But Justice Kennedy had the last, and inner-directed word, writing: "Security subsists, too, in fidelity to freedom's first principles, chief among them being freedom from arbitrary and unlawful restraint and the personal liberty that is secured by adherence to the separation of powers."

Reactions by pundits, the media, and the public were predictable. The political Right criticized the decision as dangerous and as an example of "judicial activism." The political Left praised the decision as an affirmation of American values. It is ironic that contemporary "conservatives" in American society are the ones who call for changing, bending, and softening long-held principles, while "liberals" call for adherence to traditional images of America as existing under the rule of law. Is either group being sincere, or merely jockeying for positions of power following the general election in November of 2008?

But perhaps the most disturbing reactions came from some bloggers who concluded, like the US soldiers at Operation Iron Triangle, that if "terrorists" must have rights when they are taken prisoner, it is more efficient to simply kill them rather than take prisoners. Such is the other-directed, unprincipled reaction to sentiments and opinions expressed by the US Supreme Court that even a generation ago would have been depicted as honorable and quintessentially American, namely — America is a nation of laws, not just a nation of men and women.

From an inner-directed perspective, it is clear that the abuses at Abu Ghraib, Guantanamo, Iron Triangle, Haditha, and other sites where unlawful policies and actions were tolerated or committed are connected vis-à-vis the idea that gyroscopic principles failed in the current War on Terror on a widespread scale. Adam Zagorin connects some of these issues succinctly:

> Despite years of investigation into alleged abuse and death of prisoners in US custody since 9/11, the only Americans held accountable have been the low-ranking "bad apples" convicted for the worst atrocities at Iraq's Abu Ghraib prison. No official blame has been assigned to higher-ups for abuses at Guantanamo or in Afghanistan, much less for crimes allegedly committed by US personnel in various CIA prisons around the world.... In July 2002, the office of the Pentagon's former top lawyer, William "Jim" Haynes, began to examine a program that taught US military personnel how to survive interrogation methods used by dictatorships such as North Korea and the former Soviet Union. The program, known as SERE (Survival, Evasion, Resistance, Escape), was designed to prepare US personnel to face techniques such as sensory deprivation, sleep disruption, being forced into stress positions and even "waterboarding." Haynes' office sought to borrow interrogation techniques of America's erstwhile enemies — techniques that if used against detainees, may violate US law and the Geneva Conventions.[1]

One of the exact charts of such Communist techniques used against Americans prisoners of war has been pinpointed to an article published by Albert D. Biderman in the year 1957, and is alleged to have been used verbatim as a "how to" manual by American investigators in the war on terror.[2] According to Robert Kennedy Jr. and Brendon Denelle, "despite the original study's conclusion that many of the confessions obtained through use of the 'coercive management techniques' were false, the Pentagon based is training on Communist methods that the United States long labeled as torture."[3] The other-directed type fails to see the inner-directed dilemma in the fact that Americans would postemotionally borrow techniques from their demonized enemies. As Riesman points out, the other-directed type sees the social world as divided between "good guys" versus "bad guys," and Americans are always the presumptive "good guys" who consistently win in comics, films, other sources of popular culture — and reality. Postmodernists are right to point out that the difference between narratives and reality has become blurred. If one regards the "story" or narrative of the failed mission called Operation Iron Triangle as one would approach any other story or narrative in other-directed American society, then it was a mission accomplished in every regard, from the killings in May 2006 to the subsequent convictions of the low-ranking soldiers. Riesman writes:

> Indeed, if other-directed child comic fans read or hear stories that are not comics they *will read them as if they were comics.* They will tend to focus on who won and to miss the internal complexities of the tale, of a moral sort

---

1 Adam Zagorin, "Seeking Answers on Detainee Abuse," *Time* Magazine, July 17, 2008.

2 See Albert D. Biderman, "Communist Attempts to Elicit False Confessions From Air Force Prisoners of War," *Bulletin of the New York Academy of Medicine* Volume 33 (9), pp. 616-25, 1957.

3 Robert Kennedy Jr. and Brendon Dennelle, "Unearthed: News of the Week the Mainstream Media Forgot to Report," *Huffington Post*, 11 July 2008.

or otherwise. If one asks, then, how they distinguish the "good guys" from the "bad guys" in the mass media, it usually boils down to the fact that the former always win; they are good guys by definition [p. 100, my emphasis].

Let us apply Riesman's insight concerning other-directed reasoning to the story that has been analyzed in this book. Who were the "good guys?" The immediate answer is: American soldiers, of course. Riesman adds that "morality tends to become an inference from winning" (p. 104) for other-directed types. Americans won militarily in Iraq overall and during Operation Iron Triangle in particular, so there is no need for further inquiry into motives or moral issues for the other-directed type. The "bad guys" were similarly pre-designated, pre-defined, and treated accordingly: they were the military age Iraqi males who were killed (or in the cases at Guantanamo, imprisoned and tortured), whether or not they showed hostility to Americans. According to Riesman, the other-directed type "can be strikingly insensitive to problems of character" (p. 101). When the internal complexities of the murders that were committed during Operation Iron Triangle became obvious even to the Army's own investigators, a new solution was found along the same, other-directed patterns. The "good guys" then became the officers and other commanders who issued the unlawful ROE — because these officers and commanders are, by definition, in winning roles — and the "bad guys" were, almost by definition, the low-ranking soldiers who carried out the unlawful orders. It is highly doubtful that the true, intricate, and highly complex narrative presented in this book will ever arouse curiosity, further investigation or even enthusiasm among other-directed type with regard to inner-directed principles of real honor, courage, and compliance with the rule of law.

In chapter 1, I referred to Mark Twain's sardonic criticism of General Frederick Funston's massacre of Emilio Aguinallo and his men who had surrendered to Funston during a battle in the Philippine-American War. Like Riesman, Twain writes in terms of "character" as a quality that George Washington possessed and General Funston allegedly lacked. "Washington was more and greater than the father of a nation, he was the Father of its Patriotism," writes Twain. Twain elaborates:

> Now, then, we have Funston; he has happened, and is in our hands. The question is, what are we going to do about it, how are we going to meet the emergency? We have seen what happened in Washington's case: he became a colossal example, an example to the whole world, and for all time — because his name and deeds went everywhere, and inspired, as they will inspire, and will always inspire, admiration, and compel emulation. Then the thing for the world to do in the present case is to turn the gilt front of Funston's evil notoriety to the rear, and expose the back aspect of it, the right and black aspect of it, to the youth of the land; otherwise he will become an example and a boy-admiration, and will most sorrowfully and grotesquely bring his breed of Patriotism into competition with Washington's. This competition has already begun, in fact. Some may not believe it, but it is nevertheless true, that there are now public-school teachers and

superintendents who are holding up Funston as a model hero and Patriot in the schools.

If this Funstonian boom continues, Funstonism will presently affect the army. In fact, this has already happened. There are weak-headed and weak-principled officers in all armies, and these are always ready to imitate successful notoriety-breeding methods, let them be good or bad. The fact that Funston has achieved notoriety by paralyzing the universe with a fresh and hideous idea, is sufficient for this kind — they will call that hand if they can, and go it one better when the chance offers. Funston's example has bred many imitators, and many ghastly additions to our history: the torturing of Filipinos by the awful "water-cure," for instance, to make them confess — what? Truth? Or lies? How can one know which it is they are telling? For under unendurable pain a man confesses anything that is required of him, true or false, and his evidence is worthless. Yet upon such evidence American officers have actually — but you know about those atrocities which the War Office has been hiding a year or two; and about General Smith's now world-celebrated order of <u>massacre</u> — thus summarized by the press from Major Waller's testimony:

<u>"Kill and burn — this is no time to take prisoners — the more you kill and burn, the better — Kill all above the age of ten — make Samar a howling wilderness!"</u>[1]

As previously noted, the similarities between the massacre committed by Funston and the massacre at Operation Iron Triangle, and their aftermaths, are striking. Even the "water cure" mentioned by Twain seems to resemble the contemporary technique known as "water-boarding." If the order in the Philippines was to kill all above age ten, it was simply more precise, but not more moral than the order to kill all military age males on sight in Iraq. But it is the difference between Twain's typically inner-directed attitude—to contrast Funston lack of moral principles with Washington's high regard for moral principles—versus the contemporary, other-directed approach to such war crimes that is of most import. Nowadays, few persons can expect or take seriously Twain's moral indignation, which is rooted in inner-directed social character. This is because contemporary postmodernists deconstruct Washington, Jefferson, and the other Founding Fathers and the entire nexus of ideas and values surrounding American history that surrounds them: that they held privileged moral positions, that they were admirable, even that the narratives about them in traditional history books are true. For example, postmodernists note that Washington and Jefferson owned slaves. Other postmodernists have concluded that only about a third of the Americans in Washington's time wanted independence from Britain. And so on. Once the purported moral gyroscope of the inner-directed types of the past has been deconstructed, there is no moral scaffolding left for social types such as Mark Twain and Justice Kennedy to use that can be entirely convinc-

---

1 http://www.druglibrary.org/schaffer/general/twain/deffunst.htm

ing to the contemporary collective consciousness in America. In summary, if George Washington or some other moral exemplar cannot be admired, then General Funston and the Brigade Commander at Operation Iron Triangle cannot truly be condemned for their actions. One cannot escape the over-arching issue of fake versus real sincerity: Was Washington sincere and are historical images of him sincere, or has "fake sincerity" corroded most cultural discourse?

A key point in this discussion has been and remains that scores of massacres have occurred throughout history, so that there is nothing unusual *per se* about the massacre at Operation Iron Triangle, Funston's massacre in the Philippines, the massacres at My Lai and Son Thang, or any other example. According to Riesman, in determining morality, "the test is not whether an individual's behavior obeys social norms but whether his character structure does" (p. 242). Inner-directed types committed and commit war crimes, but they judge their behavior and are judged by the juries of their peers on the basis of long-lasting character traits of courage, commitment to principles, sincerity, honor, and other values. The problem in a predominantly postemotional, other-directed society is that most people dare not commit themselves to any principle represented by Twain, Washington, Justice Kennedy, the Geneva Conventions, or any other person, principle, or event that used to be held in high esteem by a majority of American society. The reason for this cynicism is that the other-directed types "pride themselves on achieving the inside-dopester's goal: never to be taken in by any person, cause, or event" (p. 182). Indeed, to be "taken in" by Twain's argument or Justice Kennedy's judgment or any other lofty principle is as devastating to the other-directed type as failing to live up to gyroscopic principles was and is to the inner-directed type. And this sense of postemotional helplessness, cynicism, and apathy extends to all areas of contemporary social life. Increasingly, the postemotional type dares not be "taken in" by lovers, the institution of marriage, the sincerity of teachers, politicians, or most other persons and events in their lives. Witness, for example, the meteoric rise of Senator Barack Obama from an obscure first-time Senator from Illinois to Democratic Party nominee for President of the United States largely on the apparently inner-directed message he calls the "audacity of hope." In his political campaign, he promised repeatedly that he would be honest with the American people. Was he sincere, or merely more skilled at faking sincerity? Representatives of the political right wasted no time in trying to deconstruct him into a "typical" politician, which means, an artist in chicanery and fake sincerity. But even the left-leaning Jon Stewart, host of the "Daily Show," spoke for millions of other-directed types when he asked on his program, "When will Obama break our hearts?"

The central conclusion of this study is that an assessment of war crimes in the current war on terror, including the massacre committed during Operation Iron Triangle, comes down to a character struggle between inner-directed and other-directed social types in the United States, and in particularly, the struggle in distinguishing fake from genuine sincerity. The often-cited divisions in contemporary American society between liberals and conservatives, Blue states and Red states, and others, come down to a fundamental division in social character. When Riesman published his classic book in 1950, the inner-directed social types were dominant and other-directed types were just starting their ascendancy. Today, in stark contrast, the other-directed types are dominant and the inner-directed types are literally dying out. And the distinction between these two types of social character does *not* reduce itself to liberals versus conservatives or other typical divisions, but cross-cuts many other, typically used, political divisions in contemporary American society. For example, there can be and are fakely sincere Republicans as well as Democrats, conservatives as well as liberals.

In the end, this entire discussion comes down to the question: Who is the real terrorist? If Americans wage a war on terror that uses techniques, policies, and unprincipled tactics of America's past and present enemies, then the fake sincerity of the war on terror is revealed starkly. Twain's use of irony and his admiration for Washington to expose Funston's crime falls flat in contemporary times. Justice Kennedy's similar admiration for the Founding Fathers is met with similar cynicism. Other-directed views are better represented in an exchange from the more contemporary film, "Get Smart, Again." This film and other sequels to the television series, "Get Smart," focus upon the seemingly inner-directed agent, Maxwell Smart, also known as Agent 86, whose bungling is forgiven, much as Riesman predicted, because of his apparent sincerity as a "good guy" battling the "bad guys." Agents 86 and 99 are on the side of the fictional American spy organization, "Control," which battles a vaguely foreign organization called "Kaos." Toward the end of the film, Agent 99 wonders out loud whether Control is any different from Kaos. "Don't be ridiculous," Agent 86 responds, "We kill, maim, and destroy because we represent everything that is good and decent in the world." It is difficult to escape Riesman's prophesy that Americans have come to see themselves as the pre-designated "good guys" who need not be constrained by principles in their battles with pre-designated "bad guys."

What comes next? Will there be a collective soul-searching among Americans of the many false premises that have been used in waging the current War on Terror, from Guantanamo to Operation Iron Triangle and elsewhere? Is it possible to return to inner-directed standards that used to evoke respect from most people because the principles were both sincere and lawful? Or will postemotional, other-directed society eventually make films, books, and other cultural products that construct additional layers of fake sincerity in cultural discourse that make these latter-day fiascos and moral failures seem like glorious victories, on the order of the book and film, *Black Hawk Down*? These questions are important, but nevertheless America-centric. The sociological reply depends on the outcome of what Riesman called the "character struggles" between inner-directed and other-directed types within the United States. However, the metaphorical "jury of one's peers" extends internationally, and most of the world is still tradition-directed and inner-directed, even if most of America has become other-directed. And this time, the verdict of the international jury of public opinion may not necessarily be the same verdict that American society will pronounce on itself regarding this most recent war (that the good guys won). The unintended consequence of failing to follow moral principles in waging the war on terror may be that America has lost that intangible yet very real cultural capital called moral prestige that it enjoyed for decades. In Riesman's words, "the anomic person tends to sabotage either himself or his society, probably both" (p. 242). Postemotional, other-directed, anomic society sabotages itself by not being able to take a sincerely moral stand against its individual, anomic lawbreakers — going all the way up the chain of command — regardless of the empty and fakely sincere gestures it uses to pretend to exhibit hollow indignation.

INDEX